IDIOT'S GUIDES
AS EASY AS IT GETS!

Social Security

by Fred Yager and Jan Yager, PhD

ALPHA
A member of Penguin Group (USA) Inc.

This book is dedicated to our wonderful family and devoted friends.

ALPHA BOOKS

Published by Penguin Group (USA) Inc.

Penguin Group (USA) Inc., 375 Hudson Street, New York, New York 10014, USA • Penguin Group (Canada), 90 Eglinton Avenue East, Suite 700, Toronto, Ontario M4P 2Y3, Canada (a division of Pearson Penguin Canada Inc.) • Penguin Books Ltd., 80 Strand, London WC2R 0RL, England • Penguin Ireland, 25 St. Stephen's Green, Dublin 2, Ireland (a division of Penguin Books Ltd.) • Penguin Group (Australia), 250 Camberwell Road, Camberwell, Victoria 3124, Australia (a division of Pearson Australia Group Pty. Ltd.) • Penguin Books India Pvt. Ltd., 11 Community Centre, Panchsheel Park, New Delhi—110 017, India • Penguin Group (NZ), 67 Apollo Drive, Rosedale, North Shore, Auckland 1311, New Zealand (a division of Pearson New Zealand Ltd.) • Penguin Books (South Africa) (Pty.) Ltd., 24 Sturdee Avenue, Rosebank, Johannesburg 2196, South Africa • Penguin Books Ltd., Registered Offices: 80 Strand, London WC2R 0RL, England

International Standard Book Number: 978-1-61564-741-5
Library of Congress Catalog Card Number: 2014951304

17 16 15   8 7 6 5 4 3 2 1

Interpretation of the printing code: The rightmost number of the first series of numbers is the year of the book's printing; the rightmost number of the second series of numbers is the number of the book's printing. For example, a printing code of 15-1 shows that the first printing occurred in 2015.

Printed in the United States of America

Note: This publication contains the opinions and ideas of its author. It is intended to provide helpful and informative material on the subject matter covered. It is sold with the understanding that the author and publisher are not engaged in rendering professional services in the book. If the reader requires personal assistance or advice, a competent professional should be consulted. The author and publisher specifically disclaim any responsibility for any liability, loss, or risk, personal or otherwise, which is incurred as a consequence, directly or indirectly, of the use and application of any of the contents of this book.

Most Alpha books are available at special quantity discounts for bulk purchases for sales promotions, premiums, fund-raising, or educational use. Special books, or book excerpts, can also be created to fit specific needs. For details, write: Special Markets, Alpha Books, 375 Hudson Street, New York, NY 10014.

Publisher: *Mike Sanders*
Associate Publisher: *Billy Fields*
Acquisitions Editor: *Janette Lynn*
Development Editor: *John Etchison*
Cover Designer: *Laura Merriman*

Book Designer: *William Thomas*
Indexer: *Celia McCoy*
Layout: *Ayanna Lacey*
Proofreader: *Virginia Vasquez Vought*

Contents

Introduction

One of the most large-scale and popular benefits programs run by the U.S. government is Social Security—yet few people really understand just what it is or the nuts and bolts of how it works.

In short, Social Security is a benefits program the federal government provides to eligible individuals that pays monthly benefits to retirees, older workers who meet certain income or age requirements, the disabled and their dependents, and the family of retired or deceased workers.

The Social Security Act was signed into law on August 14, 1935, by President Franklin D. Roosevelt. The program has been modified over the years, but the goal has remained the same: to provide financial support and security to eligible Americans.

Social Security was never designed to be the sole source of income for retirees. However, today so many seniors don't receive pensions from their jobs and have little savings due to the economy or to lack of employment, Social Security has become a much bigger part of retirement income than it was intended to be. The reality today is that for a growing number of seniors, Social Security benefits actually represent as much as 90 percent or more of what they have to live on after they stop working.

Therefore, the stakes are high when it comes to understanding how Social Security works, deciding when to apply for benefits, and knowing whether your benefits can realistically sustain you through your retirement years.

How This Book Is Organized

Here's an overview of what you'll find in this book:

Part 1, Welcome to Social Security, lays the groundwork, beginning with how and why Social Security was established and how regulations have changed over the years. We explain how Social Security is set up, who pays for it, and what determines the amount of monthly benefits you'll collect. From there, we discuss who qualifies for Social Security and how it ties in to disability benefits. We also address the importance of protecting your Social Security card and number, handling identity theft, and replacing a lost card.

Part 2, Filing for Social Security, is where we tackle the most frequently asked question about Social Security: "When should I file?" You'll learn how to read and understand your earnings statement, upon which the Social Security Administration calculates your benefits. We'll also discuss the pros and cons of filing early, waiting until your full retirement age, or postponing benefits until you turn 70.

Part 3, Benefits for All, discusses the benefits packages for just about anyone who needs financial help to survive. You'll learn about the qualifications for the two programs that help the disabled. You'll also learn how to file an appeal if your disability claim is denied. We'll explore how divorce can impact eligibility for Social Security benefits. Finally, we'll discuss medical issues and how to apply for Medicare or Medicaid.

Part 4, Living with Social Security, ponders whether you can realistically live on just your monthly Social Security benefit check. You'll learn the best places to live if you don't want to have to pay state taxes on your benefits, as well as some of the most affordable countries and communities for those on fixed or lower incomes. There's also a chapter about continuing to work or returning to the workforce and how that could impact your Social Security benefits.

Part 5, Safeguarding Your Future, will help you prepare for your financial future, especially if you still have some time before you retire. We'll discuss how to consider ahead of time how you want to spend the rest of your life and then what steps to take to fund that lifestyle. We'll also look at many proposed changes to the Social Security program that could ensure its existence for future generations.

Finally, the appendixes include a glossary of terms and a list of additional readings and resources, including helpful websites that will further guide you along your way.

Extras

Throughout this book, you'll also find sidebars filled with extra tips, definitions of terms, warnings, and valuable quotations that we feel deserve special attention.

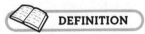

These sidebars define and explain key terms to further your understanding of how Social Security works.

Here you'll find additional key information that will help you navigate your way through the system.

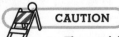

These sidebars offer warnings about potential problems or mistakes to be aware of on your journey through the Social Security process.

TIP

Here we offer a helpful piece of information or a handy suggestion we think you should know about.

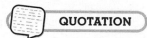

QUOTATION

These sidebars share direct quotes from experts and real-life retirees related to various aspects of Social Security.

Acknowledgments

We would like to thank all the financial advisors, retirement consultants, and other individuals—whether named or anonymous—who provided us with information, anecdotes, or examples through email communications or interviews, as well as the secondary sources and websites cited throughout the book. We want to thank Bob Diforio of D4EO Literary Agency for recommending us to write this book, as well as acquisitions editor Janette Lynn and development editor John Etchison at Alpha Books, whose editorial and production skills helped bring this project to fruition.

Trademarks

All terms mentioned in this book that are known to be or are suspected of being trademarks or service marks have been appropriately capitalized. Alpha Books and Penguin Group (USA) Inc. cannot attest to the accuracy of this information. Use of a term in this book should not be regarded as affecting the validity of any trademark or service mark.

Welcome to Social Security

What better way to introduce you to Social Security than to show you how and why it was created and how it has changed over the years as new rules and regulations were added?

Originally designed to help older Americans retire so younger Americans could get jobs during the Great Depression, it has grown into much more, providing financial assistance not only to retirees, but to disabled workers and the survivors of retired or disabled Americans.

In this part, you'll learn how Social Security works, how to qualify for it by earning work credits, and a brief overview of when is the best time to apply. You'll also learn the importance of protecting your Social Security number from would-be identity thieves, as well as what to do if you believe your identity has been stolen.

What Is Social Security?

If you ask people on the street to define Social Security, you're apt to get a variety of answers, depending on the age of the person being asked.

A typical teenager might say, "Social Security, isn't that protection so my Facebook account doesn't get hacked?"

Someone just joining the workforce might say, "Isn't that the number I have to put on my employment application?"

A person in his or her late 60s might answer, "It's the money I look forward to having direct deposited into my checking account each month that helps me pay my bills."

As these examples show, most people have either an incorrect or very narrow understanding of what Social Security really is and the role it plays in all of our lives, throughout our lives.

In this chapter, we're going to explore what Social Security is as well as how and why it came to be, and, possibly most important of all, the very basics of how to become eligible for Social Security benefits.

In This Chapter

- What Social Security is and why it was created
- How Social Security is funded, and who controls it
- How to find out if you're eligible
- An introduction to Social Security Disability Insurance (SSDI)
- The role Social Security plays in our lives

We'll also discover the ways Social Security has changed over the years, who governs it, who benefits from it, and who pays for it. The answer to the last question is actually the easiest to answer: we do. Ironically, this might be one of the biggest misconceptions of all. Social Security is *not* a "government handout"! It is the government giving back to its eligible citizens the funds they have "paid into" with a percentage of their earnings—whether salaries or self-employed income—for a minimum of 10 years (and 40 earned credits) of work.

The Third Rail

Often referred to as the *third rail* of politics—because any politician who threatens to eliminate it would probably never get elected or reelected—Social Security has grown into the largest program funded (supplemented or administered) by the federal government. It's estimated that a Social Security check is given to one in four American households each month. In 2014, an estimated 59 million people received $863 billion—close to $1 trillion—in Social Security benefits.

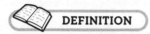

DEFINITION

The **third rail** is the rail that provides electricity to trains such as subways. When used as in terms like "the third rail of politics," it means that anyone who touches it would get politically electrocuted.

Without Social Security, millions of Americans would be living below the poverty level. For many Americans, Social Security has become their lifeline, and without it, they might as well be living in a third-world country struggling to survive.

Of course, Social Security—as you will learn in this book, and as many readers already know—is not a perfect system. Yes, there are millionaires who are getting Social Security, and even they, like every other eligible working American, earned it because they contributed to the Social Security funds.

To those who are struggling, it doesn't seem quite fair that a millionaire is also getting Social Security benefits when a hardworking retired couple in their early 70s, without a pension or any savings to speak of, are just getting by on their combined monthly benefits of $3,600. But at least that couple has that currently reliable and dependable income of $3,600, minus whatever withholding taxes they may have to pay to their state or the federal government by April 15th each year. How would they pay their rent or put food on their table without those funds now that they're no longer working?

If we are to preserve, or even improve, the amazing benefit system we call Social Security, it's in all of our best interests to understand the history and complexities of what Social Security is and how it works.

The History of Social Security

Major legislative changes rarely happen overnight in this country, and Social Security was no exception. Although it was officially created by the Social Security Act of 1935, the idea behind Social Security as a way to protect American workers if they became too old or unable to work because of disability dates back hundreds of years. Even before there was an America, in Europe in the Middle Ages there were *guilds,* which were precursors of today's unions. These guilds were formed ostensibly to protect members from employment abuse, but they also helped those who needed financial help due to illness or unemployment.

 **DEFINITION**

During the Middle Ages, a **guild** was an organization made up of people with related interests and goals who got together to maintain certain standards and to protect the interests of their members. One of the most famous of these was the Freemasons.

The colonists brought these notions with them when they settled in what was to become America. The first national pension program actually dates back to 1776, before the Declaration of Independence. Then, just after the start of the Civil War in 1861, Congress passed legislation that created a pension program providing disability benefits for soldiers, widows, and orphans. But it wasn't until 1906 that old age figured into the equation as a qualification for benefits.

Why Social Security Was Created

It was around the turn of the twentieth century that America began experiencing changes in the way people lived. In particular, there were three shifts in American life in particular that seemed to have had the greatest impact, namely:

1. A major portion of our population began moving to cities from farms and rural areas as a result of the Industrial Revolution.

2. Improvements in health care and sanitation increased the average American life span by a dozen years between 1900 and 1930 (from 46.3 for males and 48.3 for females in 1900 to 58.1 for males and 61.6 for females in 1930).

3. The stock market crashed in 1929, leading to the Great Depression and mass unemployment.

Also around this time there were a number of popular movements that related to what would become Social Security. One such movement came from the outspoken governor of Louisiana,

Huey Long. He came up with a plan that the government should seize the wealth of the nation's richest Americans and redistribute or share it with those who were less fortunate. Sound familiar?

Another movement was started by a California doctor named Francis Townsend. His plan had the government giving a pension amounting to $200 a month for every American over the age of 60. This would be funded by a 2 percent sales tax. To be eligible, there were three requirements: you had to be retired, you had to be free of any habitual criminal acts, and you had to spend the money in the United States.

Both of these plans sought to deal with the horrific economic conditions that were plaguing the lives of all but the wealthiest Americans who somehow still had at least part of their fortunes— although many of them had lost most of their money in the crash of 1929.

It was against this environment that President Franklin D. Roosevelt (FDR) issued an executive order on June 29th, 1934, creating the Committee on Economic Security. He assigned to it the task of coming up with ways to safeguard the economic security of Americans hit with what he called "the hazards and vicissitudes of life." In other words, he wanted some kind of insurance for people too old or in other ways unable to support themselves through no fault of their own.

WORTH NOTING

When FDR signed the Social Security Act in 1935 providing retirement benefits, men were not expected to live much beyond retirement age. Life expectancy was 58 for men and 62 for women. In 1935, there were only 7.8 million Americans age 65 or older.

A little over a year later, on August 14, 1935, Roosevelt—as part of his New Deal reforms— signed into law the Social Security Act. This Act would create what he called "social insurance" to help relieve economic insecurity for millions of American workers. However, not everyone was happy about this. Conservatives considered it socialism and others challenged its constitutionality.

FDR, who viewed himself as a conservative, saw the Social Security Act as a way for older people to be able to give up their jobs so younger people could find work. Keep in mind that during this period, one in four Americans was unemployed.

As predicted, the programs developed under the Social Security Act designed to aid Americans and to make life easier, got off to a rather rocky start, each facing a different set of challenges.

Who Governs Social Security?

Before any of the programs could begin, something would have to be done to create two key systems—one to operate the programs and another to pay for them.

So it was left up to Congress to supply an answer, and Congress did what it normally did during the summer: it recessed until autumn, without appropriating any funds to pay for Social Security. In fact, it took about two more years before Social Security got up and running, and even then things weren't going all that smoothly.

During the next two years, the Social Security Board was formed, along with a method to collect taxes and monitor the earnings of those workers who would one day receive benefits. In 1946, it would be named the Social Security Administration, or SSA for short.

Meanwhile, the new law had come under harsh criticism from both houses of Congress, as well as a number of legal challenges by those who questioned its constitutionality. Added to that were a number of issues that had to be dealt with related to the program, such as devising a system of record keeping. If the benefits paid to workers were going to be based on how much each worker earned, there needed to be a way to monitor that. The solution? Give each and every worker a unique number. That number would be the way the government could keep track of every penny that every worker earned, as well as what taxes were paid.

On the surface, your nine-digit Social Security number (SSN) looks like it has been drawn out of a hat. But there is actually logic to what number you're given. Each grouping of numbers—the first three, the second two, and the final four—has a specific meaning or connotation. The first three numbers are related to an area of the country. The second two represent an even more specific localization, and the last four digits are serial numbers within the group area.

Now that they had a method for creating the Social Security number, all the government had to do was get people to sign up. For help with enrollment, the government contracted with the U.S. Postal Service to help it assign and distribute the initial Social Security numbers through its estimated 45,000 local offices. More than 1,000 of the local post offices were designated as typing centers where the actual cards would be prepared.

The first cards were distributed to employers on November 16, 1936. Based on the information they received back from employers about how many employees they had, the first applications were distributed to employees by November 24, 1936. On December 1, 1936, the first block of 1,000 records were assembled in Baltimore, Maryland, at Social Security headquarters, where the master file was being kept.

So who was issued the first Social Security number and card? The closest person we have to that is a John David Sweeney, Jr., age 23, who grew up in Westchester County, New York, whom the media dubbed the first number and card recipient. Ironically he died in 1974, at the age of 61— too young to receive any Social Security benefits. But his widow, until she died eight years later in 1982, was able to receive benefits based on her late husband's work credits.

As for its constitutionality, in May of 1937 the Supreme Court ruled that the Social Security Act was indeed constitutional.

In 1937, Congress also passed the Federal Insurance Contribution Act, known as FICA, requiring workers to pay an extra 2 percent in taxes to fund the Social Security system. This money was deposited in special trust funds set up specifically for the collection of revenue and the eventual payout of benefits.

Changes to Social Security

During its early years, Social Security went through a number of changes. Between 1937 and 1940, retirees would receive their Social Security benefits in a single payment. The monthly checks didn't begin until 1942.

In 1939, amendments were made to the Social Security Act to expand benefits to include the spouse and minor dependents of a worker and also to survivors of a worker who died prematurely. These amendments also increased the amount of benefits paid.

In the 1950s, the annual Cost of Living Allowances (COLA) were introduced to try to keep benefits even with the rate of inflation.

In 1954, disability insurance was created, but it wasn't until August 1956 that the Social Security Act was amended to provide benefits to disabled workers age 50 to 64 and disabled adult children. That same year, early retirement was permitted for women at age 62. But it would be five more years before men were allowed early retirement at 62.

 WORTH NOTING

Originally, Social Security was only for retirement so older workers could leave the workforce, making way for younger workers who were having a hard time finding jobs during the Depression.

In 1965, President Johnson signed the Medicare bill, with the Social Security Administration in charge of a new program that would provide health-care coverage to anyone age 65 or older.

During the 1970s, the Social Security Administration was given a new program to run called Supplemental Security Income (SSI). This program was set up to provide financial aid to disabled adults and children who have limited income and resources.

The Social Security Amendments of 1983 provided for a gradual increase in the age for collecting full Social Security Retirement Benefits (the so-called full retirement age or FRA) beginning in 2000 and over a 22-year time period from age 65 to age 67.

In 1983 and again in 1993, laws were passed to make Social Security benefits subject to federal taxes, which previously had not been paid. (There are income thresholds and other factors that determine how much of the benefits are taxed, which are discussed in Chapter 15.)

An Introduction to Social Security Disability

Social Security Disability was created officially in July 1956 to help workers who become *disabled* before they reach retirement age. Estimates are that there are currently about 8.5 million disabled workers in America receiving Social Security Disability payments and about 2 million more who receive benefits because they're family members of a disabled worker.

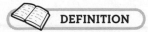 **DEFINITION**

You are considered **disabled** if you are unable to engage in any substantial gainful activity due to a medically determinable physical or mental impairment that lasts for at least 12 months or is expected to cause death.

If you don't think that's a very high number or something you should be concerned about, consider this: the Social Security Administration says you have a 30 percent chance of becoming disabled before you reach retirement age. That's almost one in three Americans.

Disability Programs

In the mid-1950s, two Social Security programs were established to provide benefits to anyone who has a mental or physical disability that prevents them from earning a living. That means if you're injured or sick and can't work, you may be eligible for disability benefits through Social Security Disability Insurance or Supplemental Security Income, which helps the disabled who already have financial challenges.

To be eligible for disability benefits, you need to be in one of two categories:

- You are disabled and under the age of 66.

- You are a family member of an eligible worker.

There are other qualifications, and we're going to explore those as we review these categories.

To qualify as a disabled worker under the age of 66, you must meet the mental or physical criteria of a disabled person, and have worked in jobs covered by Social Security long enough to have earned a specific number of work credits. That number will depend on your age at the time you become disabled. However, once you meet the criteria for being disabled and you continue to work, there is a cap on how much you can earn each year.

How Eligibility for Social Security Disability Is Determined

Under Social Security, you are deemed disabled if:

- You can't do the work you used to do.

- It is determined that you can't adjust to other work.

- Your disability is expected to last at least one year or will result in your death.

Social Security has its own list of impairments that would qualify your disability. All you have to do is prove you have the disability. To do this, you're going to need specific medical evidence, such as a professional diagnosis by a licensed physician, certified psychologist, or qualified speech-language pathologist. You will need to have a medical report that contains:

- Your medical history

- Clinical findings, such as results of a physical or mental exam

- Results of laboratory tests

- Diagnosis

- Treatment prescribed

- Prognosis

Unless you're blind, you'll also need a statement about what you can do despite your disability, such as the following:

- Sit, stand, walk, lift, carry items, hear, speak, use items such as a computer and a keyboard, write, and travel

- In terms of mental impairments, you can understand instructions, respond to supervision, and deal with everyday pressures of the workplace

If in spite of all your medical evidence the SSA still can't make up its mind, you may have to provide additional information or arrange to have a consultative examination. This can be done with your personal physician or any qualified examiner who has the necessary equipment and is willing to perform the exam. The consultative examination will then issue a report that contains the following:

- Your chief complaint or impairment

- A detailed history of the impairment

- A description and disposition of findings based on your history, physical or mental exam, lab tests, and any other information related to your impairment

- Lab results

- Diagnosis and prognosis of your impairment

- The consultant's comments regarding your impairment and a conclusion about your impairment's impact on your ability to work

In determining your claim, the SSA will also look at the effects any of your symptoms could have on your ability to work. These might include pain, shortness of breath, lack of energy or fatigue, and memory loss.

To put it mildly, the SSA doesn't hand out disability benefits without making sure whatever you say is keeping you from earning a living really exists.

What Social Security Means to You

What Social Security means to you will depend on your individual situation. For many, it's the bedrock of their economic security.

Close to 60 million Americans are currently receiving either retirement or disability benefits from Social Security. That may be anything from the majority of the income they are living on to an extra revenue stream in their retirement, because they also have a pension and savings. But for many, it's their entire retirement income.

For the majority of Americans, Social Security is something to look forward to, as well as something to continue paying into. It's the program you contribute money to today that will become available to you as a monthly benefit down the road when you either retire or become disabled.

Understanding Your Benefits

Social Security benefits are designed to provide you and your family with financial assistance when you retire, become disabled, or, for your survivors, die. The amount of your benefit is based on how much you earned from all the years you worked. There are maximums and minimums—if you earned a lot, your benefits will be in the high range, while if you were a low earner or left the workforce for a number of years, your benefits will be on the lower end.

Social Security's Role in Your Retirement

One of the biggest decisions you'll have to make that may impact how much money you receive for the next 10, 20, or 30+ years from Social Security is deciding when to retire. It's a decision you should not take lightly. In fact, there are a number of factors you should consider in making this decision, including:

- What do you plan to do after you retire?

- Are you in good health, or do you have limited time left to live because you have been diagnosed with a terminal illness?

- What is your current financial situation?

The Three Age Categories

There are three basic age categories to choose from when it comes to retirement:

- You can retire early beginning at age 62 and get retirement benefits, but the benefits will be reduced. (You will also have to abide by income caps if you want to continue working, which, if you exceed annually, will reduce the Social Security benefits you are allowed to keep.)

- You can wait until you reach full retirement age, which is usually by age 66 or 67, depending on when you were born between 1943 and 1960 and afterwards. (You will not be subject to any earnings caps.)

- You can postpone starting benefits until age 70, the maximum age at which you can begin collecting your benefits. But if you delay the start of benefits, especially if you keep working after age 66, you should see a substantial increase in benefits because of the accumulated credits you receive. (This could be as much as 32 percent above what you might have received at age 66.)

Let's break these categories down even further.

If you take early retirement and start receiving benefits as early as age 62, the amount of each check will be about 75 percent of what you would have received if you had waited until full retirement age (FRA). Another drawback to taking benefits early is the cap on earnings if you still want to work. Although this is an option that's declining in popularity, almost half of those eligible to claim benefits still apply when they turn 62.

In 2014, the income limit if you take your benefits early was $15,480. If you go over that amount, $1 in benefits will be deducted for each $2 you earn. The income limit increases substantially in the year you are due to reach full retirement, either your 65th or 66th year. During that year, the limit goes up to $41,400 and reductions of benefits, if you exceed that limit, change to $1 for every $3 earned.

But once you reach full retirement age, whether that is 66 or 67, you can earn as much as you want without any penalty or earnings cap. Different rules apply to those on disability. You have to report all earnings to Social Security no matter how much you earn.

The Least You Need to Know

- The origins of Social Security stem from the formation of guilds in the Middle Ages.
- The Social Security Act of 1935 created a program to provide income for workers who retired at age 65.
- Originally, Social Security was created to encourage older workers to retire as a way to increase employment of younger workers who had trouble finding jobs during the Great Depression.
- There are two Social Security programs: Social Security benefits for retired workers beginning at age 62, and Social Security Disability Insurance (SSDI) for disabled workers who are unable to work for one year or longer.
- When to apply for Social Security retirement benefits is a personal decision that should depend on your health, your financial situation, your projected life expectancy, and what you plan to do in retirement.

Protecting Your Number and Card

Do you ever feel as if you're just a number? Have you ever felt that your entire identity has been reduced to a series of numerals with a couple of dashes in between?

Well, guess what? It has, and it's your Social Security number—but that isn't necessarily a bad thing. It's simply the way the federal government tracks how much you've earned, how much you've paid in taxes, and therefore how much you're entitled to collect in benefits when you reach retirement age.

Your Social Security number is your connection to the vast government entity known as the Social Security Administration (SSA), which provides you retirement income from the age you start collecting your benefits (available as early as age 62, with some benefit reductions and restrictions) until you die.

In This Chapter

- Why it's important to protect your Social Security number
- Ways to keep your number from identity thieves
- What to do if someone else uses your number
- How to replace a lost card or get a new number
- How to change your name on your Social Security card

The Importance of Protecting Your Number

Your Social Security number is probably the most important number you'll ever have—unless you're a career military person, and then your service serial number is probably just as important. But for most of us, it's our Social Security number, the one number we get from the government that stays with us for life—which makes it extremely important that we protect it.

Avoiding Identity Theft

According to the FBI, identity theft has become one of the fastest-growing crimes in America. The Federal Trade Commission says 10 million Americans are defrauded every year through identity theft and other means by which thieves gain access to others' financial information.

One of the major entry points into a person's identity is through his or her Social Security number, which is why you need to be sure to protect your number. Once someone else starts using your identity, it's not that easy to get it back. Chances are it's going to take a lot of time and money, and even then your life will have been turned upside down during the process.

The number of cases involving stolen Social Security numbers has become so pervasive that the SSA has started a public relations campaign to encourage people and businesses to use other methods of identification instead of their Social Security number.

A thief who gets hold of your Social Security number can gain access to …

- Your bank or securities accounts.
- Your credit cards.
- Your driving record.
- Your tax history.
- Your medical records.

Each time you use your Social Security number, either online, on the phone, or on print applications, you open yourself up to the risk of identity theft. But if so many institutions use the Social Security number as their primary method of identification, how can you avoid sharing it?

That's beginning to change. Some businesses and schools are shifting to alternative employee or student identifiers such as a dedicated identification number issued by the employer or school, a number that always will follow the employee or student. Some are starting to use fingerprints and eye scans instead of requiring a Social Security number for identification.

The new way of thinking recommended by the SSA is to use your Social Security number only as a secondary identifier and to do this in a limited fashion, such as providing only the last four digits of your number instead of the entire number.

There are some organizations that will have to continue using Social Security numbers, and they're being asked to implement encryption software to protect this sensitive data.

Even with these changes, you're still required to use your Social Security number with the Internal Revenue Service, and with any employer, so income taxes can be withheld. But there are even ways around this. You can get what's called a Taxpayer Identification Number (TIN). This can become your alternative to using your Social Security number with employers, potential employers, and creditors.

 **CAUTION**

Here are some things you should never do with your Social Security number:

- Never list it when posting something on a public bulletin board.
- Never send it over the internet, including in an email.
- Never use it as part of a computer login.
- Never use it on an ID card.
- Never put it on a postcard.
- Never store it on an unprotected or public website.
- Never carry your Social Security card on your person, including in your wallet.

One of the newest and most sophisticated methods of stealing your personal information and your identity is through *phishing*. In this process, the phishers set up a phony website that looks just like one you've been doing business with and therefore trust implicitly. This could be a company you occasionally buy things from online, or an online bank account you access frequently. Sometimes the phishing is in the form of a contest you've supposedly won. To claim your prize, you're required to provide valuable personal information, including your Social Security number, which once again puts you at risk for identity theft.

 **DEFINITION**

Phishing is a play on the word "fishing," and it's something identity thieves do to trick you into providing them with your personal information such as passwords, credit card numbers, Social Security numbers, and anything else they can use to set up accounts in your name. They often do this by sending you an email pretending to be a person or business you trust and requesting you to supply the information they're fishing for.

Phishers may also send you an email saying your account has been frozen for some reason and you need to get in touch with them to set up a new account. If you bite and give them your information, including a credit card number, expiration date, and security code, before you know it somebody in Chechnya or Mumbai is on a shopping spree. It's especially a red flag if they ask for your Social Security number because no one should be asking for that, especially online.

Has Your Identity Been Stolen?

The Federal Trade Commission (FTC) has created an excellent guide to help you if you believe your identity has been stolen. If you're unsure, here are some tips to indicate someone else is pretending to be you:

- Money is missing from your bank account, and you did not withdraw it.
- Your credit card statement contains charges for purchases you didn't make—especially if these purchases are from overseas.
- You stopped receiving bills in the mail and you're not on a paperless billing plan.
- Vendors refuse to take your check.
- You start receiving calls from collection agencies for debts you don't recognize and you didn't incur.
- A medical claim is rejected because your health-care provider says you hit your limit.
- A data breach company notifies you that your information has been compromised.
- You get arrested for a crime someone else committed using your identity (one of the most extreme and frightening examples of identity theft).

What should you do if any of these things happen to you? Here are the first and immediate steps you should take:

- Submit a complaint to the FTC.
- File a police report and get a copy of that report or the report's number. Give the police the FTC report as well.
- Contact all three credit reporting companies—Equifax, Experian, and TransUnion—and place a fraud alert on your credit file, reporting that you have been the victim of identity theft.
- You may want to request the credit reporting companies put a freeze on your credit file, which prevents future creditors from getting access to your credit report and may prevent an identity thief from opening new accounts in your name.

- Request a free credit report from each reporting company. Go through every single item in the reports, picking out any of the fraudulent activity.

- Go through your entire bank and credit card account statements very carefully, checking for suspicious activity.

- Once you've detected any fraudulent charges, contact the businesses related to the charge and report this to their fraud department. You should also follow up in writing and send any letters by certified mail, which gives you a record that you contacted them. You might even want to include a return receipt to be sent back to you that will document that they signed for your letter.

The FTC recommends that you create an Identity Theft Report that would be attached to the report you file with the police about the identity theft. This report will be valuable as you start dealing with credit card companies, debt collectors, the credit reporting companies and any businesses that have accounts in your name. It will help you …

- Remove any fraudulent information from your credit report.

- Head off a company from collecting debts incurred through identity theft.

- Obtain information from companies about accounts an identity thief opened in your name, or your accounts that the thief simply used without your knowledge.

Replacing a Lost or Stolen Card

If your Social Security card is lost or stolen, you can replace it for free up to 3 times a year or 10 times during your lifetime.

Getting a replacement card is pretty simple:

- You'll need to complete application form number SS-5. You can find an application online by going to ssa.gov/forms/ss-5.pdf.

- You'll need to present an unexpired document, such as a driver's license or passport with your photo, which proves who you are.

- You'll have to show evidence of your U.S. citizenship, such as a birth certificate or passport.

- If you're a noncitizen but are here legally, you will need to show proof of that status.

Keep in mind that this replacement card will have the same name and number as your previous card.

Requesting a New Social Security Number

Getting a new Social Security number is not quite as easy as replacing a lost card. In fact, you need to qualify and have a good reason before the SSA will issue you a new number. Also, any new number will be cross-referenced with your old number by the SSA, so if you thought you could escape paying off old debts with a new number, you can forget about it.

How to Qualify for a New Number

The SSA will give you a new number if you …

- Can show someone else is using your number to apply for government benefits, such as welfare, food stamps, or unemployment.

- Prove you are being abused, harassed, or in grave danger by using your original number.

- Can prove someone has stolen your number and is using it to get credit cards in your name.

- Can show that your number is being used by someone trying to get a job.

- Can prove that someone else is using your number to hide illegal activities.

- Can show someone else is using your number to file fraudulent tax returns.

According to the SSA, it has issued new Social Security numbers to over 14,000 people. Many of them were the victims of domestic abuse. In fact, the SSA has created a new program to help anyone in danger get a new number. For more information on this initiative and what documents you will need to be able to obtain a new number because of domestic violence, read the publication, "New Numbers for Domestic Violence Victims," at ssa.gov/pubs/EN-05-10093.pdf.

Now, the question remains as to whether victims of identity theft should request a new Social Security number. According to the Identity Theft Resource Center, in most cases you probably shouldn't change your number because it could cause more problems than it solves. On the other hand, the SSA says if you've done all you can do to fix any problems due to misuse of your number and someone continues to use it, they may assign you a new number.

Documents Required

If you do decide to get a new number, you'll need to prove your identity, your age, and your citizenship. You'll also need to provide evidence that you're still having problems with your original number.

To prove your identity, you'll need either a U.S. driver's license, a U.S. passport, or a state-issued non-driver identification card. If you don't have one of those, you could use an employee ID card, school ID card, health insurance card (but not a Medicare card), U.S. military ID card, adoption decree, Certificate of Naturalization, or Certificate of Citizenship.

To prove your age, you'll need your birth certificate; a doctor, clinic, or hospital record; a religious record, such as a baptismal record; a U.S. passport; or school or employment records.

Any two of the above documents should suffice.

The SSA warns that even if you're given a new number, all your problems may not disappear, especially if you continue to use your original name and your same address. They add that a new number could also cause new problems because you would not have a credit history with the new number, which means you could have trouble getting credit.

Changing Your Name on Your Card

There are four good reasons to change your name on your Social Security card:

1. You got married.

2. You got divorced and now want to use your maiden name.

3. You changed your name legally.

4. Your name was wrong to begin with.

To change the name on your card, you'll need proof of identity and possibly of citizenship. The following documents should work:

- Your birth certificate

- A driver's license

- A passport

- Your marriage certificate (if this is the reason you're changing your name)

- A divorce decree (if you're changing your name back to your maiden name)

- A court order if you're changing your name legally

If you don't have a driver's license or passport, you may be able to use your military ID card, your student ID card, or a health insurance card (but not a Medicare card).

The Least You Need to Know

- There are several ways to protect your Social Security number from theft. The first way is to be really careful about providing your Social Security number to anyone.

- There are many steps you need to take if your identity is stolen, and you should take immediate action to resolve the problem.

- Phishing has become a prevalent method of identity theft by gaining illegal access to personal information. Avoid giving out such information, especially your Social Security number, to anyone or any business, especially online.

- Changing the name on your Social Security card is relatively easy with the right documentation. You can mail in the necessary documentation or take it to your local SSA office and, once the documentation is verified, your new card will be sent to you.

How Social Security Works

The answer to how Social Security works is simple: you and I, along with our employers, pay taxes under the Federal Insurance Contributions Act (FICA) that go into a trust fund that pays Social Security benefits.

Sounds pretty simple, right? In reality, to finance this vast program, the Social Security Administration (SSA) relies on a number of complex formulas and regulations that would give a nuclear physicist a headache.

In This Chapter

- Uncovering the secrets behind Social Security
- Where does all the money go?
- Who pays into the fund and who doesn't
- A brief overview of qualifying for benefits

Is It Really *Your* Money?

Many people think the money they put into the Social Security trust funds is really their money and that the government is holding on to it until they retire. If only it were that easy! Yes, you may have contributed to the trust funds through taxes, but there is no account in your name containing your contributions. There is, however, a record of how much money you earned and how much you contributed to FICA through payroll taxes.

The way this works is that the money you put in today is paying for those people who are getting benefits *today*. If you are not collecting Social Security benefits yet, someone else will be paying for your benefits down the road. So the short answer to the question "Is it your money?" is no. You are paying for someone else's benefits just as other workers will pay for yours.

Now, there is some ambiguity about those of us who collect Social Security and still pay *FICA* taxes. In that case, some of the money could be yours, but the important takeaway here is that most of us who are paying Social Security payroll taxes today are not contributing to our own benefits in the future, but to someone else's.

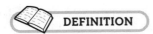 **DEFINITION**

> **FICA**, short for the **Federal Insurance Contributions Act**, is the federal law that requires payroll deductions to pay for Social Security and Medicare. Both employees and employers share the contributions; if you're self-employed, you are responsible for the entire contribution.

Another reason not to think of this as your money is your contributions actually go into two trust funds: the Old-Age and Survivors Insurance (OASI) Trust Fund and the Disability Insurance (DI) Trust Fund. Your money could just as easily be paying for someone else's disability benefits instead of for retirement because the funds are linked and are often referred to as the Old-Age, Survivors, and Disability Insurance, or the OASDI Trust Fund.

Here's another factoid that might make your head spin: the Social Security trust funds do not contain any cash or saleable assets. Then what do they contain, you might ask? This is where things get a little murky. According to the SSA, the trust funds basically represent the amount of Social Security FICA taxes that were collected beyond the amount needed to pay today's benefits. These excess funds were then converted into special Treasury bonds.

What makes these bonds special is that although they pay the same interest as other bonds the government sells to the public, these bonds can't be sold. They can only be repaid through higher taxes on future workers. Those annual surpluses that most of us thought were going to be there when the rest of us Baby Boomers begin collecting benefits are gone. They've actually been used to fund other government programs.

Still with us? Now comes the really strange part. None of this matters because the federal budget's definition of a "trust" bears little or no resemblance to the term as used in the private sector. In the private sector, trust funds invest in things like stocks and bonds or other asset-backed securities with the goal of growing the fund's revenues by maximizing earnings within a previously agreed-upon level of risk.

With the OASDI, the federal government owns the assets and earnings and it can raise or lower future trust fund collections and payments or change the purpose for which the collections are used. What this means is that the balances in the OASI and DI to be used to finance future benefit payments exist only on paper or in some digital file as a bookkeeping notation. There are no real assets here that can be withdrawn to pay for benefits.

What are they, then? Basically they're claims on the Treasury that when redeemed will have to be financed by raising taxes, by borrowing from the public, or by reducing the benefits. That's right. The Social Security trust funds contain no funds at all! They're simply a way to show how much the government has borrowed from Social Security but do not provide any methods of financing future benefits.

Who Pays into Social Security?

You and I, and our employer (if we have one), pay taxes and this money goes to the Treasury. It's up to the Treasury to estimate how much of these taxes are for Social Security through FICA and then credit the trust funds with that amount. This means the Treasury doesn't actually deposit the money into the two trust funds. It makes an accounting note that looks like the money is in the fund, but it really isn't.

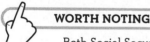

WORTH NOTING

Both Social Security trust funds are invested entirely in U.S. Treasury bonds that have special features in that they never fluctuate in value and they can always be redeemed at par.

At the end of the year, the estimates are adjusted after the actual income tax returns show how much real payroll tax was actually paid that year. We should add that the Treasury also credits the trust funds with any interest that would have been paid on its balances, along with the amount of income taxes higher-income workers paid on their Social Security benefits.

So that's what happens to the money collected. But what about the money going out? Where does that come from?

Well, the SSA tells the Treasury to pay the monthly benefits, and that amount is subtracted from the total shown on the books as being in the funds—even though the money is not really there.

Anything left over—the surplus—is, as we said earlier, converted into special-issue Treasury bonds that are basically IOUs the government gets to use when they're needed.

However, those surpluses ended in 2010, when Social Security began to pay out more in benefits than it was taking in. According to the SSA, the OASDI spent almost $44 billion more in 2013 than it brought in through the FICA payroll tax. And it expects the gap to continue growing until annual deficits grow to $153.6 billion by 2020. If that seems alarming, consider this: the SSA thinks the trust fund will run out of money in 2033.

When that happens, the Office of Management and Budget (OMB) says there are four ways Congress can repay the bonds and save Social Security:

1. Raise income taxes.

2. Authorize the Treasury to borrow the needed funds from the public.

3. Reduce spending on other federal programs.

4. If all else fails, cut Social Security benefits.

Who Doesn't Pay into Social Security?

Most of us pay Social Security taxes; however, there are a few exemptions. Some public and government employees are exempt in states that voted not to opt into a provision of the Social Security Act called the Section 218 Agreement covering public workers. This includes teachers, firefighters, police officers, prison employees, and state and local government employees. For example, teachers in Georgia don't pay Social Security taxes. But they can't apply for Social Security benefits, either.

Others exempt from paying Social Security taxes include members of some religious groups; they, too, must waive their right to receive any benefits.

Employees of foreign governments living in the United States don't have to pay Social Security taxes as long as the work they're performing is for the foreign government.

Children under the age of 18 who work for their parents in family-owned businesses don't have to pay Social Security taxes on their earnings as long as the business is solely owned or a partnership in which the child's parents are the partners. Finally, children under 21 who do domestic work, housekeeping, babysitting, and yard work don't have to pay taxes on their earnings.

FICA

For the rest of us, and the overwhelming majority of American workers, Social Security and Medicare taxes are collected under the Federal Insurance Contributions Act (FICA). These taxes represent 12.4 percent of earned income up to an annual limit. In 2014, that limit was $117,000.

In 2015, the limit increased to $118,500 Currently, 6.2 percent of your FICA tax is withheld from your income, while your employer covers the remaining 6.2 percent.

QUOTATION

"While almost all working Americans will pay into Social Security through their paychecks throughout the year, the 900 wealthiest people in the country won't. That's because the highest-earning 0.0001 percent of the U.S.—many of them corporate CEOs—made $117,000 in the first two days of the year, which is the maximum annual income that is subject to Social Security taxes under federal law."

—Alan Pike, "900 Rich People Won't Pay Into Social Security for the Rest of the year," posted on January 3, 2014, at thinkprogress.org

What If You're Self-Employed?

If you happen to be among the lucky ones who have your own business or work for yourself, estimated at 10 million Americans in 2013, or 6.6 percent of all reported jobs, according to a report from CareerBuilder and Economic Modeling Specialists Intl (EMSI), you still have to pay Social Security taxes. The only difference is that, because you are your own boss, you have to pay the entire amount, 12.4 percent, instead of the 6.2 percent paid by those who are not self-employed.

The good news, though, is that because of this you are eligible for two income tax deductions those who are not self-employed cannot get. First, your net earnings from self-employment are reduced by half of your Social Security tax. Second, you can deduct half of your Social Security tax on IRS form 1040. There are some qualifiers, however. You have to deduct it from your gross income and it can't be an itemized deduction, which means you can't list it on your Schedule C.

It's interesting to note that, according to the CareerBuilder and EMSI self-employment study, the number of self-employed has actually declined since its peak from 2001 to 2006, with the 5 percent decline since 2009 blamed on the recession. Thirty percent of those who are self-employed are 55 years of age and older.

WORTH NOTING

If you want to learn more about self-employment and Social Security benefits, access the publication, "If You Are Self-Employed," posted free online by SSA at ssa.gov/pubs/EN-05-10022.pdf. This is the 2014 version. They usually issue updated versions on an annual or regular basis.

Earning Work Credits Toward Future Benefits

The SSA determines your eligibility as well as the amount of your monthly benefits based on your work history. In order to qualify for retirement benefits, you will need at least 40 work credits, or four credits a year for 10 years. In 2014, you earned one credit for each $1,200 earned. In 2015, that increased to $1,220. The most you can earn in one year is four credits. (This topic will be discussed in greater detail in the next chapter.)

 QUOTATION

> "For many retirees, Social Security benefits represent their largest financial asset. Unfortunately, most Americans decide when to begin Social Security benefits without any advice.... Representatives at the Social Security Administration are not allowed to give advice (even if asked) and can only provide information and details on the rules. And few advisors have the training and knowledge to help a retiree select a Social Security claiming strategy."
>
> —William Reichenstein and William Meyer, Social Security Strategies, page ix.

The Least You Need to Know

- A percentage of your income taxes pay for Social Security and Medicare benefits. This is usually automatically deducted or withheld out of your paycheck before you receive what's left.

- Taxes collected today pay for those who receive Social Security tomorrow. But it's done on a general basis to those who will qualify down the road for Social Security.

- The government doesn't keep a physical account with the funds you pay into Social Security so it can give those funds to you when you retire. But it does track your earnings through your Social Security number and your income tax returns.

- The Treasury makes an accounting note that looks like money has been deposited in the Social Security trust fund, but the money really isn't there.

- You qualify for Social Security benefits by earning at least 40 work credits, which basically means you worked and paid FICA taxes for ten years. You cannot earn more than four credits in one year.

Qualifying and Calculating Your Benefits

As we've discussed, Social Security was originally created to help fund retirement, but over the years it has grown considerably to provide benefits for you and your family if you become disabled and can't work, and for your family if you should die. However, before you or anyone else in your family can receive these benefits, you have to qualify for them.

Not everyone who reaches the age of 62 or becomes disabled is automatically qualified to receive Social Security benefits. These benefits are based on how much you earned over your working lifetime. And keep in mind that not all benefits are related to retirement. Some are for disabled workers and others are for families who for one reason or another qualify under special circumstances.

In This Chapter

- How you qualify for Social Security benefits
- How retirement benefits are calculated
- Special strategies for spouses to increase benefits
- How disability benefits are calculated

Benefits for Retirees, Disabled, Children, and Survivors

The Social Security Administration (SSA) uses a complex formula to determine the actual benefit you receive. To qualify for retirement benefits you have to earn at least 40 quarterly credits, which equals 10 years' worth of payroll tax payments. You earn a credit by making at least $1,200 in a three-month period and paying Social Security taxes on that amount. So figure if you earn $4,800 in a year, you get four credits—the maximum number you can earn in one year.

The amount needed to earn a credit goes up each year, but that doesn't affect previously earned credits; once you earn 40 credits, you are permanently qualified. The level of benefits, however, is determined by your income history.

For those claiming disability, you also have to meet certain earnings credits, but that varies depending on your age at the time you became disabled. Children's benefits are based on the same formula used to calculate your retirement benefits.

If you qualify for Social Security benefits and you die, your widow or widower, if she or he is full retirement age or older, will get 100 percent of your benefits. He or she can qualify as early as age 60, but benefits would be reduced depending on age.

Survivors benefits are based on the maximum amount the worker would have received if he or she was still alive. If the worker was receiving reduced benefits because he or she took benefits early, survivors benefits would be reduced as well.

The Formula for Calculating Retirement Benefits

When it comes to determining individual benefits, the government decided to come up with one of the most complex formulas ever created. At its base, the formula is tied to your highest earnings over 35 years.

But what if you didn't work for 35 years, or had periods when you didn't work at all for a few years? Even for those years when your earnings would have been pretty low, the SSA takes 35 years of wages and creates an index called the Average Indexed Monthly Earnings (AIME).

They do this by adding up what you made each year in your 35 best years, using only those years in which Social Security taxes were paid, and then dividing that total by 420—which is the number of months in 35 years. If you worked fewer than 35 years, the missing years are filled with zeros. If you worked more than 35 years, only the highest-earning years are counted. The resulting figure is your AIME, and that's what's used to calculate your Social Security benefits. For example, let's say over those 35 highest-income years you made a total of $2 million. Divide that $2 million by 420 and you get $4,762. That's your AIME.

Once you have your AIME, there are four more steps. In 2014, you:

1. Multiply the first $816 by 90 percent

2. Subtract $816 from $4,917 and multiply that number by 32 percent

3. Subtract $4,917 from your AIME and multiply that by 15 percent

4. Total those last three numbers and then round down to the next lowest dollar. This will be your estimated monthly retirement benefit at full retirement age, either 66 or 67.

If you'd like to see what you'd get if you took early retirement at age 62, multiply your full retirement benefit by 75 percent.

What does all of this amount to? To simplify things, let's look at just three basic numbers. The first one is what is the most common Social Security benefit in 2014? The answer is that the average monthly retirement benefit for Social Security in 2014 was $1,294.

Next is the maximum you could receive if you are a high earner and you wait until your full retirement age to begin claiming your Social Security benefits, so there is no reduction in benefits. The amount of the maximum retirement benefit for a high earner beginning benefits at full retirement age in 2014 was $2,642.

Finally, what could you increase your monthly Social Security benefits to if you delay claiming your benefits until age 70, the last year there is any increase in benefits by delaying? That amount could become as high as $3,425 per month because benefits were accruing additional earning credits to the tune of around 8 percent a year between your full retirement age and age 70.

When Your Monthly Social Security Check Will Arrive/Be Deposited

If Your Birthday Falls on the ...	Wednesday Each Month
1st to 10th	2nd Wednesday
11th to 20th	3rd Wednesday
21st to 31st	4th Wednesday

Maximizing Spousal Benefits

Married people have a distinct advantage over single folks when it comes to maximizing their Social Security benefits. Beyond the fact that they get two payments a month instead of one, there are other strategies they can employ to increase the amount of at least one of those checks.

Under Social Security rules, a spouse has certain benefits, but they are restricted under the following guidelines:

- Dual entitlement, whereby a spouse, upon reaching full retirement age, is entitled to receive either his or her own benefits based on earnings, or 50 percent of the partner's benefits, depending on which is greater.

- Only one spouse can take advantage of spousal benefits.

- To receive spousal benefits, the other partner has to be already receiving benefits based on his or her own earnings.

The spousal benefit regulations are somewhat different regarding divorced spouses. Here are those rules:

- The marriage had to have lasted at least 10 years.

- The person filing for spousal benefits must still be unmarried.

- The ex-spouse is at least 62 years of age or older.

- The ex-spouse's benefit based on his or her own work record would be less than the amount he or she could receive based on their ex-spouse's work record.

- If your ex-spouse is eligible for Social Security benefits, but he or she has not yet applied for it, you can still file for spousal benefits as long as you have been divorced for at least two years.

There is also a provision in the rules to "file a restricted application." This applies if you've been divorced for more than two years. In that case, your ex-spouse is not required to have filed for benefits for you to receive spousal benefits, but he or she does have to be eligible to begin receiving benefits, which means he or she has reached age 62 and one month.

Furthermore, when it comes to divorce, it doesn't matter if the former spouse remarries. When that happens, both the current spouse and the former divorced and unmarried spouse have spousal benefits privileges related to the former spouse's work history, as well as survivor benefits for any children.

The "File and Suspend" Strategy

This one is slightly more complicated but could make sense for some couples. Here's how it works. You file for retirement benefits at the full retirement age so your spouse or dependent children can collect benefits based on your earnings record. Then you suspend your own benefits so the amount by which their benefits are calculated, and your own future benefits, will continue to increase 8 percent per year until you reach age 70.

However, now that you've filed for benefits, your spouse can claim spousal benefits, which would be 50 percent of your full retirement benefits. When you turn 70, you will begin receiving benefits as well, but at a higher amount than if you had not suspended them.

What Are Survivors Benefits?

First, reduced survivors benefits can start as early as age 60. Second, a survivors benefit is 100 percent of the deceased spouse's benefit based on whenever he or she began receiving retirement benefits. If the deceased spouse had filed for Social Security before reaching full retirement, the survivors benefits are tied to the reduced amount.

Another option is to take the survivors benefit at age 60 and then switch over to your own benefits either at full retirement or at age 70 if your retirement benefits amount to more than your deceased spouse's.

You may be eligible for survivors benefits even if your spouse did not work long enough to earn the necessary 40 credits to be eligible for Social Security benefits. Benefits may be paid to the deceased worker's children, and the spouse who is caring for those children, as long as the worker had worked for one and one-half years, earning six work credits, in the three years before his or her death.

The One-Time Death Benefit

A surviving spouse can also receive a one-time payment of $225 from the SSA if they apply for it within two years of the qualified worker's death. Note that the spouse had to be living in the same household at the time of death, or, if they were living apart, the widow or widower has to have been receiving benefits based on the earnings record of the deceased. Contact the local Social Security office to apply if you think you meet the requirements.

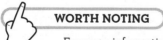 **WORTH NOTING**

For more information on survivors benefits, check out the government publication "Survivors Benefits," posted at ssa.gov/pubs/EN-05-10084.pdf.

How Are Disability Benefits Calculated?

How much you receive for disability will depend on a variety of factors. The first is whether your claim is being paid by Social Security Disability Insurance (SSDI) or Supplemental Security Income (SSI). Each program uses different methods to calculate benefits. For the purposes of this chapter, we focus on SSDI here. The SSI program is covered in Chapter 9.

Social Security Disability Insurance (SSDI)

Similar to the way retirement benefits are calculated, disability benefits are based on an average of your lifetime earnings up to the point when you became disabled. What it is not tied to is the severity of your disability. On the other hand, if you are receiving payments from other sources because of your disability—such as workers compensation—this will probably reduce the amount of your disability payment.

If you thought the retirement formula was complicated, the disability formula is even more complex! Just as in calculating retirement benefits, the SSA creates an AIME index, along with fixed percentages of different incomes they call "bend points," which are adjusted each year.

Instead of going into the formula, you can figure you'll receive somewhere between $300 and $2,600. The average payout for disability in 2014 was $1,148 a month. The maximum you could have received is $2,642 a month.

Meanwhile, when you start receiving monthly disability benefits, members of your family may also be eligible for benefits, including:

- Your spouse

- A divorced spouse

- Dependent children

- A disabled child

- An adult child disabled before age 22

Each family member may qualify for a monthly benefit equal to 50 percent of your disability amount. There's a limit, however, to the family's benefit depending on the number of family members who qualify. For 2014, the family maximum ranged from 150 percent to 180 percent of your disability benefit.

How Benefits Can Change

Just because you file for Social Security and begin receiving benefits doesn't mean your benefits can never change. In fact, what if something miraculous happens and you receive a windfall from an inheritance or win the lottery, or you decide to go back to work and begin earning enough so that you no longer need your monthly Social Security check?

If you're still under the age of 70, especially if you began getting benefits at 62 at the reduced rate, you can always withdraw your claim and reapply down the road when you have to take it, but it will be at a higher rate—possibly as much as double what you were getting.

There are a couple of stipulations you need to be aware of if you decide to withdraw your application:

- You will have to repay all the benefits you and your family have already received.

- You will have to repay any money withheld to pay for Medicare Part B, C, and D premiums.

If this is something you want to consider, you will need to file form SSA-521, which you can get online at ssa.gov/online/ssa-521.pdf. This is a request to withdraw your Social Security application. Once the SSA processes the form and you repay all your benefits, you can restart them whenever you want to.

Another way benefits can change is when you continue working and your latest year of earnings is one of your highest years. When that happens, SSA recalculates your benefit and increases your monthly payment. Although this is an automatic process, it still takes time for it to go through, typically a year. For example, if you get an increase based on your income in 2014, you wouldn't see that increase until December 2015, but it would be retroactive to January 2015.

Finally, your benefits will grow each year to keep up with inflation through something called COLA, which stands for Cost of Living Adjustment. For example, in 2015, about 64 million Americans will see a 1.7 percent increase in their monthly Social Security or Supplemental Security Income benefits.

Death of a Breadwinner

Another way your benefits can change is if your spouse dies and they were considered the principal breadwinner because they had earned more in their lifetime, which means their retirement benefit was larger.

If the deceased spouse had a higher benefit, the surviving spouse qualifies for an increase in benefits equal to what the deceased spouse was receiving. For example, let's say the surviving spouse was getting $1,000 a month, but the deceased spouse had received $2,000 a month. Now the surviving spouse will get $2,000, a $1,000-a-month increase. While that's still less than the $3,000 they received as a couple, it's much better than if the surviving spouse had been single and not qualified for any increase.

Difference in Benefits Depending on When You File

By now you realize that when you start receiving Social Security benefits will be a major factor in the size of your monthly benefit check. If you begin receiving payments at age 62, the earliest age you're allowed to collect benefits, it will be 25 percent less than if you had waited until you reached full retirement age and a whopping 76 percent less than if you had waited until age 70.

So let's begin in the section that follows with the earliest age you can retire. The SSA has a chart in one of its publications that shows how your benefit would differ depending on which age you began receiving benefits. To simplify things, it uses $1,000 as your monthly benefit at full retirement.

Benefits of Postponing Until Age 70

You can see in the following table even more clearly what a difference there is in the same benefit depending on the age at which it is initially claimed. Factor in that someone might live 20, 30, 40, or more years beyond that initial claim, and you can see the differences can add up.

Difference Age Makes in How Much You Will Receive

Age	Amount You Will Receive Monthly
62 (Earliest age to retire)	$750
63	$800
64	$866
65	$933
66 (Full retirement age)	$1,000
67	$1,080
68	$1,160
69	$1,240
70	$1,320

Earnings Caps for Those Taking Early Retirement

One thing to consider when taking early retirement benefits, if you plan to continue to work, is that there will be a cap on earnings. If you go over that cap, your retirement benefits will be reduced.

If you were born between January 2, 1943, and January 1, 1955, your full retirement age is 66. If you continue to work and are at full retirement age or older, there are no earnings caps. However, if you retire when younger than 66, the SSA will deduct $1 from your benefits for every $2 you earn (in 2014) above $15,480. (The cap changes each year, usually increasing by a small amount.)

If you reached full retirement age during 2014, during your 65th to 66th year, the income cap was raised to $41,400 and the reduction was lowered to $1 for every $3 you earn.

Another thing to keep in mind is that the way you earn your living is a factor in how these earnings caps are determined. For example, if you work for someone else, it's your wages that count toward the earnings cap. But if you work for yourself, the SSA only counts your net earnings from self-employment. They don't count any income you receive in other government benefits, any investment earnings, interest, pensions, annuities, or capital gains.

Also, when you're working for someone else, your income is calculated when it's earned, not when it's paid. That means if you have income such as sick or vacation pay or bonuses that are earned in one year but paid in the next, it's counted as earnings for the year it was earned, not the year it's paid.

However, if you're self-employed, all income counts when you receive it, and not necessarily when you earn it. The one exception is if you're paid in a year after you become entitled to Social Security and earned the money before you became eligible for those benefits.

The Least You Need to Know

- The SSA determines your benefits using a formula based on your total earnings as long as you meet the minimum of 40 work credits for 10 years of work. In any given year, you can have a maximum of four credits as long as you earn the minimum of $4,800 annually.

- There are minimums and maximums on the monthly benefits paid, based on whether you were a low or high earner, but the average monthly payment from Social Security is $1,294 for an individual.

- The maximum Social Security payment for a high-earning worker retiring at full retirement age is $2,642 a month. By delaying retirement to age 70, the maximum benefit could be as high as $3,425 a month.

- Benefits can change for a variety of reasons including the small annual increase calculated annually known as COLA (Cost of Living Adjustment).

- There's a significant difference of between several hundred and $2,000 or $3,000 in the payment you receive, depending on the age at which you begin receiving benefits. Those with low earning records who file as early as 62 may receive only $700 a month in benefits, an amount that will increase minimally each year due to COLA.

- There are earnings caps if you begin receiving retirement benefits before reaching full retirement age and you continue to work. In 2015 the earnings cap is $15,720, although it increases to $41,880 during the year you reach full retirement age.

PART 2

Filing for Social Security

Here's where we get to the nuts and bolts of the process. In this part, you'll learn how to determine your benefits as well as how to access and understand your Social Security statement. We'll also show you how to use Social Security calculators that estimate life expectancy and the amount of retirement benefits you might need to live on.

You'll learn the importance of checking your earnings record for any errors or omissions that could impact your retirement or disability benefits, and how to contact the Social Security Administration if you find errors.

Next we'll deal with one of the most important questions involving Social Security, when to file. There's no one best answer for everyone, but we'll give you the information to figure out what's best for you. In that regard, we'll go into detail about the pros and cons of taking benefits early, at full retirement age, or at age 70.

Record Keeping

There's a good reason most people believe the Social Security benefits they receive is *their* money. After all, if they worked, they paid Social Security taxes every year. Why shouldn't they think of it as their money?

Well, the government and the Social Security Administration (SSA) see things differently. What they do, however, is allow you to earn credits toward your Social Security benefits when you pay your income taxes. The number of credits you need to receive retirement benefits depends on the year you were born.

In This Chapter

- Accessing your earnings statement
- How the SSA calculates your benefits
- Reading your statement and correcting any errors
- Contacting the SSA if you find a discrepancy on your statement

Determining Your Earnings

If you were born in 1929 or later, you'll need 40 credits, which amounts to 10 years of work. (You earn a maximum of four credits per year.) For those who, for whatever reason, stopped working before the 10 years is up, those credits will stay on your Social Security record forever.

If you go back to work, you can always add more credits and hopefully reach the 40 you need to qualify. In fact, if you fail to reach that number, you will not receive Social Security retirement benefits, so it behooves you to work at least until you have achieved those 40 credits.

Setting Up Your Social Security Account

How do you find out if you qualify to collect Social Security? You have to look at your Social Security statement. To do that, you may have to set up an account online.

WORTH NOTING

Go to ssa.gov to create your personal Social Security account to help keep track of your earnings, estimate future benefits, or get a letter with proof of benefits if you're already receiving them.

The SSA has been mailing out statements to those who are eligible for Social Security and are age 60 or older. That may soon cease, however, as all of this information has been migrated online. That means in the future, most of us will have to create an account with the SSA in order to obtain access to our statements online. We suggest you create an account for yourself now.

To do this, go to ssa.gov. Click on the "my Social Security" link, which will enable you to create a new account or to sign in if you already have one.

There are four things you need in order to create your Social Security account:

1. A valid email address

2. Your Social Security number

3. A U.S. mailing address

4. To be at least 18 years old

Once you create your account and access your statement, you'll find page one contains your name and address, along with a brief message about what Social Security means to you. You'll immediately want to go to page 2 where the most important information begins. This is where you'll find out how much you'll get if you continue working until you reach your full retirement age, either 66 or 67 depending on what year you were born. You can also keep tabs on how much you'll earn by looking at this page.

Keeping Tabs on Your Earnings

Page 2 shows the breakdown of your benefits so you can better understand what you'll be receiving. First, you'll see what you'll receive each month at full retirement age. Next, you'll see what you would receive at age 70, and finally what you would get if you took early retirement at age 62. The next section deals with disability and how much you would receive if you became disabled.

After disability, you will find information pertaining to family benefits if you were to die. For example, there's a line for any children under 18 and how much they would receive, followed by your spouse who is caring for your child and what he or she would receive, and then what your spouse would receive after reaching full retirement age. The last line in this section is the maximum benefit your family could receive each month.

There's even a paragraph stating whether you have enough credits to qualify for Medicare at age 65. You should contact the SSA three months before your 65th birthday to enroll in Medicare even if you don't plan to retire until later.

You'll also see an interesting statement in bold punctuated with an asterisk (*). It states that your estimated benefits are based on current law, but that Congress can change the law any time it wants. Expect the current law covering benefits to change because, as noted previously, by 2033 the payroll taxes collected are expected to only be enough to pay for about 75 percent of everyone's scheduled benefits.

The next section of your statement explains how your benefits are estimated.

 WORTH NOTING

SSA discontinued paper statements in 2011 in an effort to save money on printing and postage. In September 2014, it announced it would resume sending out paper statements every five years to workers age 18 and over who are not receiving Social Security benefits and who have not registered for an online "my Social Security" account within three months of their birthday. Workers will receive an annual statement after age 60.

Online Social Security Calculators

This section repeats the information about your work credits, but then goes into detail about how much you need to earn for each credit. In 2014, you earned one credit for each $1,160 of wages or self-employment income. After the SSA has looked at your records and determined that you have earned the required number of credits to qualify for benefits, it begins estimating your monthly benefits based on your average annual earnings over your lifetime.

Because these are estimates, they tend to be more accurate as you get closer to retirement age. Still, it's up to you to double-check their accuracy. You can use the SSA's retirement calculator by going to socialsecurity.gov/estimator.

But you still won't be able to get your actual benefit amount until you apply for benefits. Even then, your benefits package could be impacted by a number of other issues, such as where you worked. If you were in the military, worked for the railroad, or receive government pensions from state or federal employment, what you will receive could be impacted.

The Windfall Elimination Provision

Next you'll see information on the Windfall Elimination Provision (WEP). Some of you either will be or already are receiving a pension from a job where you did not pay any Social Security taxes. These include jobs working for a state or local government, or for the federal government, as well as some nonprofit organizations and foreign jobs.

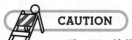

CAUTION

The Windfall Elimination Provision (WEP) reduces your Social Security benefits if you worked for an organization that did not withhold Social Security taxes.

In those cases, your benefits may be reduced by an amount dependent upon your earnings and the number of years you worked in jobs where you did pay Social Security taxes.

For example, Jane C. Owen, PhD, retired as a professor at Midwestern State University in Wichita Falls, Texas. She started taking her Social Security benefits at the age of 66. Her benefits were cut by almost 50 percent because she retired from a state position and it fell under the WEP. But she's still pleased with this extra monthly deposit to her checking account, which makes a nice addition to her pension and savings.

There are some exemptions to WEP, including the following:

- If you are a federal employee hired after December 31, 1983

- If you worked for a nonprofit organization on December 31, 1983, that did not withhold Social Security taxes at first but then began doing so

- If your only pension is based on working for the railroad

- If the only work you did that did not collect Social Security taxes was before 1957

- If you have 30+ years of substantial earnings under Social Security

- If you are receiving survivor benefits

Government Pension Offset (GPO)

Then there's the *Government Pension Offset (GPO)*. If you get a pension from the federal, state, or local government where you did not pay Social Security taxes and you qualify for Social Security benefits as a current or former spouse or a widow or widower, you will probably be impacted by GPO. GPO means your Social Security benefits will be reduced by two thirds of your government pension. Please keep in mind that depending on how much your monthly pension amounts to, your Social Security could be eliminated entirely.

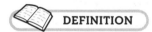 **DEFINITION**

> The **Government Pension Offset,** or **GPO,** is a law that affects spouses, widows, or widowers who receive a pension from a federal, state, or local government but didn't pay Social Security taxes. Those who fall into that category could see their Social Security benefits reduced by two thirds of their government pensions.

For example, if you receive a monthly pension of $600, two thirds, or $400, would be deducted from your Social Security benefits. Let's say you would receive a $1,000 for a widow's benefit from Social Security. If you received a government pension, you'll only receive $600 a month from Social Security.

Ensuring Your Earnings Record Is Accurate

Would you believe the government occasionally makes mistakes? Of course it does, and this is true for the SSA. Mistakes are made every day. So when it comes to your earnings record, it's up to you, your employer, and the SSA to ensure its accuracy.

The day you started working was the day the SSA began keeping records of everything you earned, or at least the reported earnings under your name and your Social Security number. New information is added annually because they update your record every time you and your employer report your earnings.

You need to look at your earnings record and make sure everything is correct. Keep in mind that some of the previous year's earnings may not yet show on your statement because the SSA is still processing that year's earnings.

How to Correct Errors

If you see any discrepancy in your earnings statement, call the SSA immediately. The number is 1-800-772-1213 and their hours of operation are between 7 A.M. and 7 P.M., Monday through Friday, local time. Remember they receive numerous inquiries, so you might have to wait to speak to someone. If possible, try to call early in the morning or later in the afternoon.

If you find an error, make sure you have your W-2 or your tax return for those years in question that confirms your claim that you had higher earnings than what your statement shows.

If you prefer to speak to someone in person about this, call your local SSA office and make an appointment. Or go to the office, and be prepared to wait an hour or two until someone is able to meet with you. Make sure you bring all the necessary documentation with you to substantiate your belief that you had higher earnings than what the statement reports.

The Least You Need to Know

- You should create an online account at "my Social Security" on ssa.gov so you can view your Social Security statement regularly to check its accuracy.
- Ensuring your earnings record is accurate is your responsibility. Take the time to go through the earnings record in your Social Security account with the information you have been compiling over the years.
- If you find a discrepancy between your official earnings record and your own calculations, assemble your W-2 earnings statements, W-9 forms, and tax returns before you call or visit your local Social Security office to dispute your earnings record.
- The Windfall Elimination Provision (WEP) and Government Pension Offset (GPO) can change the amount of benefits you earn.

When to File

When it comes to Social Security, only you can determine the best time to start receiving benefits. It is not a decision you should take lightly because it will affect your financial future. If you're not sure, ask a professional.

You could ask the Social Security Administration, but all they'll say is there is no "best time" for everyone because everyone's situation is different.

As Seth Deitchman, Financial Advisor/Portfolio Manager at The Mercury Group at Morgan Stanley in Atlanta notes, "Some great advice I would give someone or a couple looking to begin taking Social Security is to run all possible scenarios and really understand all of the benefits.

"We will go through all scenarios with our clients and discuss the client's life expectancy and health issues that may help make a decision," he adds. "Also, we will go with a client to the Social Security office to act upon their plan, that is if they are not confident enough to recite exactly what they need. The SS representative may not know the individual or couple's personal situation and handholding makes a lot of sense."

In This Chapter

- How to determine the best time to file for Social Security
- Wage caps you will face if you take early retirement
- How to apply for Social Security benefits
- Strategies to help maximize your benefits
- Eligibility requirements for disability benefits at age 65

The Minimum Age You Can Apply

You become eligible for early retirement at age 62, but should you take it at that age? The answer is "it depends." If you think you're not likely to live long enough to make it monetarily beneficial to wait, or if you're not working so the income cap is not an issue, then the answer might be yes. There are life expectancy/benefit calculators that will let you know at what age the break-even point is.

What that means is, how long do you have to live to make it more economically beneficial to delay the start of your benefits until full retirement age? (As you know by now from reading previous chapters, full retirement age [FRA] is the age, based on the year you were born, when you can get 100 percent of your benefits without the reduction caused by taking benefits early. Your FRA will be between 66 and 67, depending upon the year you were born.) Currently, that break-even age seems to be around 78. So if you think you're going to live beyond 78, you may want to postpone drawing benefits. If you don't think you'll live that long, you might be better off collecting your benefits as soon as possible.

Another reason to take your benefits early is if you're desperate and you really need the money. You may have lost your job, or you or your spouse might have medical expenses that need to be addressed. You can always suspend benefits later if the situation changes, and reapply again when things have improved and you've added more to your total earnings accumulation upon which the benefit will be based.

Wage Caps on Early Retirement

If you continue working after you take early retirement benefits beginning at age 62, and before reaching your full retirement age of 66 or 67, there are caps on how much you can earn. If you earn more than those caps, your benefits will be reduced until you reach your full retirement age. These wage caps will change year after year. As we mentioned earlier, in 2014, if you were younger than the full retirement age, the SSA would deduct $1 for every $2 you earned above the cap of $15,480. However, if you were going to reach full retirement age during 2014, the SSA would only deduct $1 for every $3 earned over $41,400.

The Benefits of Waiting Until Full Retirement Age

If you plan to continue to work or if your health history indicates you have a long life ahead of you, it may be wiser to postpone receiving payments until you reach *full retirement age (FRA)* or even later. At full retirement age, you can continue working with no earnings cap. If what you earn continues to be among your highest earnings years, the SSA will reconfigure your benefits and you will receive any increase in your monthly benefits the following year.

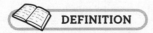 **DEFINITION**

Full retirement age (FRA) is the age, based on the year you were born, the SSA has determined you will receive 100 percent of your Social Security benefits.

How do you know if you will live to 78, 88, 98, or older? You can look at your family history as a possible indicator. How long did your mother and your father live? What's the current status of your health? Do you have any chronic life-threatening diseases that might shorten your life expectancy? Do you have a terminal disease? Or do you feel you're healthy enough that even 70 seems too young to retire? In that case, you may want to delay receiving benefits until your full retirement age of 66 or 67, or even until age 70.

The Benefits of Postponing Benefits Until Age 70

The simple reality is this: the longer you can postpone taking your retirement benefits, the larger each month's check will be. So if you can hold off until age 70, your monthly benefit will be 32 percent more than it would have been if you started benefits at the full retirement age of 66, and 24 percent higher if it is 67. In either case, that's a pretty decent raise in your monthly income. Put another way, if you wait until age 70 to start collecting, you may get a benefit that is 132 percent higher than if you started at age 62.

Financial advisors recommend holding off taking retirement benefits in a low-interest-rate environment because the 8 percent per year increase in Social Security benefits is better than the interest you would receive from U.S. Treasury bonds or some other low-risk fixed-income investment.

Sixty-seven-year-old Bob is an excellent example of someone who is postponing Social Security benefits until he turns 70. He's currently still working at his full-time educational job, which he plans to continue for at least another year or two. He will receive a generous pension from his $80,000-a-year job that he has held for more than 20 years, at that point, but he still looks forward to getting his Social Security benefits to use for travel and other expenses. It will also mean that when he dies, his wife's monthly survivors benefits will be higher because he waited till 70 to start his Social Security benefits.

Your Life Expectancy Factor

It's a fact: we're living longer today than we did in the past. That's the good news. According to the U.S. Census Bureau, the fastest-growing segment of the population is the over-90 crowd. The bad news is you could end up living as long in retirement as you did during your prime working years, with your income severely reduced. Life expectancy is one of the key factors that should determine when it would be best for you to begin taking your Social Security benefits. That is, as long as you don't have a grave financial crisis that causes you to take it as soon as you possibly can.

Life Expectancy Calculator

None of us know exactly how long we have to live, unless we are suffering from a terminal illness and our doctors have given us a life expectancy range. But there are calculators that use actuarial tables and can give us an average number of years we can expect to live.

You can find one of these calculators at the Social Security website. It's based only on gender and date of birth, but it's something to work with. For example, a male who is now age 67 and 10 months has an average life expectancy of 84.9 years. A female who is now 65 and 8 months has a life expectancy of 86.7 years.

 TIP

Just enter your gender and date of birth at socialsecurity.gov/oact/population/ longevity.html and you can find your average life expectancy. Of course, diseases, accidents, and just natural individual differences can alter this number by decades.

Retirement Estimator

If you want to know how much your Social Security benefits are going to be, the SSA website has a retirement estimator that will give you an estimation based on your earnings record at socialsecurity.gov/estimator.

The accuracy of this estimation will depend on how close you are in age to filing for Social Security, because each year you continue to work, your benefits are reconfigured depending on whether your earnings increase or decrease going forward. Other factors are the annual cost of living increase and whether the laws governing Social Security change.

You can use the retirement estimator if you ...

- Have the 40 Social Security credits needed to qualify for benefits.

- Are not currently receiving benefits.

- Are not waiting for a decision about your application for benefits or Medicare.

- Are not eligible for a pension based on work not covered by Social Security.

Too many Americans have saved nothing or very little for retirement, which means they'll be depending solely on Social Security, or, if they're lucky, pensions to help pay for the rest of their lives. But here's the wrinkle. Even the SSA is warning that those dollars may not be there at their current levels in fewer than 20 years. We'll have more in later chapters about what you can do to deal with this impending crisis.

Family Considerations

Whatever decision you make about when to start receiving your Social Security benefits doesn't just affect you. It could impact your entire family. Keep in mind that your spouse may be eligible to receive benefits based on what you receive. That's especially true if you die first. When your spouse reaches full retirement age, he or she will be eligible to receive the same amount you did. If that was a reduced amount because you took early retirement, that's what your spouse will get as well. And for couples who still have children living at home, the rules for when to apply may change a bit.

When Can a Spouse File?

Let's look at the spouses. As a spouse, at age 62 you can file and receive a benefit based on your own earnings, or use the spousal benefit and receive an amount based on your spouse's earnings. To do this, your spouse had to file. Let's say he did, and that he filed when he reached his full retirement age. You can now get 50 percent of his benefit, which could still be greater than yours.

The benefit for a survivor is even better. For example, a widow or widower can receive 100 percent of their spouse's benefit at full retirement age. But they could also begin collecting at 60 at a reduced benefit.

Couples have a number of strategies available to them to maximize their Social Security benefits. But just keep in mind, they only work under specific circumstances and often depend on the age and earnings difference between the spouses.

The Impact of a Spouse Reaching Full Retirement Age

The first strategy is sometimes referred to as the "62/70" split. In this scenario, the spouse who earns the least takes Social Security as soon as they can at age 62. The higher-earning spouse puts off filing until the age of 70, thus maximizing their benefit. Then, when the lower earner reaches full retirement age, they reapply for spousal benefits and receive half of what the other spouse is getting, which would be half the maximum.

File and Suspend Strategy

Another strategy has the lower earner taking benefits at 62, while the higher earner files at full retirement age, and then suspends the benefits. This allows the lower-earning spouse to collect the spousal benefit earlier based on the higher earner's record. This is called the "file and suspend" strategy, and is discussed in more detail in Chapter 8.

Survivor's Strategy

There's a third strategy for survivors. Let's say you have to deal with the sad reality that your spouse dies. You can begin collecting survivors benefits as early as 60 years old. At the same time, you can put off receiving your own retirement benefits until you turn 70. That way you'll be receiving your survivors benefit while your own retirement benefit continues to grow. If you take it at age 70, it will be 32 percent higher than if you took it at your full retirement age.

These strategies work only if the ages and earnings numbers work. Since every situation is unique, and these are just general strategies to be aware of, you should definitely consider consulting with a financial advisor or at least your accountant before trying them out.

Filing for Spousal Benefits If You're Divorced

You can also file for Social Security spousal benefits beginning at age 62 if you are divorced but your marriage lasted at least 10 years and you remain unmarried. (Or you can wait until full retirement age to file for spousal benefits so the benefits will not be reduced.) The benefits will be based on your spouse's earnings record, and the same rules used to calculate spousal benefits will be used here. For example, if you receive the benefits at age 62, the amount will be 75 percent of what you would have received at full retirement age. Also, if you wait until your full retirement age, you can receive benefits based on your spouse's benefits and delay receiving your own retirement benefits until age 70, at which time they will be 32 percent higher.

Children's Benefits

You can apply for Social Security benefits for a child if you are retired or disabled and they are:

- Under the age of 18, or 19 if they're still in high school
- Unmarried
- Older than 18 but disabled, with the disability starting before the age of 22

When you do apply, this is what you'll need:

- The child's birth certificate
- You and your child's Social Security numbers

If you're applying for survivors benefits for the child, you'll need proof of your spouse's death. If you're applying for benefits for a disabled child, you'll need the medical evidence proving the disability.

How to Apply for Social Security

Now that you've made the decision about when to apply for Social Security benefits, you're ready to take the big step and actually apply.

The easiest and fastest way to apply, as long as you have already done your homework and do not have any questions you need answered, is to do it online at ssa.gov. If you already have created your own online account at the Social Security website, you can apply directly through your account.

You could also set up an appointment with a representative at a local SSA office if you wish to apply in person. Alternatively, you could apply over the phone.

What to Expect in the Online Application

For efficiency, you may want to use the online application method. But please note, as you read through the following sample application, that you will be asked at one point if you agree with your Social Security statement earnings history.

This is very important! If you have not yet located and reviewed your Social Security statement, do so before you go online to apply. You want to check over that statement and take care of any inaccuracies that need to be adjusted before applying.

If you are approved for benefits, you will be told that your monthly benefits are directly tied to the formula the SSA will apply to your earnings history. Make sure your history is accurate or you may unwittingly reduce the size of your monthly benefit payment.

You also will be asked to include direct deposit information right in your initial application. If you do not yet have a checking account that enables you to make direct deposits, or you have a checking account but you are unsure of the information you need for making a direct deposit, find it out before applying. (You will need your account number and the routing number for the bank.)

You will be asked the following information in your online application:

Applicant name

Social Security number

Gender

Date of birth

Contact information

Mailing address

Phone and email

Language preferences

Birth and citizenship information

Place of birth

U.S. citizen? (yes/no)

Type of U.S. citizenship

Other Social Security numbers and names

Other names

Disability

During the last 14 months, were you unable to work because of illnesses, injuries, or conditions that have lasted or are expected to last at least 12 months or can be expected to result in death? (yes/no)

Blind? (yes/no)

Marriage information

Currently married? (yes/no)

Spouse's name

Spouse's Social Security number

Spouse's date of birth

Marriage date

Place of marriage

Marriage type, such as valid ceremonial, common law, etc.

Prior marriages

Children

Any children who became disabled prior to age 22? (yes/no)

Any unmarried children under age 18? (yes/no)

Any unmarried children age 18 to 19 still attending elementary or secondary level (below college level) full time? (yes/no)

Military details

Military service prior to 1968

Employment details

Worked or will work for an employer in (current year)

First employer's name

First employer's address

First employer—Date employment began

First employer—Date employment ended

Self-employment details

Supplemental information

Worked outside the U.S.

Spouse worked outside the U.S.

Agree with earnings history as shown on Social Security statement? (yes/no)

A corporate officer of employer? (yes/no)

Related to a corporate officer of employer? (yes/no)

Receive earnings from a family corporation or other closely held corporation? (yes/no)

Permission granted to contact employer(s) if necessary? (yes/no)

Total earnings

Total of all wages and tips including net income from self-employment (in current year)

Earned wages, tips, and net income from self-employment (amount) or performed substantial services in self-employment in all months of (current year)

Months of (current year) when earnings were less than ($1,220 or current year's amount)

Total earnings (include any special payments paid in one year but earned in another)

Other pensions/annuities

Ever worked in a job where Social Security taxes were not deducted or withheld? (yes/no)

Spouse worked for the railroad for 5 years or more? (yes/no)

General

When to start retirement benefits

Benefits should start in (date)

The specific reason this start date was selected

Direct deposit details

Account type

Routing number

Account number

Other benefits information

Any previous application(s) for Medicare, Social Security, or Supplemental Security Income Benefits (yes/no)

Remarks:

Electronic signature & submission for (your name)

The Next Step—Awaiting the Decision

When you fill out your retirement benefit application, you will get a confirmation number. You will be advised to guard this number carefully. This is the number you will need when you want to check on the status of your application.

You will be advised that you can check on the status of your application after five business days. At that time, go to socialsecurity.gov and select "Check the Status of Your Application." You will be asked to enter your confirmation number (the one we just advised you to safeguard).

Once you receive the decision and you are satisfied with their decision, you don't have anything else to do except begin receiving your payments. The decision will state whether you have been approved to start receiving benefits; if yes, how much it will be; and the date and day of the month to receive your benefits.

What If Your Application Is Denied or You Disagree?

If your claim has been denied or you disagree with the amount the SSA has stated you will receive, you will have 60 days to appeal the decision. The 60 days begins the day you are notified of the decision, whether that's online or through a letter.

You have to ask for an appeal in writing. You will be asked to sign a Form SSA-561-U2, called "Request for Reconsideration." If you need help, contact an SSA office. You might also want to contact a lawyer or a benefits expert for help. There also are advisors who will not charge unless you win your appeal. If you do plan to hire someone to help with your appeal, SSA asks you to let them know because they have to approve the fee before the advisor can collect it.

Qualifying at Age 65 Under Disability

There are quite a few of you who are over the age of 65 but have no plans to retire, either because you're financially strapped and can't afford to, or you simply love the work you do and never want to stop. But then life intervenes and you become disabled or somehow physically or mentally impaired to the degree that you can no longer continue working. In other words, you've been forced into retirement through no fault of your own.

Recognizing that, the SSA created a program to help you receive *disability* benefits that will be converted to retirement benefits once you reach full retirement age.

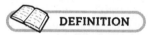 **DEFINITION**

> A **disability** is a physical or mental condition that prevents you from doing any kind of work and will last for at least one year or will lead to your death.

Eligibility Requirements for Disability over 65

Basically, there are two ways for you to qualify for Social Security disability benefits if you're over 65:

- You must meet or equal a disability found in Social Security's "Blue Book" list of impairments. Even though today most people access this information online, the list is still referred to as the "Blue Book," because the cover of the printed version was blue.

- You can receive a Medical-Vocational allowance based on your limitations, age, level of education, and work history.

Since you're over 65, Social Security gives you some slack in determining whether you meet or equal one of these listings. For example, since you would be less than one year away from qualifying for full retirement under Social Security, you no longer have to be disabled for at least 12 months to be eligible for disability. Moreover, examiners or judges are not allowed to dismiss age-related impairments such as arthritis or vision, hearing, or memory loss that are not included in the Blue Book listings.

Also, if you're over 65 and fail to meet or equal a listing in the Blue Book, but are still unable to work, Social Security will examine how your diminished capacity could affect the workplace.

Social Security's Blue Book of Impairments

The list of physical and mental impairments considered serious enough to qualify you for disability payments includes such conditions as:

- Musculoskeletal problems, including back injuries
- Cardiovascular conditions such as coronary disease
- Vision and hearing loss
- Respiratory illnesses such as asthma
- Mental disorders such as depression, anxiety, and schizophrenia
- Neurological disorders such as multiple sclerosis
- Digestive tract illnesses such as liver disease or Inflammatory Bowel Disease (IBD)
- Cancer
- Kidney disease
- Immune disorders such as HIV/AIDs and lupus

 TIP

The Blue Book has an extensive list of mental impairments that include schizophrenia, retardation, anxiety-related disorders, depression, bipolar disorder, substance addiction, and autism.

If you have a condition such as rheumatoid arthritis that is not on the Blue Book list, you can still apply for disability. You just have to show that this condition is so severe it prevents you from performing those functions required for work.

Medical-Vocational Allowance

Let's say you don't meet the equal of a listing requirement. Does that mean disability is out of the question? Not necessarily. You could still qualify if you receive what's called a Medical-Vocational Allowance.

Here's how that works. Social Security has created grids or profiles that take a number of factors into account to determine whether you're disabled and unable to do any job. If you're over 65, there are two categories that will qualify you for disability benefits. These are:

- If you have no work experience, an eleventh-grade education or less, and haven't worked in the past 15 years.

- If you were an unskilled but strenuous physical laborer for at least 35 years, with a sixth-grade education or less, and with no other training.

If you don't qualify under either of these categories, you'll be put into the grid for those 60 years of age and up and will be eligible for a Medical-Vocational Allowance if you meet the following criteria:

- You have a *residual functional capacity (RFC)* for sedentary or light work that requires no heavy lifting and for which you sit most of the day.

- You haven't finished high school, or if you finished high school, it was so long ago that you are unable to do skilled work, or you lack any transferrable skills such as typing.

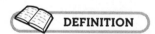 **DEFINITION**

> A **residual functional capacity** is the most you can still do because of your limitations. The SSA will assess your residual functional capacity based on all the relevant information in your case record.

On the other hand, if you have an RFC for medium-level work, which requires some level of lifting, standing, or walking most of the day, you will be found disabled if you:

- Have no prior work experience or any transferrable skills.

- Have an eleventh-grade education or less, no other significant training, or are illiterate or unable to communicate in English.

These qualifications are generalizations and are by no means the only ways you can qualify for disability under the Medical-Vocational Allowance rules.

In fact, if you're suffering from a mental illness that isn't on the Blue Book list but prevents you from doing your job, you can still apply for disability. In this situation, the examiner will look at your residual functional capacity to determine whether you understand how to carry out specific tasks, remember instructions, and interact effectively with other employees; are able to concentrate or focus on the task at hand; or have the ability to reason and no impaired judgment.

Another way around the grid is to show how you're unable to even perform sedentary work due to what are called "exertional" and "nonexertional" limitations. Under the exertional limitations, the Social Security Administration includes the following:

- Unable to lift 10 pounds
- Unable to stand or walk for more than two hours a day
- Using medically required handheld devices to walk (such as walkers, crutches and canes)
- The need to keep one leg elevated
- Unable to use an arm due to amputation above the elbow
- Unable to sit for six hours out of an eight-hour workday

As for nonexertional limitations, the following would apply:

- Need to alternate sitting and standing throughout the day
- Need to rest or lie down during the workday
- Unable to stoop or bend
- Reduced use of hands and fingers
- Need to take frequent sick days
- Unable to balance even on level surfaces
- Visual limitations
- Unable to work in noisy environments

In each of the previous situations, the vocational expert who examines your claim will determine if your limits would truly prevent you from doing any type of sedentary job. Because these decisions are so subjective, it's advisable to seek out a disability attorney to help you navigate what can be an extremely complex and complicated process. To find an attorney in your area, the Social Security website has a disability attorney locator.

TIP

There are two easy ways to find a lawyer who specializes in Social Security and disability benefits. The government's Social Security website (socialsecurity.gov) has an attorney directory, as does nolo.com, an online network of legal information sites.

The "Worn-Out Worker" Rule

Some people qualify for a little-known provision in Social Security's vast ocean of regulations called the "Worn-Out Worker" rule. This rule doesn't mean that if you're simply tired of working, you can apply for assistance. In fact, this rule has some fairly strict requirements. Here are a few:

- You have to have a marginal education, meaning you dropped out of school before starting the seventh grade.

- You worked at least 35 years performing unskilled hard labor, such as working in a mine or on a farm, or building roads and bridges.

- You're not able to perform hard labor due to physical or mental impairments that are expected to last more than one year.

Qualifying for disability under the Worn-Out Worker rule isn't easy. If you do apply to use this regulation, go to a disability lawyer for help. Too many claims examiners are not familiar with the rule and make mistakes in their determinations because they didn't think the type of work the applicant performed was strenuous enough or unskilled enough to be eligible. To prevent something like that from occurring you need to be prepared going in, and a disability attorney would be able to provide the help you need.

CAUTION

You have a better chance of winning a claim through appeal than filing a new application. You can find forms for a Request for Reconsideration and the Disability Report-Appeals at secure.ssa.gov/apps6z/iAppeals/ap001.jsp.

If your claim is denied, you can still appeal and even win if you can show how the grid rules shouldn't apply to you. Let's say you were denied because the SSA determined you have transferrable skills. If you're able to show you have certain problems such as tremors, poor posture, or even memory problems due to age that prevent you from using those transferrable skills, you can file an appeal and possibly win. Just make sure you file for appeal within 60 days of your claim being denied. Otherwise you have to reapply and begin the process all over again.

The Least You Need to Know

- The best time to file for Social Security is different for each individual or couple. Some key considerations are whether you intend to keep working, your health, your life expectancy, and whether you need the benefits now or you can wait as many as eight years, from age 62 to 70.

- If you're married or divorced and still unmarried you can apply for spousal benefits based on your spouse or ex-spouse's full retirement age (FRA) benefit.

- There are special requirements for claiming disability at age 65.

- The Social Security's Blue Book of impairments lists medical conditions that qualify as disabilities, such as musculoskeletal problems; cardiovascular conditions; vision and hearing loss; respiratory illnesses; mental disorders; cancer; and kidney disease.

Filing for Benefits Before Reaching Full Retirement Age

What is the number one question people ask about Social Security? "When should I take my Social Security?" says Angela S. Deppe, CPA, who runs Social Security Central (socialsecuritycentral.com), a website that offers educational tools including a simple benefit maximization calculator. "It's a personal decision that should be based on multiple variables including your marital status, longevity, benefit amount, necessity of income, desire to continue working, and taxes. It's especially important for married couples to make their decision jointly as your individual decision can impact your spouse long after you're gone."

Because deciding when to start taking Social Security benefits is one of the most important financial judgments you'll ever make, we're going to devote two entire chapters to this single decision. In this chapter, we'll discuss the pros and cons of taking benefits early. We'll provide you with information that will help you decide whether you *should* start taking your Social Security benefits early, at any age from 62 until you reach your full retirement age (FRA). In Chapter 8, we'll probe the pluses and minuses of starting your Social Security benefits at your FRA or even as late as age 70, when monthly benefits reach their maximum amount.

In This Chapter

- Consequences of taking benefits before your full retirement age
- When taking early retirement is a good idea
- Break-even age points for receiving benefits early
- The impact on your spouse and dependents if you receive benefits early

Making the Decision

No matter what your FRA, you can start collecting Social Security benefits as early as age 62, at least for now. This may change if Congress decides to vote on a number of proposals that would increase the minimum retirement age beyond 62. But until that happens, the starting age at which you can file to begin receiving benefits is 62.

But should you take your benefits that early? One thing we can't do is make that decision for you. We also aren't advocating taking Social Security retirement benefits early, starting them at your full retirement age, or waiting until age 70. This is a very personal decision based on many factors, and one only you should make.

However, we can provide you with examples of what others have done, either on their own or with advice from a financial advisor. Some took Social Security early, and you'll see how it worked out for them. You'll learn how some of those who were married used strategies to maximize those early benefits by switching to spousal benefits when they reached full retirement age. You'll also see how, if you're divorced after being married for 10 years and have not yet remarried, you can receive spousal benefits from your ex-spouse, even if his or her current spouse is also receiving spousal benefits.

What Is Your Full Retirement Age?

One of the first factors you should be aware of in making this decision is your full retirement age. Your FRA varies from age 65 to 67, depending upon the year you were born. If you're unsure what your FRA is, the following table can help you figure it out.

Age When You Can Receive Full Social Security Benefits

Year of Birth*	Full Retirement Age (FRA)
1937 or earlier	65
1938	65 and 2 months
1939	65 and 4 months
1940	65 and 6 months
1941	65 and 8 months
1942	65 and 10 months
1943-1954	66
1955	66 and 2 months

Year of Birth*	Full Retirement Age (FRA)
1956	66 and 4 months
1957	66 and 6 months
1958	66 and 8 months
1959	66 and 10 months
1960 and later	67

The Social Security Administration (SSA) notes that anyone born on January 1st of any year should use the previous year to find their FRA. Also, for anyone born on the 1st of the month, the SSA computes your FRA as if your birthday occurred during the previous month.

There are numerous variables to consider when making the decision about whether to begin getting your Social Security retirement benefits as early as age 62.

How common is it for men and women to start their Social Security benefits at age 62? As Brian O'Connell points out in his September 23, 2014, article at Mainstreet.com, "Why 80 percent of women take Social Security too early," "… more than half of Americans start collecting Social Security at 62—and four out of five women."

Pros and Cons of Taking Benefits Early

Perhaps the most important negative variable you need to consider is that you'll have a reduction in the monthly benefit you receive. This reduction will be calculated on what you would have received at your full retirement age, and will be lowered a certain percentage for every year prior to your full retirement age you began receiving benefits. For example, according to the SSA, if your full retirement age is 66 and you start your benefits at age 62, they will only be reduced by 25 percent. At age 63, the reduction is about 20 percent; age 64, 13.3 percent; and at age 65, it is around 6.7 percent.

At full retirement age your Social Security benefit would be 100 percent of its value based on your individual cumulative earnings, which were derived using the complicated Social Security formula described earlier in this book. (See "The Formula for Calculating Retirement Benefits" in Chapter 4.)

Let's say you would be eligible for a $1,000 per month benefit if you wait to start collecting at your FRA of 66. But for a number of reasons, most of all that you are not working and need money to pay off debts, you decide to take your retirement benefits at age 62.

By beginning your benefits at 62, your monthly check will be reduced by 25 percent so you will receive only $750.

Unless you're married and can switch over to spousal benefits when you reach your FRA, that reduced rate could continue for the rest of your life.

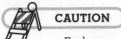

CAUTION

Each year you delay between 62 and your full retirement age, the amount of your monthly benefit increases until it reaches 100 percent at your FRA. Stated another way, the closer you are to your FRA when you begin collecting your Social Security retirement benefits, the smaller the reduction from the 100 percent of the amount at your FRA.

The following table shows you how your benefits will be decreased, based on the age before your FRA you begin taking Social Security.

Benefit Reduction if Your FRA Is 67, Based on the Age You Actually Start Benefits

If you start benefits at age ...	The percentage of reduction is ...
62	–30%
63	–25%
64	–20%
65	–13.3%
66	–6.7%

Since you've been contributing to Social Security your entire working life, reclaiming this money as soon as possible is extremely tempting, especially if you're not working and your previous work history gives you enough credits to start receiving Social Security retirement benefits.

But before you file early, carefully consider whether this is the best financial decision for you at this point in your life, especially if you're the higher earner of a married couple. You must take into account several key factors:

- Your health
- Whether you're working
- If you plan to continue working
- Whether you plan on returning to work
- Your estimated life expectancy

Don't go by what your neighbor or your Uncle Ned did, or is doing. Their situations may not have any resemblance to yours. Everyone is unique. Even married couples have different decisions to make about when to begin benefits. These could be based on which partner is the higher earner, the age difference between spouses, income differences, and expected life spans.

The following table shows the financial impact of taking Social Security benefits at age 62 on a typical $1,000 per month benefit. It shows the impact on you as well as on your spouse, if he or she is getting a spousal benefit, of taking your benefits at 62 based on the year you were born, your full retirement age, and the months between age 62 and your FRA.

Full Retirement and Age 62 Benefit by Year of Birth*

Year of birth	Full (normal retirement age	Months between age 62 and full retirement age	A $1000 retirement benefit would be reduced to ...	The retirement benefit is reduced by ...	A $500 spouse's benefit would be reduced to ...	The spouse's benefit is reduced by ...
			At Age 62			
1937 or earlier	65	36	$800	20.00%	$375	25.00%
1938	65 and 2 months	38	$791	20.83%	$370	25.83%
1939	65 and 4 months	40	$783	21.67%	$366	26.67%
1940	65 and 6 months	42	$775	22.50%	$362	27.50%
1941	65 and 8 months	44	$766	23.33%	$358	28.33%
1942	65 and 10 months	46	$758	24.17%	$354	29.17%
1943-1954	66	48	$750	25.00%	$350	30.00%
1955	66 and 2 months	50	$741	25.83%	$345	30.83%
1956	66 and 4 months	52	$733	26.67%	$341	31.67%
1957	66 and 6 months	54	$725	27.50%	$337	32.50%

continues

Full Retirement and Age 62 Benefit by Year of Birth* (continued)

Year of birth	Full (normal retirement age)	Months between age 62 and full retirement age	At Age 62			
			A $1000 retirement benefit would be reduced to ...	The retirement benefit is reduced by ...	A $500 spouse's benefit would be reduced to ...	The spouse's benefit is reduced by ...
1958	66 and 8 months	56	$716	28.33%	$333	33.33%
1959	66 and 10 months	58	$708	29.17%	$329	34.17%
1960 and later	67	60	$700	30.00%	$325	35.00%

The SSA says people born on January 1st are considered to have been born in the prior year, so if you were born on January 1st of 1960, your birth year would be 1959.

Table courtesy of the Social Security Administration.

 QUOTATION

"Most people are taking Social Security earlier than later, but they probably would have done things a little bit differently in hindsight if they had talked to an advisor. To me it's a choice of when to take it. What can I do to make sure that I can wait for as long as possible? Is my job secure? Can I put more money into my 401K plan? Planning is key. Saving now rather than waiting. In general, you should wait to take your benefits as long as you can, but because of individual circumstances, there may be an income need to take it earlier."

—Daniel Fisher, financial planner, Fisher Financial Group, Northbrook, Illinois

There are both pros and cons related to taking Social Security retirement benefits as early as 62, and most of them are related to your health and your financial situation at this particular time in your life. In the next few pages, we're going to explore a range of these situations and considerations so you'll see what factors you should also be reviewing, on your own or with a financial advisor.

Health Considerations

In terms of deciding to start taking Social Security benefits at age 62 or any other age before reaching your full retirement age, which could range from 65 to 67 depending on when you were born, the state of your health and your family's history regarding longevity are paramount.

If you've been diagnosed with a terminal illness and given a finite number of years to live, taking Social Security as early as age 62 might make the most sense. On the other hand, your condition might make you eligible for disability if your illness impairs your ability to work. In that case, it may be more beneficial to apply for disability and postpone your retirement for as long as possible to allow you and your spouse the benefit of a larger monthly payment because you waited. (If you think this describes your situation, please refer to Chapter 9.)

 **CAUTION**

Your family's health history will show if you are more likely to inherit a medical condition that could dramatically shorten your life span, in which case you might take that into consideration when you decide when to start taking your benefits.

Of course, no one really knows how long he or she is going to live. But you can make an educated guess based on a number of factors, such as your health history. Are you obese? Do you have high blood pressure? Do you have diabetes, heart problems, or a history of cancer?

Another health consideration is if the job you have is actually making you sick. Sometimes a job can be emotionally or physically debilitating to the point that remaining in that position might even shorten your life. In this case, retiring as early as possible and taking Social Security benefits could actually be just what the doctor ordered. Ironically, taking earlier retirement and receiving Social Security benefits from age 62 might actually extend your life.

Longevity is always a factor in deciding when to begin receiving retirement benefits. Consider this: in 2014, the average life span for a man 65 years old was another 19.3 years to age 84.3, and for a woman of the same age another 21.6 years to age 86.6. (For a more extensive discussion of life expectancy, see the section "Determining Your Life Expectancy" in Chapter 8.)

Armed with this information, you may want to rethink taking Social Security benefits too early. On the other hand, other factors, such as your current financial situation, could dictate the need for receiving those benefits as soon as possible.

TIP

If you're in dire financial straits, you have been diagnosed with a terminal illness, you have a family history of premature death due to heart problems or cancer, and you no longer want to work but your company pension, savings, or other sources of income are not enough, taking Social Security as early as age 62 may be a better option for you. Weigh your options carefully and, if you have one, consult your financial advisor to discuss your plans.

Retiring Without Enough Saved

If you can afford to, and your health is excellent with a long life expectancy, most financial experts recommend you wait as long as possible to take Social Security benefits. If you can't afford to retire, the next consideration becomes whether you need to start taking your benefits early purely for economic survival because you aren't earning enough to cover your bills. If you need the funds just to make ends meet, you may have to start collecting benefits before you reach your FRA.

Here are some typical scenarios for those who took Social Security before their FRA:

Sixty-seven-year-old Bill began taking his Social Security benefits at age 63, when he returned from an out-of-town job that ended after three years. He decided to use his relocation with his wife back to his hometown as an opportunity to retire. He began receiving benefits early because he wanted that additional monthly benefit, which he used to supplement his company pension. That extra money each month made retirement economically feasible for him.

When she was 62, Beverly began her Social Security benefits because she was only working part-time making less than the income cap on those who take benefits early, which in 2014 was $15,480. Her husband is the higher wage earner and began receiving his own benefits at his FRA. Taking her benefits early made economic sense for Beverly because when she reaches her FRA, she'll be eligible to switch to receiving spousal benefits, which will be one half of what her husband receives, a higher amount than her own reduced benefit. At that point, an income cap will also no longer apply to Beverly's earnings, if she continues to work and her earnings situation improves.

Let's reconsider Bill's example. Some financial advisors recommend that someone in Bill's situation first consider all the 401(k)s, IRAs, investment income, and any other economic sources they might have to fund those couple of years until full retirement age rather than file early. For every year you don't take your Social Security benefits from age 62 to your FRA, and even until age 70, you could get a return that equals as much as $100,000 or more if you don't file early.

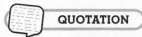

Considerations If You're Still Working

If you're still working, you have to consider your income and the fact that you're continuing to contribute to Social Security through FICA, which will also increase your monthly benefit once you claim it.

Consider this: once you leave a good-paying job, returning to work at something that pays as well when you're older is going to be extremely difficult. So you might want to hold on to the job you've got as long as possible.

But what if your job is physically or emotionally demanding? Let's say you're a construction worker or you work on an oil rig. Are you going to be able to, or even want to, perform that job at age 62, especially if you don't qualify for disability? Under those conditions, it might make sense to start collecting your retirement benefits early.

There's another factor that those who file early have to consider: the cap on their annual income.

Annual Income Caps

Many people are not aware that there's a cap on the amount of income they can earn when they file for Social Security early. In 2014, the income limit for someone already receiving Social Security benefits is $15,480. For every $2 you earn over that limit, you have to pay back $1. That means if you earned $23,480, or $8,000 over the limit, you would have your benefits reduced by $4,000. If your normal benefits would have been $9,600 for the year, you would receive only $5,600.

Things change in the year you're supposed to reach full retirement age. The income cap for that year dramatically rises. Let's say in November of 2014 you reach your FRA of 66. At the start of that year, you only have to deduct $1 for every $3 earned over a much higher income cap of $41,400.

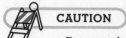

There's a special rule for the first year you claim retirement benefits. This was established because some people will retire at some point during the year and may have already earned more than the earnings cap. Under this first year rule, your Social Security check will not be reduced for any whole month you're retired even if prior earnings that year were above the cap.

For example, let's say you retire at age 62 on October 30, 2014. Up to that point, you earned $45,000. Starting in November, you decide to take a part-time job that pays $500 a month. So even though your earnings for the year far exceed the annual cap of $15,480 (or $1,290 per month) you will still receive your regular monthly retirement benefit checks for November and December because your part-time job paid less than the monthly cap of $1,290. However, the amount will be reduced due to early filing, and the regular annual cap will apply starting January 2015.

If you're receiving retirement benefits before your FRA and are self-employed, things are a little different. The SSA looks at how much work you do in your business. If you work more than 15 hours a month and are self-employed, the government may not consider you to be retired.

Determining Your Break-Even Point

By now you know that when you take Social Security before reaching your full retirement age, you'll be reducing your monthly check. That reduction amounts to about 8 percent for every year you receive benefits before you reach full retirement age. And that's the amount you're going to be getting for the rest of your life (except for the very minimal COLA adjustments for inflation) unless you stop your benefits and repay what you've received up to that point. If you do that, you can re-apply for benefits at a later date.

Let's say you start taking Social Security at age 62. You will receive about 25 percent less than if you had waited until your FRA of 66, or 33 percent less if your FRA is 67.

Still, receiving less each month could be better than waiting four more years, when you consider how long it will take to reach your *break-even point*.

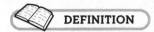 **DEFINITION**

The **break-even point** is a specific age, based on taking retirement benefits at age 62, at your full retirement age, or at age 70. For example, the break-even point between collecting at 62 and at full retirement age is the age at which you will have received the same amount of benefits from either choice (so you will break even).

According to the SSA, someone who receives $750 a month at 62 would instead have received $1,000 a month if they had waited to begin claiming their benefits at a full retirement age of 66. So by starting retirement as early as possible, you would actually earn $3,000 less per year. But by the time you reach age 66, you would have received $36,000 in benefits. It will take you another 12 years, to age 78, to make up that difference.

Therefore, age 78 becomes your break-even age if you began receiving benefits at age 62. If you're expecting to live a lot longer than that, you should probably wait to take your benefits because they'll be a lot higher. The longer you live, the more money you're going to need down the road, especially if medical bills start to pile up and if you don't have "gap insurance" to cover the 20 percent that Medicare does not cover. However, if you have a family history of a shorter life expectancy of only 60 or 70, it might make sense for you to start your benefits earlier.

Spousal Privileges

Keep in mind that taking Social Security early will also reduce the amount of benefits your spouse can receive under spousal benefits or as a survivor if you die first.

Here's an example shared by Michael Turner, MBA, Managing Director of Charlotte, North Carolina–based Franklin Chase Wealth Management. Turner helped one of his clients understand how taking Social Security benefits early would impact his wife's future spousal benefits:

"About a year ago, I met with a client to discuss retirement plans. He felt it was wise to file for Social Security at age 62. His rationale was the earlier he got the benefit, although reduced, it would result in more money over the long haul. I asked him how he felt taking benefits early would impact his wife. She is seven years younger than him and since he was the major breadwinner, she would receive his benefit upon his death. He didn't feel it would be a large impact. I was able to illustrate to him that impact: if he died at age 77, his wife would receive about $10,000 a year less by him taking Social Security at age 62 as opposed to at age 66 [his full retirement age]. If he waited until age 69, it grew to about $20,000 a year less. He went to the Social Security Administration the next day to cancel his submission for benefit!"

What Are Spousal Benefits?

When it comes to Social Security spousal benefits, they apply to three categories of spouses: a current spouse, an ex-spouse (in the case of divorce), and a widowed spouse.

If you're collecting a spousal benefit before you reach full retirement age, your monthly benefit check will remain at that reduced level for the rest of your life. And if your spouse also took his or her Social Security early, your spousal benefit will be cut even more.

In order to avoid this, many married couples use different strategies and coordinate the timing on when they begin collecting Social Security.

However, if your finances demand that both spouses file as soon as possible, just be aware of the consequences of filing early.

WORTH NOTING

Because Section 3 of the Defense of Marriage Act (DOMA) was declared unconstitutional on June 25, 2013, by the Supreme Court, Social Security can now consider same-sex couples for eligibility for spousal benefits. For more information, go to ssa.gov.

How to Qualify

Not every ex-spouse or widow qualifies for spousal benefits. If you are divorced, you'll need to have been married for at least 10 years and must currently be unmarried. However, it doesn't matter if your ex-spouse has remarried or not, only you. The only other qualification is that you must be at least 62 years of age to file.

Widows or widowers, on the other hand, can begin receiving survivor benefits as early as age 60. Also, a widow or widower only needs to have been married for nine months. If you're caring for a disabled child or a child under the age of 16 who is also your ex-spouse's child, you may be eligible for more benefits.

According to the SSA, the amount a widow or widower will receive is based on four criteria:

1. The amount the deceased spouse would have received at their full retirement age

2. Whether the deceased spouse had begun collecting benefits

3. Whether the deceased spouse had reached their full retirement age before dying

4. Whether the surviving spouse has reached their full retirement age

If your deceased spouse had started receiving benefits before they reached their full retirement age, you will receive at least 82.5 percent of what they would have received at full retirement age, even if they started collecting benefits at age 62. The rule was put into place to protect surviving spouses from having a lower income for the rest of their lives.

If the deceased spouse died before they had begun receiving Social Security benefits, the widow or widower is eligible to receive 100 percent of what the deceased spouse would have received at their full retirement age. For example, if your spouse died at age 65 but still hadn't collected any benefits, you would receive what he or she would have received at their full retirement age even though their death preceded it.

Benefits for a widowed ex-spouse are similar to a widowed current spouse, except that you would have needed to have been married for at least 10 years and to be currently unmarried.

 TIP

Keep in mind that you can take a spousal benefit while letting your own retirement benefit continue to grow.

File and Suspend Strategy

If you take Social Security early, you'll also lose the opportunity to use the file and suspend strategy for your spouse, which is only available to those who file when they reach their full retirement age.

Here's how it works. You file your Social Security claim when you reach your full retirement age, but then you suspend receiving any benefits. Why would you do that, you ask?

Well, the main answer is to allow your spouse to apply for the spousal benefit so she receives 50 percent of your full retirement age benefit. This works whether your wife was a stay-at-home mom or if she was a low wage earner for most of her working life. It even works if your spouse earned a salary similar to yours, because she can take the spousal benefit and delay applying for her own Social Security until later as well, allowing both spouses to get a larger monthly benefit check for delaying collecting the benefit.

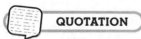 **QUOTATION**

"You can get a 'do-over' where the Social Security Administration permits you to repay all benefits received and make a new claim in the future. But you can only do this once and it must be done prior to receiving 12 months of benefits."

—Michael Turner, Management Director, Franklin Chase Wealth Management

The Least You Need to Know

- The earliest age at which you can start receiving Social Security benefits is 62.

- If you take benefits before reaching your full retirement age, your benefits will be reduced by a certain percentage for every year before your full retirement age.

- Taking retirement as early as possible might make sense if you need the money or if you don't expect to live a long and healthy life.

- There are income caps you need to know about if you take early retirement benefits and still plan to keep working. The income cap in 2015 is $15,720. If you exceed that, for every $2 you earn, Social Security will hold back $1 in benefits. During your full retirement age year, the income cap rises to $41,880. Once you reach your full retirement age, there is no income cap.

- You will not be eligible for the file and suspend strategy for your spouse if you take retirement benefits early.

Filing at Full Retirement Age or Beyond

When you begin receiving your Social Security benefits can mean the difference of hundreds of thousands of dollars over your lifetime, and your spouse's or survivor's lifetime. Therefore, it's in your best interest to find out as much as possible about this key decision.

In Chapter 7, we looked at the advantages and disadvantages of filing as early as age 62. In this chapter, we'll explore the pluses and minuses of waiting to file at your full retirement age (FRA) or beyond, to as late as age 70. That's the final age limit to any financial benefit of delaying the start of your Social Security retirement payments. Your benefits won't go any higher if you delay taking them beyond age 70.

The concept of FRA can be confusing because these days it has nothing to do with anyone being fully retired. In reality, it's just an age selected by the Social Security Administration (SSA) to determine when you are eligible to begin receiving your full retirement benefits. By "full" retirement benefits we mean that your benefits will not be reduced as they would by starting them as early as age 62, the earliest you can start receiving benefits.

In This Chapter

- Pros and cons of taking benefits at full retirement age or later
- Increasing benefits with strategies not available to early filers
- How waiting until age 70 can significantly increase benefits
- Why you should not put off collecting benefits after 70

There are increased advantages to delaying when you start receiving your benefits to beyond your FRA. In fact, the value of your benefits increases by as much as 8 percent per year between your FRA and age 70, which some are now calling the "new" age for retirement.

Pluses and Minuses of Filing at Full Retirement Age

There are advantages and disadvantages to waiting until you reach your FRA to start taking your Social Security benefits. On the plus side, the amount you receive each month will be larger than if you had started taking your benefits earlier. As noted in the previous chapter, your benefit can be reduced by as much as 25 to 30 percent if you take retirement benefits at age 62.

By waiting until your FRA, you'll get 100 percent of your benefits. In addition, for those who are still working, you also will no longer have an income cap on earnings. That means you can continue working at your job, whether your salary is $25,000, $50,000, or more per year without having to return any income above a certain amount.

On the minus side, if you had started taking the somewhat reduced benefit amount earlier, you would have been receiving those benefits all those months and years until you reached your FRA. That means you're going to have to live for at least another 12 years to make the waiting worthwhile. As discussed earlier, the break-even point is between 74 and 78, depending on when you started your early retirement benefits and what your FRA is computed to be. If you don't live at least that long, you'll lose money. Still, the actuarial tables are on your side should you decide to wait until your FRA or even later to start taking your benefits.

Determining Your Full Retirement Age

What your FRA is depends on what year you were born. For example, if you were born before 1938, your FRA is 65. If you were born between 1943 and 1954, it's 66. Your FRA then goes up incrementally two months each year until 1960, when it becomes 67.

There are so many benefits to waiting to file for Social Security at your FRA. Please refer back to the table "Age When You Can Receive Full Social Security Benefits" provided in Chapter 7.

TIP

The SSA suggests that you apply for your Social Security benefits three months before the date you want them to start. So if you want to start benefits at your full retirement age, make sure you have the correct date for your age group.

Determining Your Life Expectancy

The good news is that, in general, we're all living longer these days. The average life expectancy for a 65-year-old man in 2014 was another 19.3 years, and for a 65-year-old woman, it's an additional 21.6 years. Both of these are well beyond the break-even age for taking Social Security at age 62, which is around age 78.

But remember that those are general predictions. No one has a crystal ball that shows what your exact life expectancy is going to be! All any of us can do is to make some estimated predictions. The stakes of predicting correctly have some very real financial consequences, especially when it comes to Social Security benefits.

If you want a quick way to determine your life expectancy, check out the SSA's free online calculator at socialsecurity.gov/oact/population/longevity.html. Just enter your gender (male or female) and your date of birth (month, day, and year) and you'll find your ballpark life expectancy.

However, this simple calculator doesn't take into account such pivotal additional factors as:

- Family or personal history of heart disease

- Family or personal history of cancer

- Whether you have high blood pressure

- Your cholesterol levels

- Whether you're obese or overweight

- Whether you have diabetes

- Whether you exercise or are completely sedentary

- Your stress level and how you deal with stress

- Whether you smoke cigarettes, and if you do, how many packs daily

- Whether you drink alcohol, and if you do, how many drinks daily

- How many close family or friends you have in your life

- If you work at a job with a higher death rate (such as fishermen, loggers, law enforcement, roofers, pilots, farmers, or ranchers)

Nor does it predict whether you'll get an infection that could become fatal, or if you'll get into an accident or a natural disaster that causes fatality before your estimated life expectancy.

There are other, more detailed life expectancy calculators you can fill out to help you come up with an estimate of expected life span, which could help you in your retirement planning. As you've learned, for each year you delay starting Social Security after your FRA, you get an increase of about 8 percent due to delayed retirement credits.

Once again, computing your life expectancy with any calculator is all conjecture based on how straightforward you are in your answers and any other unforeseen circumstances.

Check out this more comprehensive online calculator at livingto100.com/calculator/age. This longevity estimation tool was created by Thomas Perls, MD, MPH. Although it's free, it does require that you sign up by providing your email address and creating a password so you can get occasional information about some of the health or education topics that are suggested.

Co-author Jan was quite pleased by the 95.5 estimated life expectancy the livingto100.com calculator gave her based on her responses to the myriad questions that were asked. However, she's actually hoping the estimate is on the low side and that she makes it to 110 or more, and in the best of health!

There's also another free life expectancy calculator to try out at the Bankrate.com site: bankrate. com/calculators/retirement/life-age-expectancy-calculator.aspx. This calculator asks the usual questions about age, height, weight, and gender, but it also asks about how much alcohol you drink daily. Much to her surprise, Jan discovered that by changing her answer from "none" for how much alcohol she consumes—since she usually doesn't drink at all—to "never more than 2 drinks a day" her estimated life expectancy went up by two years!

That prediction of a two-year longevity increase, upon further investigation, is borne out by research. For example, a 2010 study of 1,824 older male and female adults conducted by researchers at the University of Texas at Austin tied moderate consumption of one or two drinks a day to longevity for middle-aged and older persons.

However, one of the study's researchers, psychology professor Dr. Charles Holahan, cautioned in a press release from the university: "Older persons drinking alcohol should remember that consuming more than two drinks a day exceeds recommended alcohol consumption guidelines in the United States and is associated with increased falls, a higher risk of alcohol use problems, and potential adverse interactions with medications."

Other Longevity Factors

When considering what your life expectancy might be, remember that the variables are not just gender-related. In general, women live a few years longer than men, but these factors apply as well:

- Race/ethnicity
- Geographic region or state where you live

According to the National Center for Health Statistics, in 2011, the overall life expectancy for all races was 76.3 years for males and 81.1 years for females in the United States. When they divided that information by race, however, the life expectancy was 76.6 for white males and 81.3 for white females; for black males it was 72.1 years and for black females 78.2 years.

However, the SSA provides much higher life expectancy predictions at their website (ssa.gov/planners/lifeexpectancy.htm). The SSA states that the average man, regardless of race, reaching the age of 65 can expect to live to 84.3 years, and the average woman reaching the age of 65 can expect to live to 86.6. But they also are quick to point out that these are just averages. For some, the life expectancy is even much higher. As they note, 1 in every 4 65-year-olds will live past 90, and 1 out of 10 will live past 95.

What state you live in also impacts your life expectancy by as much as five years. As you'll see in the list of life expectancies by state posted at the Henry J. Kaiser Family Foundation website (kff.org/other/state-indicator/life-expectancy), the estimated life expectancy is 75 for someone living in the state of Mississippi, 79.4 if you live in Florida, 80 for Wyoming residents, 80.5 for New Yorkers, and 80.8 for those who live in Connecticut and California.

One thing, however, that none of the calculators take into consideration is the likelihood that technological advances in health care will prolong our lives even further. People over 90 are the fastest-growing segment of our population, according to the latest Census Bureau statistics. So if longevity is the strongest factor in your decision making, waiting until 70 to take retirement benefits seems like the smartest move.

No More Income Caps

Another plus for waiting until you reach your FRA is that if you're still working, there are no earnings caps once you reach that age. That means you can continue working, earning whatever income you can generate and contributing to FICA, which could even increase your monthly Social Security benefits, especially if your earnings are in your top 10 earning years.

Strategies to Help You Increase Your Benefits

One of the biggest pluses to waiting until you reach your FRA or older to start taking Social Security is it makes you eligible for a number of strategies aimed at boosting your ultimate benefits. Note that these strategies are not available to anyone who takes early retirement.

Everybody's situation is different, so these strategies depend on whether you're married or single, and the age difference between you and your spouse, along with whether you and your spouse are both working, and whether you are earning high or low incomes.

One strategy to maximize benefits is the following: When two spouses earn the maximum benefit, it makes sense for one spouse to file and suspend his benefits, and then have his spouse take a spousal benefit based on his earnings while deferring her retirement benefits for as long as possible. That way they each get their own full benefit while receiving Social Security benefits under the spousal benefit rule.

Let's say you're 66 and you file for full retirement benefits, but then you immediately suspend those benefits. By filing, you allow your wife to take a spousal benefit based on your full retirement age. Meanwhile, you've suspended your benefits, so your benefits will continue to grow because they've been deferred. With this strategy, your own benefit continues to go up, and your wife begins collecting 50 percent off of your full retirement benefit.

Now you've got Social Security money coming in. But later on, your wife can switch and file for her own retirement benefits. Since your wife's benefits were also deferred, that amount also continued to grow. Then, when both of you are ready, you can start taking your benefits, which will be at a higher rate than they would have been if they had been taken at your FRAs. In fact, both spouses' benefits could be as much as 32 percent higher even though one of them had already started collecting.

 QUOTATION

"The most common error people make when it comes to Social Security is starting to collect their benefit too early. Yes, it's tempting to take the money and run. But before you do, carefully weigh your options. On further scrutiny, you are likely to find that you will get the best return on your money by postponing and allowing your monthly draw to increase."

—Carrie Schwab-Pomerantz, "When Is the Best Time to File for Social Security Benefits?" posted at schwab.com

Not a lot of couples are taking advantage of the file and suspend strategy, probably because most people aren't even aware it exists.

Should You Wait to Take Social Security at 70?

There are three key factors to consider besides life expectancy if you are going to file at your full retirement age or beyond your health, your economic situation, and the current interest rates.

Just as your health was one of the factors that went into deciding whether to take Social Security at age 62 (early retirement benefits, beginning at age 62, the earliest age you can claim your benefits) you need to consider your health when deciding if you'll file at your FRA or wait so your benefits will increase annually until 70. This is a consideration beyond your general life expectancy, as this means you need to seriously and objectively look at your current health and whether you have any illnesses or conditions that might shorten your life.

Another factor is your financial situation. If you lack a pension or retirement savings and you need your Social Security benefits to pay your mortgage or rent, you may not have the luxury of delaying your benefits.

Assuming your FRA is 66, here's a chart that Carrie Schwab-Pomerantz posted at schwab.com as part of her article, "When Is the Best Time to File for Social Security Benefits?"

Delay	Benefit Increase
Age 62–63	6.66%
Age 63–64	8.38%
Age 64–65	7.6%
Age 65–66	7.2%
Age 66–67	8%
Age 67–68	8%
Age 68–69	8%
Age 69–70	8%
Beyond age 70	None

Schwab-Pomerantz also points out that interest rates are a consideration in determining whether to start Social Security at your FRA or delay until 70. She notes that a 2012 study by economists John Shoven of Stanford University and Sita Slavov of Occidental College determined that "delaying Social Security is most advantageous when real interest rates are 3.5 percent or lower." Here's the excellent example she shares to illustrate this point:

> "Let's say you're 64 and trying to decide whether to tap into your 401(k) savings or collect Social Security. If part of your 401(k) is invested in Treasuries, in 2013 you're effectively earning no interest after inflation. You'll get a better return by withdrawing those funds and allowing your Social Security benefit to grow."

As Alicia H. Munnell, director of the Center for Retirement Research at Boston College and the Peter F. Drucker Professor of Management Sciences at Boston College's Carroll School of Management, points out in the October 2013 Center bulletin article "Social Security's Real Retirement Age is 70,", "… 70 has become the new 65."

As Munnell notes, when Social Security started in the 1930s, the retirement age was typically 65, which was the same age most public and private pension plans used. In the late 1950s and early 1960s, Congress changed the law so that first women and then men as well could file as early as age 62. The reduction in benefits for those filing early was adjusted so that, over a person's lifetime, the amount that could be received would even out with those who had filed at the regular retirement age.

But in the early 1970s, Congress introduced the Delayed Retirement Credit. Depending on the year you were born, there is a yearly increase in the benefit you receive. The following SSA chart explains how much that increase will be, based on the year you were born:

Increase in Social Security Benefits for Delayed Retirement

Year of Birth*	Yearly Rate of Increase
1933–1934	5.5%
1935–1936	6.0%
1937–1938	6.5%
1939–1940	7.0%
1941–1942	7.5%
1943 or later	8.0%

If you were born on January 1st, refer to the rate of increase for the previous year.

Why Everyone Should Take Their Benefits by Age 70

No matter how long you want to work, the oldest age your Social Security benefits are tied to is age 70. That doesn't mean you have to file at age 70, but waiting beyond 70 isn't going to earn you any more benefits. Whether you take Social Security at 70 or later, your benefit amount is going to be the most you'll ever receive.

Many financial advisors are recommending that if you can afford it and you're in good health, postponing your benefits until age 70 will give you 32 percent more cash each month than if you took it at your full retirement age.

The so-called break-even age for waiting until 70 to take Social Security is age 84. But longevity shouldn't be your only determining factor. You should also consider your spouse in that by waiting to receive the maximum benefit, it also helps him or her when they apply for spousal benefits.

WORTH NOTING

Compare the economic consequences of taking your benefit early versus at your full retirement age or at age 70. Let's say your FRA benefit was $1,800. If you take retirement at 62, that monthly benefit would drop to $1,350. But if you wait until 70, it jumps to $2,376, almost double what you would have received at 62.

The Advantage of Delaying Benefits Until Age 70

As noted before, your Social Security benefits go up 8 percent annually from your full retirement age until age 70. The following SSA table illustrates the difference each month makes if you delay your benefits beyond your FRA.

How Delayed Retirement Affects Your Social Security Benefits

If you start getting benefits at age ...	Multiply your full retirement benefit by ...
66	100%
66 + 1 month	100.7%
66 + 2 months	101.3%
66 + 3 months	102.0%
66 + 4 months	102.7%
66 + 5 months	103.3%
66 + 6 months	104.0%
66 + 7 months	104.7%
66 + 8 months	105.3%
66 + 9 months	106.0%
66 + 10 months	106.7%
66 + 11 months	107.3%
67	108.0%
67 + 1 month	108.7%
67 + 2 months	109.3%
67 + 3 months	110.0%
67 + 4 months	110.7%

continues

How Delayed Retirement Affects Your Social Security Benefits   (continued)

If you start getting benefits at age ...	Multiply your full retirement benefit by ...
67 + 5 months	111.3%
67 + 6 months	112.0%
67 + 7 months	112.7%
67 + 8 months	113.3%
67 + 9 months	114.0%
67 + 10 months	114.7%
67 + 11 months	115.3%
68	116.0%
68 + 1 month	116.7%
68 + 2 months	117.3%
68 + 3 months	118.0%
68 + 4 months	118.7%
64 + 5 months	119.3%
64 + 6 months	120.0%
64 + 7 months	120.7%
64 + 8 months	121.3%
64 + 9 months	122.0%
64 + 10 months	122.7%
64 + 11 months	123.3%
69	124.0%
69 + 1 months	124.7%
69 + 2 months	125.3%
69 + 3 months	126.0%
69 + 4 months	126.7%
69 + 5 months	127.3%
69 + 6 months	128.0%
69 + 7 months	128.7%

If you start getting benefits at age ...	Multiply your full retirement benefit by ...
69 + 8 months	129.3%
69 + 9 months	130.0%
69 + 10 months	130.7%
69 + 11 months	131.3%
70 +	132.0%

It All Depends on Life Expectancy

When all is said and done, however, one of the greatest determining factors on when you should start receiving Social Security benefits is your life expectancy. Now there are other factors to consider, such as financial need, but your estimated longevity will usually help you decide when to take benefits. If you expect to live well into your 80s or beyond, you should consider waiting until 70, when you will receive the maximum benefit, if you can afford to.

Filing Details

You can file for your Social Security benefits on your own or you can choose to have someone help you file, such as a financial advisor. There are three ways to file for the first time: online, by phone, or in person.

Filing by Yourself

To apply online, go to secure.ssa.gov/iClaim/rib and complete the online application. The website estimates it will take 10 to 30 minutes to complete the online application. Please note, if you haven't reviewed your earnings history associated with your Social Security number, you should do that in advance of filing because the accuracy of those amounts will impact how much money you'll receive monthly. (For more details on what's asked on the application, refer back to Chapter 6.) Your completed application then will go directly to SSA. Within a week or so, you'll be notified of their decision.

If you want to call and speak to someone, you can phone the SSA at 1-800-772-1213 (TTY 1-800-325-0778) from 7 A.M. to 7 P.M. Monday through Friday.

If you want to talk with someone in person, you can go to your local Social Security office. It's recommended that you call in advance to make an appointment because you could wait as long as a couple of hours if you decide to just drop in.

The financial advisors we interviewed pointed out that when you go in person to your local office, you should know in advance that they are not authorized to advise you about what age would be best for you to begin taking Social Security because it's such a personal decision.

Having a Financial Advisor Present

You do have the right to bring a financial advisor with you to your meeting if you choose to confer with an advisor before making the decision about whether to file for benefits at that time.

Seth Deitchman, Financial Advisor for Atlanta's The Mercury Group at Morgan Stanley, shared the following:

> "A benefit of bringing an advisor with you is that you won't be pushed into doing something that you don't need to do. You'll also have the arsenal of knowledge and experience of the advisor, especially if the advisor has been there several times with other clients. For example, a client was brought to the Social Security office. Her husband had passed on six months prior. She was going to file for herself. Instead, we advised her to file for survivors benefits so her own benefits could accrue. Now, instead, she will take her own benefits at 70, giving up the survivors benefits, but we helped her get the best case scenario. She would have taken hers at a much lower rate for the rest of her life. So our assistance and presence was a great value to the client. Thousands upon thousands of dollars that she might not have gotten she will now receive."

The Least You Need to Know

- Your full retirement age is based on the year you were born. It's 65 if you were born before 1938. If you were born between 1943 and 1954, it's 66. From 1955 it goes up incrementally two months a year until 1960, when it becomes 67.
- There are benefits to waiting to collect Social Security until you reach your full retirement age. If you file before your full retirement age, your benefits will be reduced permanently, and you will have income caps.
- The file and suspend strategy is available to married couples to allow both partners to delay taking benefits on their own earnings record to help potentially maximize their benefits.
- Choosing to wait until after your FRA, even late as age 70, enables your Social Security benefit to reach its maximum value. Your benefits will increase 8 percent each year from your FRA to age 70.

Benefits for All

Over the years, Social Security evolved from just a retirement benefits package to offering financial assistance to disabled workers as well as survivors of deceased retired and disabled workers. Part 3 details how the various benefits packages work, how to qualify for them, and how to apply for them. This also is where you'll find information about Medicare and Medicaid.

There's a section on disabilities and information to help you determine if you have one of the more than 200 medical problems that could qualify you to receive disability benefits. You'll learn all about how to earn work credits the Social Security Administration uses to determine whether you're eligible for benefits. We'll discuss benefits for the family, as well as divorced ex-spouses and their rights.

Finally, we'll go through the application process for filing for disability, retirement, and survivors benefits. You'll see how the SSA makes its decisions, and how you can appeal those decisions if they deny your claim. You may even want to get help from a representative or disability lawyer, and we'll show you how to do that, too.

Applying for Disability Benefits

What is the Social Security Disability program? It's a government-run plan that offers financial help to people who are unable to work for at least a year because of severe mental or physical impairments or disabilities.

According to the Social Security Administration (SSA), in December 2013 there were a total of almost 9 million disabled American workers—4,600,000 males and 4,300,000 females—with an average monthly benefit of $1,146.43. At the same time, there were an additional 2 million spouses and children of disabled workers receiving on average $338.86 in monthly disability benefits.

How likely is it that you or someone you depend on could become disabled and unable to work for at least a year or longer? The SSA notes that one in every four American workers will probably become disabled before they reach age 67.

In This Chapter

- The two types of disability benefits
- How the SSA determines your eligibility
- How to apply for disability benefits
- What happens if you return to work?

Just like retirement benefits, disability payments are administered by the SSA, but there are two different programs:

- Social Security Disability Insurance (SSDI)

- Supplemental Security Income (SSI), which is for people with limited income and resources

The SSA will decide if you are eligible for disability payments under one of these two programs, depending on whether you meet certain requirements it has established. Each program has its own requirements, and we'll discuss what those requirements are in this chapter.

Three Ways to Apply

There are three ways you can apply for both of these disability benefits:

- Apply online at socialsecurity.gov.

- Call the SSA's toll-free number, 1-800-772-1213, to make an appointment to file a disability claim through your local office.

- Call SSA's toll-free number and arrange for someone to take your claim over the telephone at a specific time.

An interview by phone or in person will last about one hour. If you're deaf or hard of hearing, you can call a special TTY number—1-800-325-0778—between 7 A.M. and 7 P.M. on business days to schedule an appointment.

Once you schedule an appointment, the SSA will send you a Disability Starter Kit, which is also available online at socialsecurity.gov/disability/disability_starter_kits.htm#sb=.

 WORTH NOTING

If you become disabled, apply for benefits as soon as possible because it usually takes from three to five months just to process your claim.

Social Security Disability Insurance (SSDI)

Because most people receiving disability do so under the Social Security Disability Insurance program (SSDI), we'll examine that first.

Under SSDI, in order to receive disability payments you had to have made contributions to Social Security by paying those FICA taxes if you were employed, or Self-Employed Contributions Act (SECA) taxes if you were self-employed.

Just as with retirement benefits, SSDI may also be available to spouses and dependent children, but first you have to meet certain qualifications.

WORTH NOTING

One of the main differences between Social Security Disability Insurance (SSDI) and Supplemental Security Income (SSI) is that you can get SSI without having paid Social Security taxes, but you can't with SSDI.

Depending on your age, you should have worked in jobs where you contributed to Social Security through FICA or have a self-employed business that contributes through the SECA tax. You also should have worked enough years to earn the necessary number of work credits for your particular age group.

For example, if you were disabled between ages 31 and 42, you would need 20 credits, which means you worked at least five years. (You receive 4 credits per year.) The number of credits needed goes up from there, until age 62 when you would need 40 work credits.

TIP

You can check on the number of work credits you've accumulated by going online and filling out a request for a Social Security statement form at ssa.gov/myaccount/SSA-7004.pdf or by contacting your local SSA office.

After you determine that you have enough work credits to qualify, you have to have a mental or physical condition that meets the SSA's definition of a disability. To qualify, this condition typically would have to prevent you from working for at least one year.

Benefits can be retroactive and, once approved, you'll receive them for as long as necessary until you're able to return to work. There are even special work incentives that will offer continued benefits and health-care coverage to help you in your transition back to the workforce.

If your disability lasts until you reach your full retirement age (FRA), your disability benefits automatically switch over to retirement benefits at the same amount you had been receiving for disability.

Definition and Duration of Disability

The SSA has its own definition of disability. SSA considers you disabled if:

- Your condition prevents you from doing the work you used to do.

- You can't adjust to any other work because of your condition.

- Your disability will last at least one year and/or will result in death.

That definition doesn't leave much wiggle room. In other words, you have to pretty much be totally disabled to qualify. Short-term problems won't cut it. Even if you seem to have a condition that fits their criteria, the SSA makes very sure you meet their definition of disabled before approving your claim.

Here are five questions SSA will ask you immediately:

1. **Are you still working?** This is a biggie. If you're still working and earning more than $1,070 monthly, you probably will not qualify as disabled. If you're not working, your application then goes to the Disability Determination Services (DDS) office, which will make a decision based on your mental or physical condition.

2. **Is your condition severe enough that it interferes with your ability to work?** Your condition must be so severe that it prevents you from continuing your job daily.

3. **Is this condition found in the list of disabled conditions?** In the next section, we list the 14 categories of potential disabilities that include some 200 possible medical problems that could qualify for disability.

4. **Can you perform the work you did before you were disabled?** If your condition isn't on this list, you'll be asked if you can do the work you did before becoming impaired. If your condition is severe enough to prevent you from doing your job, an examiner will review your condition, and you might still qualify for disability even if your illness isn't among the conditions listed.

5. **Can you do any other kind of work?** If you can't perform your previous job, the examiner may ask if you could do something else, or if you can possibly adjust to a different, possibly less physically or mentally taxing job. In this case, they'll look at your medical condition and your age, education, and past work experience for any transferable skills. If you can't adjust to any other work, they'll probably approve your claim. If you can, they probably won't.

The Blue Book's List of Impairments

Now let's look at what medical conditions the SSA considers when determining a disability claim. Sometimes referred to as the "Blue Book" list of impairments, the SSA has 14 different categories of illnesses that apply to adults 18 and over, in addition to those that apply to some children under 18. Here are the 14 illness categories:

1. **Musculoskeletal system conditions:** Includes any loss of function due to bone or joint disorders (such as amputations, fractures, disorders of the spine), and soft-tissue injuries (such as burns).

2. **Special sense and speech disorders:** Includes visual disorders (such as blindness and loss of visual efficiency), loss of speech, and loss of hearing.

3. **Respiratory system illnesses and impairments:** Includes chronic pulmonary insufficiency, asthma, cystic fibrosis, pneumoconiosis, bronchiectasis, lung infections, sleep-related breathing disorders (such as apnea), and lung transplants.

4. **Cardiovascular system illnesses or impairments to your heart and circulatory system:** Includes chronic heart failure, heart disease, recurrent arrhythmias, symptomatic congenital heart disease, heart transplants, aneurysm of the aorta or its major branches, chronic venous insufficiency, or peripheral arterial disease.

5. **Digestive system disorders:** Includes gastrointestinal hemorrhages, liver disease, inflammatory bowel disease, short bowel syndrome, and malnutrition.

6. **Genitourinary impairments:** Includes impairments to renal function (such as chronic renal disease, diabetic nephropathy, or glomerular disease), kidney failure, and osteoporosis, to name a few.

7. **Hematological disorders:** Includes blood disorders such as anemia, sickle cell disease, coagulation defects, and hereditary telangiectasia, or hemorrhages requiring transfusions at least three times during a five-month period.

8. **Skin disorders:** Includes extensive skin lesions, skin tumors, or infections caused by autoimmune disorders such as lupus or HIV infection, burns, or any type of skin disorder the SSA considers severe enough to prevent you from working.

9. **Endocrine disorders causing hormonal imbalances:** Including pituitary gland disorders that can disrupt and affect your endocrine glands, as well as water and electrolyte balance in your kidneys possibly leading to adult onset diabetes. It also includes thyroid gland disorders, which impact your blood pressure and heart rate; parathyroid gland disorders, which can cause osteoporosis, cataracts, and kidney failure; and adrenal gland disorders, which impact your blood pressure, your body's metabolism, and your mental status.

10. **Congenital disorders:** Includes disorders that affect different systems of your body, with the most common being Down syndrome.

11. **Neurological disorders:** Including epilepsy, trauma to the central nervous system, brain tumors, Parkinson's disease, cerebral palsy, spinal cord or nerve root lesions, multiple sclerosis, muscular dystrophy, Huntington's disease, and any disorder related to the brain and nervous system.

12. **Mental disorders:** Includes such psychotic disorders as schizophrenia and paranoia, intellectual disabilities, anxiety-related disorders (such as post-traumatic stress syndrome [PTSD]), autism, personality disorders, substance addiction disorders, and other pervasive developmental disorders.

13. **Malignant neoplastic diseases:** Includes soft tissue tumors; lymphoma; Kaposi's sarcoma; HIV; leukemia; myeloma; cancers of the breast, lung, bone, nervous system, stomach, esophagus, small and large intestines, pancreas, liver, gallbladder, ovaries, testicles, marrow, or any other type of cancer that would prevent work or lead to death.

14. **Immune system disorders:** Includes disorders such as lupus, sclerosis, HIV, AIDS, and severe inflammatory arthritis, to name a few.

  TIP

The SSA has special rules if you are legally blind, which means your vision can't be corrected to better than 20/200 in your better eye, or if your visual field is 20 degrees less than in your better eye. If this is the case, and if you don't have enough work credits based on your own earnings, you may be able to get disability benefits based on your parents' or spouse's earnings.

When deciding on a claim based on one of these illnesses or impairments, the SSA considers your medical and legal issues. SSA officials review your claim to make sure you legally qualify for the benefits by having earned the prerequisite work credits and contributed to FICA. Then they'll review your medical records regarding your impairment to make sure it prevents you from doing your job or transferring your skills to another job.

Earning the Required Credits

To qualify for Social Security disability payments, you need to earn a certain number of work credits. Similar to the credit rules for retirement benefits, you can earn up to four credits annually. Because you can become disabled at any time during your working career, the number of work credits required for disability payments will depend on how old you are when you become disabled. That means the younger you are, the fewer work credits you'll need to qualify for disability.

For example:

- If you become disabled before the age of 24, you only need to have earned six credits over a three-year period prior to when you became disabled to qualify.

- If you become disabled between the ages of 24 and 31, you would only need credits for working *half the time* between age 21 and the year you became disabled. For example, if you became disabled at age 27, you would only need credit for half of those six years worked, which is three years or 12 credits.

- If you become disabled between the ages of 31 and 42, you will need at least 20 credits, and those credits could have been earned anytime in the 10 years prior to your becoming disabled.

- If you become disabled between the ages of 44 and 66, the credits will start accumulating at 22 and grow at 2 credits every two years until age 62, when they cap at 40. Ages 62 to 66 still only need 40 credits to qualify.

Qualifying for Disability as a Family Member

Some family members of an eligible worker may also qualify for Social Security disability benefits. They include the following persons:

- Your spouse, if he or she is 62 or older.

- Your spouse if he or she is caring for your child age 16 or younger; or if the child is also disabled, your spouse is eligible at any age.

- Your unmarried child, including any adopted child or in some cases stepchildren or grandchildren, if the child is 18 years or younger and in elementary or secondary school full time.

- Your unmarried child who is 18 or older and has a disability that began before age 22. (The child's disability must meet the requirements of a disability for an adult.)

In certain circumstances, a divorced spouse may also qualify for benefits based on your earnings, if he or she was married to you for at least 10 years, is currently unmarried, and is at least 62 years old.

There are also benefits for the parents of a worker if:

- Your child was an insured worker who died.

- You are at least 62 years old.

- You are divorced, widowed, or unmarried, and have not married since the death of your child.

- You were receiving at least one half of your support from your child at the time of his or her death and you can provide evidence of that support.

Citizenship or Residency Requirements

There are specific citizenship or residency requirements in order to qualify for Social Security disability benefits. You must be a U.S. citizen or a permanent legal resident living in the United States or abroad.

However, even if you aren't a citizen or permanent legal resident, you may still qualify if you can show that you are lawfully present in the United States and meet certain other requirements, which we discuss later in this chapter in the section "Citizenship and Residency Requirements."

Income or Resource Limits

Just as with retirement benefits, your disability benefits will be based on your average lifetime earnings. It isn't, as some people think, based on how bad your disability is or how much income you have.

There are reasons you may receive a reduction in disability payments, such as if you're receiving payments from some other disability program like workers compensation.

When the SSA calculates your average lifetime earnings, it will exclude any periods when your income dropped because of your disability.

As usual, the formula the SSA uses to calculate disability benefits is just as complicated as the one they use for retirement. First, they determine your average indexed monthly earnings (AIME). Your AIME is then used to calculate your primary insurance amount (PIA), which becomes the number the SSA uses to determine the actual amount of your monthly benefit.

Here's where it gets tricky. Your PIA is made up of fixed percentages of predetermined amounts of your AIME. Those dollar amounts go up each year; however, the percentages do not.

In 2014, the monthly PIA benefit for a disabled worker looks like this:

90% of $0 to $816

32% of $817 to $4,917

15% of anything above $4,917

Let's say your AIME is $8,000. This means your PIA comes out to …

90% of $816 is $734.40

32% of $4101 is $1,312.32

15% of $8,000 - $4,917 or $3,083 is $462.45

Which totals $2,509.20 when rounded to the nearest .10.

Eligibility for Supplemental Security Income (SSI)

The SSI program makes monthly payments to people who have low income and few resources, who are age 65 or older, or who are blind or disabled. Children who are disabled or blind may also receive SSI if they meet certain criteria. The primary requirements here are limited income and resources and being disabled. Simply put, if you make more than a certain amount of money, you will not receive SSI even if you are disabled.

In 2014, the basic monthly SSI payments are $721 for one person or $1,082 for a couple. As noted in the government booklet "You May Be Able to Get Supplemental Security Income (SSI)," if you receive SSI, you're also expected to apply for any other cash benefits available to you, including Medicaid to pay doctor and hospital bills and Supplemental Nutrition Assistance Program (SNAP), which assists in paying for food. You can download this free booklet at ssa.gov/pubs/EN-05-11069.pdf.

What Is the Definition of Being Disabled?

Under SSI, being disabled means you can't participate in any gainful employment due to a physical or mental impairment as an adult. For children, being disabled means a child's physical or mental impairments result in extreme limitations.

Duration of Disability Requirements

The duration of disability means the impairment had to have lasted, or is expected to last, for at least one year or result in your death, such as having terminal cancer. The 12-month period doesn't necessarily mean you have to have been severely ill or impaired for a year *before* applying for benefits. You only have to expect the impairment to last at least one year to be able to apply.

The SSA will deem a qualified impairment eligible if it hasn't improved after three months. Sometimes it can be awarded sooner in situations where it's obvious you are going to be impaired or unable to work because of a condition for a protracted period of time (if you broke your back or lost the use of your legs, for example). In those cases, the SSA can make an immediate ruling.

Income Limits

There are strict income limitations for receiving SSI. For nonblind people, couples cannot earn more than $1,082 a month in 2014 (around $12,984 annually). If you're single and not blind, the amount drops to $721 a month (around $8,652 annually). This is known as the Federal Benefit Rate (FBR).

The FBR also sets the maximum amount you can receive in an SSI payment. These payments are typically supplemented by state funds in all but a few states. The states not providing additional financial support are Arizona, Arkansas, Mississippi, North Dakota, Oregon, Tennessee, and West Virginia. All other states allow higher SSI payments than the federal maximums.

Resource Limits

Income isn't the only thing being considered to qualify for SSI. Your assets must also not exceed a certain level. Assets are considered anything that can be converted into cash. This means if you own property that you don't live on, it can be considered a sellable resource.

Resources are categorized as either liquid or nonliquid. Liquid assets are cash or anything that can be converted into cash within 20 working days, which includes savings and checking accounts, stocks, bonds, mutual funds, promissory notes, and some kinds of life insurance. Nonliquid assets would include property such as land or a house or co-op you don't live in; and personal property, such as cars, clothing, jewelry, silverware, musical instruments, etc. In 2014, you would not be eligible for SSI if your assets exceeded $2,000 for a single person or $3,000 for a couple.

The SSA will exclude certain assets, such as your primary residence, some restricted Indian land, household goods, and personal effects up to $2,000. Also excluded are wedding and engagement rings of any value; necessary health aids such as wheelchairs or prosthetic devices; one car;

grants, fellowships or scholarships used to pay tuition; life insurance with a face value of $1,500 or less; burial plots worth up to $1,500; disaster relief; and housing assistance you receive under the U.S. Housing Act, the National Housing Act, or the Housing and Urban Development Act.

Citizenship and Residency Requirements

Unlike SSDI, SSI disability payments are usually only given to U.S. citizens. But there are a few exceptions under which a noncitizen would qualify, such as:

- During the first seven years after you entered the United States, you became a legal resident as a refugee, have been granted asylum, or under certain conditions you entered as an Amerasian immigrant, or have been granted status as a Cuban or Haitian entrant.

- You legally entered the United States.

- You were honorably discharged from the U.S. military or are on active duty in the U.S. military; or are the spouse of a veteran or person on active duty, the unmarried dependent child of a veteran or person on active duty, or the surviving spouse of a deceased veteran or person who died on active duty and you are still unmarried.

- You were lawfully residing in the United States and receiving SSI benefits on August 22, 1996.

- You were lawfully residing in the United States on August 22, 1996, and you are blind or became disabled.

- You are lawfully residing in the United States and are a Native American who was born in Canada.

- You have been battered or subjected to cruelty by a family member while in the United States.

The Application Process

There are three ways you can apply for disability benefits: online, by scheduling an appointment to apply at the local SSA office, or by speaking over the phone with an SSA employee.

But before you contact SSA and begin your application, you should do your homework to ensure your claim is presented accurately so it can be processed properly and in the shortest amount of time. It is extremely important to keep detailed records and documents related to your impairment in order to show how it impacts your ability to work.

Documenting Your Symptoms

One of the first things you should do is keep a daily record of your symptoms—of how you feel, both physically and emotionally—and keep track of anything you're no longer able to do. Keep in mind, however, a Social Security Administration fact sheet notes, "The medical condition(s) must be shown to exist by means of medically acceptable clinical and laboratory findings. Under the law, symptoms alone cannot be the basis for a finding of disability, although the effects of symptoms may be an important factor in our decision whether a person is disabled."

Necessary Information and Documents

Gather together all your pertinent medical records from doctors, therapists, hospitals, clinics, and any laboratory results (both positive and negative) to support your claim of being disabled. (If you are applying for disability for an adult child who is unable to work, have all the notes and any other records from all doctors' visits.) You'll also need the following:

- A summary of where you worked and the kind of work you performed for the past 15 years.

- A copy of your most recent W-2 Form, or if you are self-employed, your federal tax return from the previous year.

- Your Social Security number.

- Your birth certificate or some other proof of age, such as a driver's license, state ID, or passport.

Field Office Observations

If you decide to apply in person at a local Social Security field office, a field office representative will be observing you while you're there. That means she will be watching as you fill out the application form(s), and will keep notes on how you do in terms of reading, writing, answering questions, hearing, sitting, using your hands, breathing, seeing, walking, and anything else that might bear upon your claim.

There won't be any medical exams because the person taking your application isn't a doctor or nurse. But she will keep a record of what she observed.

The SSA examiners will read these observations and consider them, along with all the other data you provided, in deciding for or against your claim. For example, if the field officer wrote that you had no problem walking, but your claim indicates you do, it could raise some questions. It doesn't automatically mean your claim will be denied, only that the examiner will be looking more closely at your ability to walk.

Processing Your Application

The agency that determines whether your impairment is bad enough to keep you from working and qualify you for benefits is called the Disability Determination Service (DDS). This is a state agency funded either by the federal government or the state, and the SSA will send your claim there once it determines that you meet all the nonmedical requirements for eligibility.

Most claims for disability benefits are handled through a network of state DDS offices. The DDS office informs the SSA of their decision. If the DDS reaches a favorable decision, SSA administers sending out the disability benefits.

The DDS will go over your medical records and may even contact your doctor(s) for more information. They may also contact your employer or visit your business if you are self-employed to verify your work activities.

If more information is needed, they will also contact you and may request further medical examinations or lab tests. If they do, the SSA pays for it. This is called a consultative examination and it can be performed by your regular doctor, or the SSA can arrange for an independent doctor to perform it. SSA pays for it no matter who performs the exam.

The Impact of Other Disability Payments on Social Security Benefits

If you receive workers compensation or benefits from a different publicly funded disability program, it could impact your Social Security benefits. Examples of these would be civil service disability benefits, state temporary disability benefits or state or local government retirement benefits that are based on disability.

If you receive workers compensation or any other public disability benefits the total amount of these benefits cannot exceed 80 percent of your average current earnings before you became disabled. If the total amount of these benefits exceeds 80 percent of your average current earnings, the excess amount is deducted from your Social Security benefit.

For example, for a family of four, if before you became disabled your average earnings were $4,000 a month, you, your spouse, and two children would be eligible to receive $2,200 a month in Social Security disability benefits. Then, if you also receive $2,000 a month from workers' compensation, your family's Social Security benefits would be reduced by $1,000 because the total amount from both benefits, $4,200, is $1,000 more than 80 percent of your average earnings of $3,200.

Fortunately, the SSA will deduct legal, medical, and rehabilitation expenses from any workers compensation award before decreasing your Social Security disability benefit.

Some payments have no impact on your Social Security disability payment. These include:

- Veteran's Administration (VA) benefits
- Federal benefits (if the work you did to earn them was covered by Social Security)
- State and local government benefits (if the work was covered by Social Security)
- Private pension plans or insurance benefits
- Supplemental Security Income (SSI) payments

How the SSA Makes Its Decision

There are a number of factors that go into determining whether the SSA approves your disability claim or rejects it. First, if you're currently working and earning income, the SSA may consider you gainfully employed, or in their terms, engaged in substantial gainful activity (SGA). If that's the case, your claim will be denied.

Second, if you are not engaged in SGA, the SSA looks at the severity of your illness or impairment. Again, if your problem is not deemed bad enough to significantly limit your ability to work, they will deny your claim.

This means that even if you have one of the medical problems listed in the Blue Book list of impairments, it may not be enough. Your impairment has to be so severe that you are unable to work in your job or any other job where your skills are transferrable.

Furthermore, if your impairment is deemed severe enough, the SSA then determines whether the impairment is expected to last at least one year or lead to death. If the answer is no, your claim will be denied. If the answer is yes and you have all the previous requirements, your claim probably will be approved.

In 2006, the SSA initiated what's called the Quick Disability Determination (QDD). QDD is used with claimants who meet both the legal and medical eligibility requirements and are definitely disabled, including those who are blind, suffering from metastatic cancer, have kidney failure to the point they need dialysis, or are no longer able to walk. In these cases, your claim could be approved within two to three weeks.

Receiving Benefits

Now that you've been approved, you'll receive a certificate of award that spells out what you'll be receiving in terms of disability benefits. Unfortunately, these payments won't start immediately. In fact, you won't begin receiving disability payments for five months after the date you're declared disabled, which is called the "established onset date" (EOD).

On the positive side, you'll be paid retroactively back to your EOD even if you didn't apply for disability until a few weeks or months after you became disabled. There is, however, a maximum of 12 months of retroactive benefits.

Disability Benefit Payments

Once approved, SSA will first notify you to tell you how much you will be receiving each month in disability benefits as well as when your payments will begin. If any family members are eligible for benefits based on your work credits, they will receive a separate notice and booklet. Your payments will usually begin in your sixth month of disability.

Payments will continue for as long as your medical condition prevents you from working. But don't expect your benefits to last forever. Science and medicine are constantly working to come up with new techniques that improve and hasten rehabilitation, allowing more and more people to recover from disabilities caused by accidents or illnesses. You should expect the SSA to review your case every so often just to make sure you still qualify for disability benefits.

Currently, monthly payments are made electronically using your bank's routing number and the checking account number you provided when you applied.

If you didn't provide this information, you should contact the SSA and provide it as soon as possible to receive payments electronically. Otherwise, the Treasury Department may send your payments through what's called the Direct Express card program. With Direct Express, payments are made directly to a debit card account, which can be used like a regular bank debit card. You can sign up for the Direct Express card by calling the U.S. Treasury's electronic payment solution contact center at 1-800-333-1795. You can also sign up online at GoDirect.org.

There's also a third option to receive the funds called an Electronic Transfer Account. This is a low-cost, federally insured account that allows you to receive automatic payments. You can contact the SSA or go online at eta-find.gov for more information about the Electronic Transfer Account.

Receiving Medicare Benefits After 24 Months

After receiving disability benefits for 24 months, you become eligible to receive both Part A (Hospital Insurance) and Part B (Medical Insurance) from Medicare. Sometimes you might even qualify for Medicare before then. For example, if you have permanent kidney failure requiring dialysis on a regular basis or a transplant, or you have amyotrophic lateral sclerosis (Lou Gehrig's disease), you could qualify for Medicare almost immediately.

Returning to Work

If you return to work, take a job, or become self-employed, you need to notify the SSA. They'll want to know how many hours you expect to work and when your work starts and stops. You need to do this no matter how little you're paid.

However, just because you're working again doesn't automatically mean your disability payments will stop. In fact, if you're still disabled, you'll be eligible for a Trial Work Period (TWP), and you can continue receiving benefits for up to nine months.

 TIP

Some work will not count toward the nine-month period also known as the Trial Work Period (TWP). For example, if you earn less than $780 per month (in 2015) no matter how many hours you worked, it will not be counted.

You also need to tell the SSA if you have any distinct work expenses because of your disability, such as specialized equipment like a wheelchair, or whether you have to continue taking prescription drugs.

Ticket to Work Program

The SSA has what's called the Ticket to Work Program. It's designed so you can use it to obtain services to help you go back to work or to earn more money. It's open to anyone from age 18 to 64 who is getting Social Security Disability Insurance (SSDI) or Supplemental Security Income (SSI). Through this program, SSA offers free employment services including career counseling, job placement, job training, and vocational rehabilitation.

You used to get a ticket in the mail and you would take that physical ticket to your state's vocational rehabilitation agency or to an employment network that has agreed to work with Social Security to provide employment services to people with disabilities. But Social Security discontinued sending out paper tickets through the mail. Instead, whatever service you choose to work with, such as job placement and training, vocational rehabilitation, or career counseling, will confirm that you are eligible to participate in the program.

This program is purely voluntary and participation is free. For more information, ask the SSA for Publication No. 05-10061, "Your Ticket to Work," or you can download the free booklet at ssa. gov/pubs/EN-05-10061.pdf. You'll find more information on Ticket to Work at ssa.gov/work.

Ticket to Hire Program

The Ticket to Hire program provides services to employers, employment networks, and state vocational rehabilitation agencies. It's an outreach referral service that links employers with people receiving disability benefits who want to work or earn money.

The Ticket to Hire program helps increase the opportunities for disability recipients by ensuring successful job placements through employer participation. The program provides resources and solutions within the full range of disability employment issues, and it reduces barriers to employment. It also serves as a one-stop place for employers to recruit, hire, and retain qualified workers with disabilities.

The Least You Need to Know

- A disability is a severe mental or physical impairment that prevents you from working for at least a year.
- There are two disability benefits programs available: Social Security Disability Insurance (SSDI) and Supplemental Security Income (SSI).
- You need to provide your Social Security number and birth certificate, medical records, and employment information when applying for disability.
- To be eligible for disability, you must have worked long enough to earn a certain number of work credits based on your age.
- Ticket to Work is a free and voluntary program that provides those receiving disability benefits who are eligible with employment services such as career counseling, job placement, vocational rehabilitation, and job training.

Filing an Appeal with Social Security

Whether you're filing a claim for disability or for retirement benefits, you have the right to appeal the Social Security Administration's decision if your claim is denied or you disagree with your benefit amount.

That means that if you think the SSA's decision to deny your disability claim is wrong, or the amount of your monthly Social Security retirement benefit is lower than you're entitled to based on your own computations, you have the right to plead your case and explain why they should revise their decision.

The clock on your decision to appeal begins ticking as soon as you receive SSA's decision or the Notice of Award for Retirement, Survivors, and Disability Insurance.

Once you receive this notice, you have only 60 days, beginning on the day you received the letter, to request an appeal in writing. If you take longer than 60 days, the SSA may still consider your appeal, but you'd better have a good reason for delaying, otherwise they may not.

In This Chapter

- How to appeal if you disagree with the SSA's decision
- Why many disability claims are denied
- The four levels of the appeal process
- How to find a good disability attorney

You must ask for an appeal in writing by filling out the SSA's Form SSA-561-U2, known as the Request for Reconsideration form. You can get this form online at socialsecurity.gov/forms/ssa-561.html, or you can call and request that a copy be mailed to you. Or you can visit one of SSA's local field offices to obtain a copy.

When you request an appeal, the SSA will review their original decision and if they determine an error was made and their original decision was wrong, they will change it. However, you will have to make a strong case as to why they were initially wrong in their decision.

When and How to File an Appeal

The first step in the *appeal* process is to submit a Request for Reconsideration form. Directions for how to submit the form are in the letter you receive from Social Security denying your claim. This letter will spell out what you need to do if you want to appeal the SSA's decision.

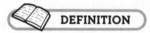 **DEFINITION**

An **appeal** is a four-level process beginning with a simple Request for Reconsideration and ending with taking your case to federal court, if necessary. You can file an appeal if you receive a determination from the Social Security Administration that they're denying your initial request for benefits for either retirement or disability or if, once you're receiving benefits, they reevaluate your situation and decide to stop paying them.

Appealing a Disability Claim Denial

The easiest and fastest way to appeal is to go to the Social Security website at socialsecurity.gov/disability/appeal. If for some reason you are unable to do that, you can either call and talk to someone over the phone or visit your local Social Security field office in person. Someone there can help you with your request for reconsideration.

There are, of course, a lot of reasons for a disability claim to be denied. According to the SSA, of the more than 2.3 million disability claims that were filed in 2013, 31 percent were denied for purely technical reasons. These technical reasons included:

- The claimant's income was higher than the SSA's limit.

- The claimant lacked the necessary work credits to be eligible for disability.

- The claimant was unable to prove a relationship to a disabled person.

- The claimant lacked the necessary information requested in the application.

- The claimant's application included errors.

Out of all the people who were eligible to apply and completed applications for disability benefits, only 38 percent of those under consideration were awarded benefits. The remaining 62 percent had their claims denied.

According to the SSA, less than half (48 percent) of those who have their claims denied file an appeal or a Request for Reconsideration. Usually the claimants don't believe they have a chance or they give up too easily. Sometimes they file too late, or worse, they file a new claim and start the process all over again. The SSA says this is usually a mistake; claimants would have had a better chance if they had appealed the original claim. Without resolving or dealing with the reasons the initial claim was resolved, it's likely that the newly filed claim will also be denied.

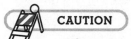 **CAUTION**

Filing a new application if your first claim is denied is usually a waste of time because chances are you'll be denied again for the same reason your first application was denied. You stand a better chance if you resolve the reasons the first claim was denied and then appeal that decision.

The bottom line is that if you feel the SSA has made a mistake or you simply do not agree with the decision, you should ask the SSA to reconsider. Plus, filing an appeal is free, so you have nothing to lose.

Appealing Incorrect Retirement Benefits

Your right to appeal extends to your retirement benefits as well. If you disagree with a decision made on your Social Security retirement benefits claim—either your claim was denied or you think the amount you were awarded is insufficient based on your verified calculations—you can appeal that, too.

For an explanation of the steps you should take, ask the SSA for a copy of the "The Appeals Process" (Publication No. 05-10041) or read it online at ssa.gov/pubs/EN-05-10041.pdf.

You can handle your own appeal with free help from the SSA or you can choose to have a representative help you. For more information about selecting a representative, ask the SSA for "Your Right to Representation" (Publication No. 05-10075) or read it online at ssa.gov/pubs/EN-05-10075.pdf.

Keep in mind that even if your request for reconsideration is rejected, there are a total of four possible levels to the appeal process available to you:

1. A request for reconsideration

2. A hearing by an administrative law judge (ALJ)

3. A review by the Appeals Council

4. A federal court review

Let's take a look at each step.

The Request for Reconsideration

When you request reconsideration, there will be a complete review of your original claim. This review will be conducted by someone who wasn't involved in making the initial decision to deny your claim. The new examiners will review all of the evidence and information in the original claim, plus any new information you wish to add that was not included in your original submission.

Note that the request for reconsideration can refer to an appeal for two different points in the benefits process. There is the request for reconsideration of the initial claim—you were denied either Social Security retirement benefits or disability benefits, or you're appealing the amount of the award. But there is a second type of request for reconsideration: when you're already receiving benefits, but the SSA reevaluates your claim and your benefits are stopped. You can appeal that decision as well.

 WORTH NOTING

There are 10 states that have a streamlined appeal process in which the initial appeal goes directly to an administrative law judge. These states are Alabama, Alaska, California, Colorado, Louisiana, Michigan, Missouri, New Hampshire, New York, and Pennsylvania.

Usually, the review of your files is done without you needing to be there. However, there are some instances in which your presence is required. For example, if you're appealing a decision that you are no longer eligible for disability because your impairment has improved, you could meet in person with a Social Security representative to show that you're still disabled or to explain why you're still unable to work.

There are three different forms you may have to fill out, all of which are available online. These forms are:

- Request for Reconsideration (Form SSA-561-U2, socialsecurity.gov/forms/ssa-561.pdf)

- Disability Report-Appeal (Form SSA-3441-BK, socialsecurity.gov/forms/ssa-3441.pdf)

- Authorization for Source to Release Information to the SSA (Form SSA-827, socialsecurity.gov/forms/ssa-827.pdf)

Sometimes you only have to fill out the first form. The second two are in case you have additional information to add regarding your medical condition that was not included in your first claim. If you need to authorize the release of further medical information, the third form is required.

After filling out all the forms you need and attaching copies of any evidence showing how the denial of the original claim is incorrect, mail all your forms in a standard business envelope to your local Social Security field office. Make sure you keep a copy of everything you send. You might also consider sending it by priority mail, which is relatively inexpensive and doesn't require a signature, but provides you with a tracking number so you can follow up and see if your envelope actually arrived. You may also, of course, send your claim by certified mail, or with a return receipt requested, or overnight it with or without a signature required.

Your request for reconsideration review doesn't take place at your Social Security office. It occurs at Disability Determination Services (DDS), which is a state office funded by the federal government or by your state. Your request is reviewed by another examiner who wasn't involved in your original claim. The medical consultant will review all the evidence submitted and make a determination. If your claim is again denied, you still have the right to appeal by requesting a hearing before an administrative law judge (ALJ).

Requesting a Hearing

If you continue to disagree with the reconsideration decision, you can request a hearing before an ALJ. The ALJ will be someone who had no role in the original decision or the reconsideration of your case. But before that happens, the SSA will probably ask you to provide more evidence or to clarify some of the information in your original claim. Again, you'll have 60 days to file a second appeal to request a hearing, plus an extra 5 days to account for mailing time.

The hearing is usually held within 75 miles of where you reside. You'll be notified by the ALJ assigned to your case of the time and place of your hearing.

To request an ALJ hearing, you'll have to fill out three forms, which you can find online:

- Request for Hearing (Form HA-501-U5, socialsecurity.gov/forms/ha-501.pdf)
- Disability Report-Appeal (Form SS-3441-BK, socialsecurity.gov/forms/ssa-3441.pdf)
- Authorization for Source to Release Information (Form SSA-827, socialsecurity.gov/forms/ssa-827.pdf)

At the hearing, the ALJ will question you and any witnesses you bring. These witnesses may include medical or vocational experts. You and any authorized representative you bring will also be allowed to question these witnesses.

WORTH NOTING

You may be able to receive benefits during the appeals process if you file your Request for Reconsideration within 10 days of receiving your Continuing Disability Review (CDR) Notice of Benefits Cessation along with a request for continuing cash benefits and Medicare. However, if you lose your appeal, you may have to repay the SSA for those continued benefits.

If you can't attend the hearing, you must let the SSA know why as soon as possible. There's always the chance the ALJ could decide your presence is not needed and, if that's the case, then you won't have to go. However, you should always have a good reason why you are unable to attend the hearing in person.

In some circumstances, the hearing can be held via video conference rather than in person. The SSA will notify you in advance if this is to occur. Video hearings are typically arranged to make the hearing more convenient to you in terms of time and traveling distance. Usually, a video conference can be scheduled sooner than an in-person appearance, and it can also be closer to your home. Plus, a video conference can make it easier for your witnesses to attend.

After the hearing, the ALJ makes a decision based on all the information in your case, including any new information provided at the hearing. This decision will be to either continue to deny your claim or overturn the previous decisions. The SSA will send you a letter and a copy of the judge's decision.

If your claim is again rejected, you can still go to the next level in the appeal process, the Appeals Council.

The Appeals Council Review

If you disagree with the ALJ's decision, you can appeal this to the Appeals Council by asking for a review of your claim. To take this action, you need to fill out yet another form (Form HA-520-U5, socialsecurity.gov/forms/ha-520.pdf). You have 60 days to file this appeal, with 5 days for the mailing time.

The Appeals Council will look at your request and may decide to turn it over to another ALJ for further review. On the other hand, it may deny your request if it believes the decision by the ALJ was correct.

If the Appeals Council denies your request for review, the SSA will send you a letter explaining why. However, if it decides to review your case and renders a decision, it will send you a copy of that decision.

Federal Court

If you disagree with the Appeals Council's decision, or if the Appeals Council decides not to review your case, you can still argue your case in federal court. You do this by filing a lawsuit in which you will be suing the Social Security Administration in U.S. District Court.

Again you will receive a letter with the Appeals Council's decision, along with how to go about filing a lawsuit in federal court if you wish to consider pursuing the matter.

According to the SSA, less than 1 percent of disability claimants take this action, which isn't free. In fact, one reason more people don't do this is because of the legal fees and time involved. It can take years for your case to wind its way through the federal court.

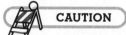
CAUTION

> Usually, taking your case to federal court is the final step you can take to appeal your claim. You can, in some circumstances, take your case as high as the U.S. Supreme Court. However, that will occur only if the high court determines the case should receive special consideration, meaning that its outcome could impact other claimants or in some way have constitutional implications.

Will Your Benefits Continue During the Appeal Process?

There's a chance your benefits will continue during the appeal process, but you may have to request this by asking the SSA to continue paying them while it decides on your appeal. You can ask for a continuation of benefits when:

- You are appealing the SSA's decision that you can no longer receive Social Security disability benefits because your medical condition has improved so much it no longer prevents you from working.

- You are appealing the SSA's decision that you are no longer eligible for Supplemental Security Income (SSI) payments or that your SSI payments should be reduced or suspended.

If you want your benefit payments to continue, you must request that within 10 days of the date you receive the SSA's letter. Just keep in mind that if your appeal is rejected, you may have to return any money you received that you were not eligible to get.

Your Right to Representation

There's no rule that says you have to go through this process alone. You have the right to hire a lawyer or someone else who is knowledgeable about these matters, or even to have a friend there for you, acting as your authorized representative during the appeal process.

The SSA is more than willing to work with you and your authorized representative. Keep in mind that this representative must first receive the SSA's approval before he or she can charge or collect a fee out of your disability benefits. Once designated, your representative is able to act on your behalf in most issues regarding your appeal and will receive a copy of all SSA correspondence.

However, just because you have the right to representation doesn't mean you're going to need someone other than yourself to represent you. In fact, the only reasons for appointing an authorized representative to handle your disability claim are …

- You don't feel capable of handling the claim yourself.

- Your impairment actually prevents you from doing everything you need to do to represent yourself.

- You don't have the time necessary to fill out all the required forms or to attend any hearings.

In addition to those reasons, however, you might just find that dealing with the various state or federal government agencies is difficult for you, especially if you have not done so before. Relying on an expert, such as a lawyer with experience in handling disabilities or Social Security Administration appeals, could be a wise investment—especially if the outcome could mean tens of thousands of dollars over your lifetime.

How to Find a Representative

There are typically two groups of authorized representatives: those who are attorneys and those who are not. Your local SSA field office should be able to help you find an authorized representative, or you can go to socialsecurity.gov/forms/ssa-1696.html for more help.

When choosing a representative, he or she should be a person in good standing, be able to help you with your claim, and meet certain standards set by the SSA. The SSA has been known to disqualify someone from serving as an authorized representative for one of the following reasons:

- They've knowingly falsified information.

- They've charged an unauthorized fee.

- They've previously been suspended or disqualified to be an authorized representative.

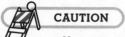
CAUTION

Your representative cannot charge or collect a fee from you without first receiving written approval from the SSA.

How to Find a Lawyer to Help with Your Appeal

Many people feel more comfortable letting an attorney deal with another attorney when it comes to the appeal process. This may especially be the case once you've reached the administrative law judge level of the process.

According to nolo.com, a network of websites that has been offering legal advice to consumers dating back more than 40 years, statistics show the chances of being approved for disability benefits increases for those claimants who are represented by an attorney who specializes in disability cases.

Nolo.com has a directory of disability lawyers at its website (nolo.com/lawyers/disability) organized by state. They also are associated with DisabilitySecrets.com, which offers information about disability.

Another method for finding a lawyer to help with your appeal is through referrals. If you know someone who received disability benefits after filing an appeal through an attorney, or who received benefits after receiving a revised decision on a Social Security retirement benefits appeal, you may want to have a consultation with their attorney and decide if you want to hire him or her.

Here are some things to consider asking when interviewing possible lawyers:

- Will they give you a free consultation?

- Are they courteous and professional?

- How much experience do they have with the SSA appeal process?

- Do they make exaggerated promises, or do they provide an honest and realistic assessment of your case?

- What is their approval rate?

- How many years have they been in practice?

- Are they licensed to practice in your state?

- How long have they practiced in this area?

The reason you ask the last question is to establish whether they have experience with the administrative law judges who could hear your case if it gets to that level of the appeal. A knowledgeable lawyer may know how to tailor their arguments when dealing with a particular ALJ if he or she has had past experience with that specific judge.

> **TIP**
>
> If you want more information about representatives, you can download Publication No. 05-10075 "Your Right to Representation" at ssa.gov/pubs/EN-05-10075.pdf.

Deciding If You Need an Attorney

Only you can determine whether you can handle your appeal on your own or if you need a representative. Most people don't use a representative until they reach the hearing stage of the appeal process. However, keep in mind that, statistically speaking, those who use an attorney experienced with appeals, including disability cases, fare better than those who don't.

Once you reach the hearing level of an appeal, an attorney will help you by making sure you have everything you need before appearing in front of an administrative law judge. They will check that you have all of your medical records and any medical or vocational opinions, and perhaps most importantly, they will prepare you for questioning to ensure you are ready to answer any and all questions the judge is likely to ask.

Moreover, as we mentioned previously, a disability attorney is more likely to be familiar with your ALJ's way of thinking. He or she will know what arguments will work best with the ALJ, as well as any weaknesses in your case that need strengthening before your hearing occurs.

The Least You Need to Know

- If your Social Security disability claim is rejected, your retirement benefits have been denied, or your benefits seem lower than you think they should be, you can appeal the decision.
- There are many possible reasons why a disability claim may be rejected, including technical errors or incomplete information on the application.
- The four possible levels of the appeal process are: request for reconsideration of the initial claim; hearing by an administrative law judge; review by the Appeals Council; and review in a federal court.
- Hiring a lawyer or other representative to help you during the appeal process may improve your chances of winning your claim.

CHAPTER 11

Special Circumstances

There are several special situations that can impact your Social Security benefits. In this chapter, we review two of the most common ones, widowhood and divorce, as well as two unique situations that impact hundreds of thousands of Americans every year: living outside of the United States or under incarceration.

For each of these situations, there are specific conditions and requirements that must be considered in terms of qualifying for Social Security benefits. Whether you qualify or not will depend on such things as how long you were married, your age, and most important of all, if you or your spouse met the minimum work credit requirements to be eligible for Social Security benefits.

In This Chapter

* Social Security protection if you're divorced or widowed
* How to maximize your spousal benefits
* What happens to your benefits if you live outside the United States
* The impact on Social Security benefits if you're incarcerated

Social Security and Divorce

Among the most overlooked benefits are the ones offered to ex-spouses, provided they meet certain criteria. For example, you need to have been married at least 10 years at the time of the divorce, be divorced for at least 2 years, and be at least 62 years old when you file for spousal (or, in this case, ex-spousal) benefits. Also, your ex-spouse needs to be at full retirement age (FRA) and eligible for Social Security benefits. Your ex-spouse, however, does *not* have to file for Social Security for you to be able to file for ex-spousal benefits. You can do an independent filing. Nor will your ex-spouse have to be told that you are filing for ex-spouse benefits based on his work record.

 TIP

If you're at your FRA, which will be 66 or 67 depending upon the year you were born, it might be possible the Social Security Administration (SSA) will make an exception to the rule of having a 2-year delay between the divorce and filing for ex-spousal benefits as long as you were married for 10 years before the divorce, you have not remarried, and your ex-spouse qualifies to receive benefits.

How Benefits Are Affected by Divorce

Just because you're divorced doesn't mean you can't collect spousal benefits based on the work record of your ex. As stated, it depends on a number of factors, including your age, your ex-spouse's age, and whether you have remarried.

If your ex-spouse has remarried, it will not impact whether you can also claim ex-spousal benefits. It's you who must not have remarried, because that would disqualify you from claiming ex-spousal benefits.

Criteria for Collecting Ex-Spousal Benefits

Here's a summary of the conditions you have to meet in order to be able to receive benefits based on your ex-spouse's earnings record even if he or she has remarried:

- Your marriage lasted at least 10 years.
- You're still unmarried.
- You're age 62 or older.
- Your ex-spouse qualifies for Social Security benefits (either retirement or disability).

- It's been at least 2 years since your divorce (although SSA might make an exception to this if you've reached your FRA).

- The benefits you would receive based on your own earnings record is less than one half the benefits you would get based on your ex-spouse's earnings record.

WORTH NOTING

If you remarried after your divorce, you can still be eligible for benefits based on your first ex-spouse's earnings record if your second marriage ended in death, divorce, or annulment, and you meet all of the other criteria. You currently must be single to apply for ex-spousal benefits, and if you had multiple ex-spouses, you can only claim ex-spousal benefits on one of them. However, you can choose the one with the higher benefits when applying for your ex-spousal benefits.

How Much Will an Unmarried Divorced Spouse Receive?

The amount you can receive as a divorced spouse depends upon a variety of factors. For example, if you're entitled to retirement benefits based on your own earnings record, the SSA will pay you that amount first. However, if one half of your ex-spouse's benefit is higher than yours, you'll receive a combination of both your and your ex's benefits equal to the higher amount.

WORTH NOTING

The benefits you could receive don't include any delayed retirement credits your ex-spouse may receive by postponing his or her benefits beyond full retirement age. However, if you have reached your own FRA, you can choose to receive only your divorced spouse's benefits now and delay receiving your own until the maximum age of 70. Doing so will enable you to receive higher benefits at a later date, based on accruing delayed retirement credits on your own earnings.

Some other things to consider are that if you apply for benefits as a divorced spouse before you reach your FRA, your benefit will be at a reduced rate just as it would be if you applied for your own benefit as a single person. You would see about an 8 percent per year reduction. The reduced rate, as noted previously, is based on the fact that the rates are reduced unless you postpone receiving your Social Security benefits until your FRA.

If you continue to work while receiving ex-spousal benefits, there will be a cap placed on how much you can earn if you are receiving those benefits before reaching your FRA. These are the same earnings caps for anyone who is still working before their FRA and receiving Social Security benefits. If you receive a work pension not covered by Social Security, such as pensions for working for the government or in a foreign country, your benefits can also be impacted.

Applying for Benefits Based on an Ex-Spouse's Work Record

You can apply for Social Security benefits based on your ex-spouse's work record either by going in person to a Social Security field office or by going online to socialsecurity.gov and following the prompts for your particular situation. You can also apply over the phone by calling 1-800-772-1213.

The key is to make sure you first have gathered the necessary information to complete your application. This includes the following:

- Your ex-spouse's Social Security number

- Your own birth certificate or proof of birth

- Proof of U.S. citizenship or lawful alien status if you weren't born in the United States

- Your marriage certificate to that ex-spouse

- Your final divorce decree

In addition to those items, the SSA will ask you for the following:

- Your own Social Security number

- Your name at birth (if it has changed)

- Whether you or anyone else has ever filed for Social Security benefits on your behalf

- Whether you have ever used any other Social Security number

- Whether you receive any benefits from military service or a federal civilian agency

- Whether you or your spouse have ever worked for the railroad

- Whether you have earned Social Security credits under another country's Social Security system

- Whether you receive or expect to receive a pension or annuity from the federal, state, or local government

- Whether you are currently married

- The names, ages, and Social Security numbers of any other former spouses

- Dates and places of each marriage, and how and when each marriage ended

- The names of any unmarried children under age 18, ages 18 to 19 and in secondary school, or disabled before the age of 22

- The names of employers, or if self-employed, your earnings for this year, last year, and projected earnings for next year.

Furthermore, the SSA may need to ask you even more questions, depending on the information you provide.

You may also want to have your checkbook handy or at least your bank's routing number and your account number so you can sign up for direct deposit to expedite the payment process once your benefits start.

Social Security and the Death of a Spouse

There are few periods in an adult's life as traumatic as the death of a spouse. Emotionally it is devastating, but if that spouse was also the primary wage earner, his death can throw the surviving family members into financial turmoil. Fortunately, there's some relief available from the SSA in the form of survivors benefits.

Survivors Benefits

Survivors benefits are benefits the SSA pays to certain eligible family members of a deceased worker. This can include widows and widowers, as well as divorced widows and widowers, children, and in some cases, dependent parents.

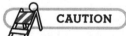 **CAUTION**

> In general, you need to have been married at least nine months to be eligible to collect Social Security survivors benefits based on your deceased spouse's work record. Exceptions may include if the deceased's death was a job-related accident, if you had a child or adopted his/her child, or if the death occurred in the line of duty in active uniformed service.

Here's a breakdown of eligibility requirements for the different types of survivors:

- If you're a widow or widower, you may be eligible for full benefits at your FRA, which at this time is 65 to 67, depending on when you were born. (If you need help computing your FRA, refer back to the age table in Chapter 7.) Reduced widow (or widower) benefits are available for you beginning at age 60. If you're disabled, you can begin receiving benefits at age 50. In addition, if you're caring for a child who is also receiving Social Security benefits and is younger than 16 or disabled, you can receive survivors benefits at any age.

- Unmarried children who are younger than 18, or between 18 and 19 and still attending secondary school, can also receive survivors benefits.

- Children who are disabled before turning 22 can receive benefits at any age. There are also circumstances in which stepchildren, grandchildren, step-grandchildren, and adopted children can also receive benefits.

- If your dependent parents are 62 or older, they may also be eligible to receive survivors benefits. However, in order for them to qualify as dependents, the deceased would have to have been providing at least one half of their support.

- If you are a surviving divorced ex-spouse, you can begin receiving benefits at age 60, or 50 if you are disabled, as long as your marriage had lasted at least 10 years. If you are caring for your ex-spouse's child under the age of 16 or a disabled child, you can collect at any age.

 WORTH NOTING

If you remarry *before* reaching age 60, or age 50 if you are disabled, you are ineligible to receive survivors benefits during your new marriage.

However, if you remarry *after* reaching age 60, or after age 50 if you are disabled, you are still eligible for survivors benefits on your deceased spouse's work record.

How to Apply for Survivors Benefits

As with most things related to Social Security, timing is key in applying for survivors benefits—the sooner, the better. Keep in mind, however, benefits are usually paid from the time you apply and *not* from the time your spouse or ex-spouse died.

To apply for survivors benefits (if you are not already receiving Social Security benefits), call or visit your local Social Security field office. Bring the following information or documentation with you:

- Proof of death. Usually the funeral home will provide you with the official death certificate. (If possible, get multiple originals so you always have at least one or two originals in your files. Note, you likely will have to pay for each one.)

- Your Social Security number as well as the Social Security number of the deceased.

- Your birth certificate.

- Your marriage certificate.

- Your divorce papers if applying as a divorced widow or widower.

- The deceased worker's W-2 forms or federal self-employment tax return for the most recent year.

- Your bank's routing number and your account number so that your benefits can be deposited directly into your account.

If you're already receiving Social Security benefits based on your spouse's work credits when you report his or her death, the SSA will change your payments to survivors benefits. If they still need more information to process your application, they'll get in touch with you.

If you're receiving benefits based on your own work history, contact the SSA and ask them to check to see if you could receive more as a widow or widower. If you can, then you'll receive a combination of benefits that equal the higher amount. In this case, you'll have to complete an application form to switch to survivors benefits and the SSA will want to see your spouse's death certificate.

Calculating What Survivors Benefits You're Due

Your amount of survivors benefits is determined by how long the deceased worked as well as their age at the time of death. The younger that person was, the fewer years he would have had to work to become eligible for any Social Security benefits.

Basically, survivors receive a payment calculated upon the average lifetime earnings of the deceased, just like retirement benefits. That means the more the deceased earned, the more their survivors will receive. To determine this figure, check the Social Security statement of the deceased, which should give you an estimate of what your survivors benefits will be.

Please note: you will not be able to use the retirement calculators at the Social Security website to estimate what you might receive as a survivor. These calculators only estimate your benefits. Contact your local Social Security office or call their toll-free number (1-800-772-1213 or 1-800-325-0778 for the hard of hearing) to find out how much you might receive on your deceased spouse's work record.

There are a number of variables to consider when calculating your survivors benefits. For example, if you are a:

- Widow or widower at full retirement age or older, you will receive 100 percent of your deceased spouse's benefit.

- Widow or widower between age 60 and your FRA, you will receive between 71 to 99 percent of your deceased spouse's benefit.

- Disabled widow or widower age 50 through 59, you should receive 71.5 percent.

- Widow or widower of any age and caring for a child under the age of 16, you will receive 75 percent.

- Child under the age of 18, 19 and still in high school, or disabled, you will receive 75 percent of your deceased parent's benefit.

- A surviving dependent parent of a deceased worker, age 62 or older, you will receive 82.5 percent.

- Two surviving dependent parents of a deceased worker age 62 or older, you should each receive 75 percent.

- Surviving divorced widow or widower, you should receive the same amount as a widow or widower.

You might also be eligible for a lump-sum death benefit, which we will talk about in a bit.

Maximum Family Amount

You should keep in mind that there's a limit to what a family can receive each month. Although the limit varies, the maximum amount any one family can receive is between 150 to 180 percent of the worker's basic benefit rate.

For more information on the maximum family amount, you can call Social Security's toll-free number at 1-800-772-1213, visit your local field office, or go to socialsecurity.gov.

 TIP

Even if a worker has worked for only one and one-half years in the three years prior to his/her death, under a special rule survivors benefits can be paid to the deceased worker's children and the spouse who is caring for the children.

Government Pension Offset

If you receive a government pension from working for the federal, state, or local municipal government where you did not pay Social Security taxes, your survivors or ex-spouse's benefits may be reduced by something called the Government Pension Offset.

Typically, this reduction will amount to two thirds of your government pension. For example, if you receive a monthly civil service pension of $1,000, then two thirds or $666 of that pension would be offset or deducted from your Social Security benefits. If you are also eligible for a spouse's, widow's, or widower's benefits, those benefits would be reduced by $666 or be offset by your government pension.

Applying for the One-Time $255 Death Benefit

Survivors can apply for a one-time Lump Sum Death Benefit (LSDB) payment of $255 when their spouse dies, provided the deceased spouse worked long enough to be eligible for Social Security benefits.

The LSDB was actually included in the original 1935 Social Security legislation, although the average amount paid back in 1939 was $96.93, according to a document prepared in 1996 and updated in 2006 by Larry DeWitt of the SSA Historian's Office.

The LSDB was originally included in the legislation, according to DeWitt, because there was initially no survivors benefit option. The LSDB was supposed to amount to 3.5 percent of the worker's earnings that were covered by Social Security; at that time, it was a maximum of $3,000 per year.

There were amendments over the years to LSDB, but the $255 amount has been the same since a 1954 Amendment. It might not sound like a lot of money to some, but when you consider that in 2012 there were 770,000 LSDB payments made, the total added up to $220 million.

The LSDB payment is made only to a surviving spouse of a deceased worker eligible for Social Security benefits, or to a dependent child if there is no surviving spouse at the time of the eligible worker's death, if they meet certain criteria and apply within two years of the deceased's death. The following criteria must be met to receive the $255 LSDB:

- The surviving spouse was living with the deceased worker when he or she died.

- If the surviving spouse was living apart from the deceased worker, he or she had already begun receiving retirement benefits at the time of death or became eligible for benefits at the time of death.

- If there is no surviving spouse, the LSDB can be paid to a surviving dependent child or children if, during the month the worker died, the child or children had already begun receiving retirement benefits on the worker's record or became eligible for benefits at the time of the worker's death.

If You Are Living Outside the United States

You are considered to be living outside the United States if where you reside is not one of the 50 states or in any of these additional districts: the District of Columbia, Puerto Rico, Guam, American Samoa, or the Northern Mariana Islands.

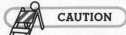 **CAUTION**

The SSA considers you living outside the United States if you have been in another country for at least 30 days in a row. Until you return and live in the United States for 30 consecutive days, you are technically still considered living outside the United States.

Many people on Social Security choose to live abroad because their money goes farther, and they can live a more luxurious lifestyle where the cost of living is lower. For example, there is a large contingency of retired Americans living in Baja, Mexico, because the cost of living is lower there.

There are, however, some countries where the SSA will not send benefit payments, such as Cuba, North Korea, Azerbaijan, Belarus, Georgia, Kazakhstan, Kyrgyzstan, Moldova, Tajikistan, Turkmenistan, Ukraine, Uzbekistan, and Vietnam.

The SSA has a booklet that contains detailed information on how living outside the United States will impact your payments, as well as what information you need to report to the SSA to ensure your payments are kept up to date and protected. This booklet is titled "Your Payments While You Are Outside the United States" and you can access it for free online at ssa.gov/pubs/EN-05-10137.pdf.

In most situations, if you're living in countries such as Austria, Belgium, Canada, Chile, Czech Republic, Finland, France, Germany, Greece, Ireland, Israel, Italy, Japan, South Korea, Luxembourg, the Netherlands, Norway, Poland, Portugal, Spain, Sweden, Switzerland, and the United Kingdom, you will receive payments without any restrictions.

On the other hand, if you're living in South America or other European and Asian nations not on the no-restrictions list, there are additional requirements you will have to meet. Again, read the previously mentioned booklet to get information about your specific country.

The same rules apply to survivors or ex-spouses as to primary Social Security beneficiaries.

There are other rules that apply to anyone who is not a U.S. citizen. These rules in such specialized circumstances are noted in the SSA booklet.

If you do work or own a business outside the United States, you should notify the U.S. Embassy in the country in which you are living if you have not already done so. If you don't, you could be penalized and possibly lose some of your benefits.

Incarceration

Currently 2.4 million Americans are incarcerated in state and federal prisons. Almost 700,000 Americans are released from prison, including local jails, each year. How does incarceration impact your Social Security benefits?

If you're in prison, you're not eligible to receive Social Security benefits during your incarceration. If you're receiving Social Security benefits when you are sentenced, those benefits will be suspended if you are incarcerated for longer than 30 days due to conviction for a crime. Your benefits will be reinstated one month following your release. Your spouse or children, however, will be able to continue receiving benefits as long as they are eligible.

As soon as you are released and you have reached age 62, or your FRA, or age 70, you may apply for Social Security retirement benefits as long as you worked enough years to acquire the necessary 40 work credits and you paid into Social Security *before* you were incarcerated. Even if you aren't eligible for Social Security retirement benefits, you may still qualify for Supplemental Security Income (SSI) if you are 65 or older, blind, have a disability, or have limited or no income and resources. None of this is automatic, however, which means you're going to have to apply for it if you think you deserve it.

To help you in this matter, the SSA has produced a booklet titled "What Prisoners Need to Know." It contains everything you should know about applying for Social Security, disability, or SSI once you leave prison. You can access this free publication at socialsecurity.gov/pubs/EN-05-10133.pdf.

Remember, you will not be paid for your time in prison, nor will this time count toward your required work credits.

In order to receive benefits once you're released, you'll need to contact Social Security and give them a copy of your release documents.

The Least You Need to Know

- You can apply for spousal benefits even if you're divorced as long as you meet certain criteria.

- You can receive survivors benefits beginning at age 60, or at 50, if you're disabled. If you're caring for a dependent child, you can begin immediately receiving survivors benefits.

- Survivors benefits start when your application is approved, not upon the death of the eligible worker.

- A surviving spouse can apply for a Lump Sum Death Benefit (LSDB) of $255, but it must be applied for within two years of the eligible worker's death.

- With some exceptions, such as Cuba and North Korea, you should still be able to collect your Social Security benefits even if you reside outside the United States.

- Social Security benefits stop when you're incarcerated for 30 days or more, but begin again upon your release. You must apply for a reinstatement of your benefits and you'll need release papers for the application.

Family Benefits

When you start receiving Social Security benefits either for retirement or disability, some members of your family could also be entitled to benefits based on your work history. These family benefits are also called auxiliary benefits and will not impact what you receive each month, but could add a significant amount to your family's funds overall.

Provided they qualify, your child or spouse could receive monthly benefits that total up to 50 percent of your benefit. These benefits are available to eligible family members when you retire, become disabled, or die. The fact that these benefits are available to eligible family members could help you decide when to start taking your benefits.

In This Chapter

- Who qualifies for family benefits
- The SSA's definition of family
- Benefits available for qualified children
- How to get the maximum family benefits

Dependents and Spouse Benefits

Over time, the amount your family members will receive could total hundreds of thousands of dollars. Some financial advisors have compared family Social Security benefits to having a six-figure life insurance policy.

Who's in the Family

When the Social Security Administration (SSA) uses the term *family*, it's a little different than the common definition. In Social Security parlance, "family" means anyone who receives benefits that are tied to an insured worker's primary insurance amount (PIA). What does that mean? Well, if you and your spouse are retired and are both receiving benefits based on each of your own work credits, you will be counted by the SSA as two families. But if one spouse is taking spousal benefits because he or she didn't accumulate the necessary work credits, the couple are counted as one family.

Relationship to the Retired or Disabled

To further complicate things, the SSA has three categories of families and a total of 24 distinct family relationship types. Here's how they break out.

A family with a retired worker could include:

- A single retired worker who's at least 62 years old.

- A married retired worker and spouse, both of whom are at least 62 years old.

- A married retired worker and spouse of at least 62, who have one or more children.

- A married retired worker, young spouse with either a child under the age of 16 or a disabled child in his or her care, and one or more nondisabled children.

- A married retired worker, young spouse, and two or more nondisabled children.

- A retired worker with one or more nondisabled children.

- Any family with a retired worker.

A family with a disabled worker could include:

- A disabled worker only.

- A disabled worker and a spouse who's at least 62 years old.

- A disabled worker, spouse 62 or older, and one or more nondisabled children.

- A disabled worker, young spouse with either a child under the age of 16 or a disabled child in his or her care, and one or more nondisabled children over 17.

- A disabled worker, young spouse, and two or more nondisabled children.

- A disabled worker and one or more nondisabled children.

- Any family with a disabled worker.

A survivor family could include:

- One or more children of a deceased worker with the children under the age of 18, a high school student under the age of 19, or a child who has become disabled before the age of 22, in addition to a surviving spouse who is not receiving a benefit.

- A 60+-year-old widow or widower, where the marriage lasted at least nine months. There are exceptions, however: for example, if the insured worker was expected to live nine months but accidentally died before that time was up, and his death was caused by an accident not more than three months after the bodily injuries occurred, with the exception of suicide, or death in the line of active military duty.

- An aged widow or widower with one or more dependent children.

- A disabled widow or widower who is at least 50 years old.

- A young widow or widower with a child under the age of 16 or a disabled child in his or her care and one or more nondisabled children.

- A young widow or widower with two or more nondisabled children.

- Any surviving family.

WORTH NOTING

Since the SSA has no fewer than 24 family relationship types that could qualify you, your spouse, or children as a family, check to see if you fit into any of the definitions of a family. For same-sex relationships, what SSA defines as a family for the purpose of retirement or disability benefits is more complicated. Check with your state and then with SSA for your particular circumstances.

Age Qualifications

By now it's become apparent that the SSA has established age qualifications for nearly every benefit. Here's a brief rundown of some of the more common age qualifications or requirements anyone seeking any kind of Social Security benefit is likely to encounter:

- The earliest age you can receive retirement benefits is 62.

- Retirement benefits for widows and widowers begin at 60.

- If widows or widowers are disabled, they can begin receiving retirement benefits at age 50.

- You can begin receiving your personal Social Security statement online if you are a worker 18 years of age or older. This statement is an important tool to help you plan for your financial future by providing estimates of what your benefits will be at different retirement ages, as well as what disability benefits you can receive if you become disabled and are unable to work. Go to ssa.gov to create an account. Your full retirement age (FRA) depends on when you were born. If you were born before 1944, your FRA is 65. For those born between 1943 and1954, it's 66, and for those born after 1960, it's 67.

- Retirement benefits will increase 8 percent annually after your FRA until you reach age 70. This annual increase is known as the delayed retirement credit.

- If you are receiving retirement benefits, your spouse age 62 or older can also receive spousal benefits.

- Spouses who are younger than 62 and are taking care of a child who is younger than 16 or is disabled may also qualify for spousal benefits.

- Former spouses who remain unmarried and are age 62 could qualify for spousal benefits if they were married for 10 years or more and it has been at least 2 years since their divorce before they filed for benefits.

- Children up to the age of 18, or 19 if still in high school, are eligible for family benefits.

- Children who became disabled before the age of 22 are eligible at any age.

Maximum Family Benefits

There is a maximum amount your family can receive above your Social Security benefit no matter how many dependent children you have. This maximum ranges between 150 and 180 percent of your total monthly benefit payment.

Of course, there's a special complicated formula for determining what your particular family maximum benefit is, but we'll try to keep this as simple as possible. It's similar to the formula the SSA uses to determine the benefits amount you receive at your FRA (or what they call your Primary Insurance Amount [PIA]).

If you remember from earlier in the book, the formula used to compute your PIA takes percentages of four different sections of your PIA. These sections are called "bend points."

For 2014, the bend points are:

- 150 percent of the first $1,042 of your PIA.

- 272 percent of your PIA between $1,042 and $1,505.

- 134 percent of your PIA between $1,505 and $1,962.

- 175 percent of your PIA over $1,962.

For the family of a disabled worker, it's a little different. In that situation, the family maximum is either 85 percent of the worker's average indexed monthly earnings or 150 percent of the worker's PIA if one is available.

How a Spouse Can File for Auxiliary Benefits

Auxiliary benefits are those benefits that are paid to eligible family members. You can apply for auxiliary benefits by calling SSA's toll-free number at 1-800-772-1213, or by visiting a local field office and applying in person. When you do, here is a list of some of the documents you should have handy:

- If you're filing for yourself or your child, you'll need all your birth certificates or other proof of birth.

- Your proof of marriage to the worker.

- Proof of U.S. citizenship or your lawful alien status.

- U.S. military discharge papers, if relevant.

- W-2 forms and/or self-employment tax returns for the last year.

If you're applying for disability benefits for an adult child disabled before the age of 22, there are two special forms you'll need to complete:

- The Adult Disability Report (SSA-3368).

- Authorization to disclose information to the Social Security Administration (Form SSA-827).

Chances are the SSA representative will ask you to provide the following information:

- Your name and your Social Security number.

- The worker's name and his or her Social Security number.

- Date of birth, Social Security number, and relationship to the worker (such as each biological or adopted child, stepchild, or dependent grandchild) for each child listed on the application.

- The child's citizenship status.

- If any child 17 years or older is a student or is disabled.

- If any child is the worker's stepchild in addition to when and where the worker and the child's parent were married.

- Whether you are the child's natural or adoptive parent.

- Whether the child has a legal guardian.

- If the child has been adopted by someone other than the worker.

- Does the child live with you and did he or she live with the worker during each of the last 13 months?

- If the child has ever been married, and if so, the dates and locations of the marriages and how and when those unions ended.

- Whether you or anyone else has ever filed for Social Security benefits, Medicare, or Supplemental Security Income (SSI) on behalf of the children. If so, the SSA will ask for information about whose Social Security record was used for the previous application.

- If the child worked, the amount of each child's earnings for this year, last year, and projections for next year.

- Dates of any adoption of any children by the worker.

- Whether you have been convicted of a felony.

- Whether any child age 13 or older has any unsatisfied felony warrants for arrest or unsatisfied federal or state warrants for arrest for any violation of the conditions of their parole or probation.

- Whether you have ever served as a representative payee for someone's Social Security benefits.

If the worker is deceased and you are filing as a survivor, you will be asked for:

- The worker's date of birth and his or her name at birth if different from the name at death.

- The worker's date and place of death.

- State or foreign country of the worker's fixed permanent residence address at the time of death.

- Whether the worker was unable to work due to illness, injuries, or conditions at any time in the 14 months prior to death. If the answer is yes, you will also be asked for the date he or she became unable to work.

- Whether the worker was in active military service before 1968 or ever worked for the railroad. If the answer is yes, you will also be asked to provide dates of service and whether he or she received a pension from the military or a federal civilian agency.

- Whether the worker earned Social Security credits under another country's Social Security system.

- Whether the worker was employed or was self-employed between 1978 and last year.

- How much the worker earned in the year of his or her death and the previous year.

- Whether the worker ever filed for Social Security benefits, Medicare, or Supplemental Security Income. If yes, you will be asked for information about whose Social Security record he or she applied on.

- Whether each child was living with the worker at the time of death.

Filing for Disability Benefits for Dependents

When you become eligible for disability benefits, some of your family members (such as your spouse and dependent children) may also qualify for auxiliary benefits.

Filing for auxiliary benefits for your spouse and dependent children is similar to the process of filing for yourself, with a few additional steps.

To receive auxiliary disability benefits, your spouse must be under the age of 62 and be the joint caregiver of your children age 16 and under. If your spouse divorces you, he or she may still qualify for auxiliary disability benefits as long as you were married for at least 10 years.

For children to qualify, they must be dependents, under the age of 18 unless enrolled in school full time, and unmarried.

Dependent children who are legally adopted are also eligible, along with dependents who do not live with you, such as a child for whom you provide child support. A disabled child is considered a dependent if he or she became disabled before the age of 22.

How Can a Spouse Receive Disability Benefits?

Your spouse or ex-spouse may be eligible for disability benefits once you qualify for disability benefits. He or she must meet certain criteria, such as:

- The spouse must be caring for your child who is under the age of 16 or disabled and receiving Social Security benefits.

- Your spouse is old enough to receive retirement benefits at age 62 or older or survivors benefits as a widow or widower starting at age 60.

WORTH NOTING

Your spouse also can get disability benefits, which is usually around 50 percent of the benefits you are receiving based on your work record, if he or she is over 62, you are receiving disability benefits, and/or he or she is caring for a dependent child under 16 or a disabled child. One or more of your children may also receive benefits. However, there is a maximum family benefit, which is approximately 150 to 180 percent of your monthly benefit.

Reasons for Denying Spousal Benefits

There are only a few reasons why a spouse is denied benefits. Here are some of those reasons:

- He or she is not over the age of 62.

- He or she is not the joint caregiver of any dependent children you have with either your current spouse or ex-spouse.

- An ex-spouse wasn't married to the worker for at least 10 years.

- Two years have not yet passed between the divorce and the filing for ex-spousal benefits by the ex-spouse.

- For retirement benefits, the spouse or ex-spouse does not have enough work credits to qualify for Social Security retirement benefits or has not yet reached their FRA.

- For survivor benefits, the spouse or ex-spouse did not have enough work credits to qualify for Social Security retirement benefits. Although there is the special ruling that benefits can be paid to the worker's children and the spouse caring for the children if the worker worked for only one and one-half years in the three years prior to their death.

- For survivor benefits, the widow or widower wasn't married to the eligible worker for at least nine months prior to the worker's death.

- If a surviving spouse remarries before the age of 60 or before the age of 50 if disabled, they cannot receive survivors benefits as long as they are remarried. (However, if they remarry *after* the age of 60 or after the age of 50 if disabled, they can qualify to receive benefits on the Social Security work record of the deceased spouse.)

As previously mentioned, if your spouse is 62 years old or older, she doesn't need a child to care for in order to qualify for Social Security benefits based on your earnings. From the age of 62 and older, spousal benefits are available to your spouse on the basis of age alone. But you must have reached your FRA for your spouse to apply for spousal benefits, which will usually be computed at 50 percent of your retirement benefit at your own FRA. If your spouse is still working, he or she needs to consider the income caps on their earnings, or their Social Security benefits will be reduced according to the formula the SSA created. In 2014, the income cap was raised to $15,480, which was a $360 increase over 2013.

Here's how it works. From the age of 62 until the year you reach your FRA, if you earn more than that income cap, Social Security will withhold $1 in benefits for every $2 you earn over that limit.

However, in the year you reach your FRA, the income cap rises to $41,400. If you go over the income cap during that year, Social Security will withhold $1 in benefits for every $3 you earn over that cap. As you know, there is no income cap once you reach your FRA.

In addition, you can also continue putting your own earnings into the pool for your benefits. Then when you reach age 70 you can switch from spousal benefits (50 percent of your spouse's benefit) to 100 percent of your own benefits, which would have increased by 8 percent each year you delayed taking your benefits after reaching your FRA.

However, you cannot switch from spousal benefits to your own benefits if you had already begun receiving your own benefits at an earlier age. The rate at which you began taking retirement benefits is the same rate that will remain for the rest of your life. So if you started receiving your benefits at age 62, the rate (or amount) you receive will remain at that reduced rate forever.

You can, however, pay back Social Security all the benefits income you received before switching to spousal benefits, and then restart your own at a later date for higher benefits.

Check with your local Social Security office to see if this option is available to you. If it is, find out what amount you would be required to repay if you want to pursue this higher benefits option beginning at age 70, based on your own work credits and earnings record.

The break-even point for taking Social Security at 70, which could be as high as $3,500 a month, is between ages 83 and 84. So you will have to live at least until that age to make it financially beneficial to wait until 70 to take your benefits. If you die before then, you've lost the advantage of starting your benefits at a later date.

Do You Have Parental Responsibility?

According to the SSA, you must have parental control and responsibility for a dependent or disabled child in order to be eligible for parental benefits. That means you must …

- Show a strong interest in properly raising the child.

- Oversee the child's activities.

- Be actively involved in making important decisions about the child's needs and welfare.

- Have control in the child's upbringing and development.

- Be responsible for cleaning, feeding, and dressing a disabled child.

- Manage the activities of a physically disabled child.

- Be physically present with the child because of the disability.

You will lose your parental benefits if you no longer meet these "in care" requirements. This can happen when a child grows up or overcomes his or her disability. For example, if you and the child no longer live together, you will not be able to receive parental benefits.

Here are some other reasons you'll lose benefits if you and the child no longer live together:

- You become mentally disabled.

- You and your spouse separate or get divorced, and you lose custody or give up your right to either directly or indirectly control the child.

- You lose care and custody of the child due to a court order.

- You give up care and custody of the child to another person or agency.

- The child is physically disabled and 16 years or older and you have been separated from him or her for more than six months.

- The child is under the care of a court-appointed guardian besides you.

Other Issues Involving Family Benefits

Because there are so many issues involving family benefits, you should contact the SSA by phone or by visiting a local office in person with any questions you may have that are not addressed in this book. Everyone's situation is different, and the laws regarding qualifications for receiving benefits are changing all the time.

Same-Sex Couples

Speaking of important changes in the law, on June 26, 2013, the Supreme Court ruled Section 3 of the Defense of Marriage Act unconstitutional, which meant the SSA was no longer prevented from recognizing same-sex marriages to determine Social Security benefits.

In fact, it has published new rules that allow the agency to process claims involving same-sex relationships. They have published an extensive Q&A of 13 frequently asked questions about same-sex relationships and how it impacts Social Security benefits at faq.ssa.gov/link/portal/34011/34019/ArticleFolder/452/Same-Sex-Couples.

If you're in a same-sex marriage, the surviving spouse of a same-sex marriage, or even a non-marital legal same-sex relationship, you can still apply for benefits including Social Security retirement benefits, survivors or ex-spouse benefits, and even the $255 Lump Sum Death Benefit (LSDB).

However, you should also be aware that the SSA follows state guidelines when it makes its determinations about same-sex marriages or nonmarital same-sex relationships and their impact on eligibility for Social Security benefits.

Social Security recommends you contact your local Social Security office or call their toll-free number at 1-800-772-1213 if you have questions about how your same-sex marriage or non-marital same-sex relationship may impact your benefits.

 QUOTATION

"Two same-sex individuals are married for SSI purposes if they are legally married under the laws of the state where they make their permanent home.

NOTE: We will **not** recognize that a claimant and a same-sex individual with whom he or she lives are married for SSI purposes because they are …

- entitled to Title II benefits, based on a marriage or other nonmarital legal relationship; or
- holding themselves out to the community as a married couple."

Source: Social Security website (https://secure.ssa.gov/poms.nsf/lnx/0500501150)

How a Child's Benefits Change with Age

Benefits to children typically end when a child reaches 18 years old or leaves high school. But if the child is disabled, that's another story. Payments can continue into adulthood if the child's disability occurred before the age of 22 and continues to be a major impairment to the ability to support him- or herself financially.

An adult who was disabled before age 22 may also continue to be eligible for child's benefits if a parent is deceased or starts receiving retirement or disability benefits. The SSA considers it a "child's" benefit because it's paid on the earnings record of a parent.

The adult child, even an adopted child, stepchild, or grandchild, must be unmarried and have been disabled since before the age of 22.

If the child is 18 or older, the SSA will evaluate his or her disability the same way it evaluates the disability for an adult. An application is filed and the SSA sends it to the Disability Determination Services (DDS) in your state.

Caring for Sick Children or Relatives

If you are the parent or caregiver for disabled children under the age of 18, you could be eligible for Supplemental Security Income (SSI) payments or Social Security Disability Insurance (SSDI) benefits payments. The child must first have to meet the SSA's definition of disability for children.

When applying for benefits for your child, you will be asked for detailed information about your child's medical condition and how it affects his or her ability to function on a daily basis.

You will also be asked to give permission to doctors, teachers, therapists, or any other professional who might have information about your child's condition to provide that information to SSA.

It usually takes the Disability Determination Services (DDS) about five months to decide if your child is disabled enough to qualify for benefits. However, there are some conditions that will get a faster response, such as if your child …

- Has an HIV infection.
- Is totally blind.
- Is totally deaf.
- Has cerebral palsy.
- Has Down syndrome (DS).

- Has muscular dystrophy.

- Has a severe mental or intellectual disorder.

Chances are, if your child has one of these conditions, he or she will receive payments much faster. Once your child begins receiving benefits, the SSA will review the child's condition about every three years to verify that he or she is still disabled.

The Family and Medical Leave Act (FMLA)

The U.S. Department of Labor, which is responsible for the nation's labor laws, has a provision to help families burdened with medical problems. It's called the Family and Medical Leave Act (FMLA), and it gives you the ability to take unpaid leave without worrying about losing your job when you need to deal with family and medical issues.

Eligible employees can take off up to 12 weeks during a 12-month period to …

- Give birth and care for a new baby.

- Care for a newly adopted infant or child.

- Care for a spouse, child, or parent with a serious medical condition.

- Care for yourself if you have a serious medical condition that prevents you from performing your job.

- Deal with any qualifying situation related to a spouse, child, or parent in the military and on active duty.

You're also eligible for 26 weeks of leave during a 12-month period if your spouse, child, or parent is a service member and suffers a serious injury or illness while on active duty and you are their caregiver.

There is currently a bill in Congress that would establish the Office of Paid Family and Medical Leave within the SSA. It would provide family and medical leave insurance benefit payments for each month you are on unpaid leave. As of this writing, the bill, sponsored by Representative Rosa DeLauro, a Connecticut Democrat, was still in the House Ways and Means Committee.

Benefits for Severe Medical Conditions

There are some medical conditions the SSA deems so severe it is willing to provide benefits as quickly as possible to anyone suffering from one of them. These benefits are called Compassionate Allowances (CAL). Basically, CAL is the SSA's way of identifying specific diseases and other medical conditions that immediately qualify you as being disabled.

To see a full list of CAL conditions, go to ssa.gov/compassionateallowances/conditions.htm. Here are a few of the more common conditions:

- Acute Leukemia
- Adrenal Cancer
- Breast Cancer
- Bladder Cancer
- Child Non-Hodgkin Lymphoma
- Heart Transplant Graft Failure
- Liver Cancer
- Lung Cancer
- Pancreatic Cancer
- Prostate Cancer
- Stomach Cancer
- Thyroid Cancer

 TIP

CAL is not a separate program; it's part of the SSA's disability benefits considerations. It enables a quicker response to those who apply so they can be considered for disability benefits. For more information on disability, see the free publication titled "Disability Benefits" at ssa.gov/pubs/EN-05-10029.pdf.

The Least You Need to Know

- Family members who qualify may be eligible for Social Security benefits.
- The maximum benefit any family member can receive varies between 150 and 180 percent of your monthly benefit payment.
- The Social Security Administration recognizes same-sex marriages in those states where it is legal.
- Your survivors may be entitled to 100 percent of your Social Security benefits after you die.

Medicare

Medicare is a somewhat complicated and often misunderstood federal health-care insurance program funded by two trust funds the U.S. Treasury holds: the Hospital Insurance (HI) Trust Fund and the Supplementary Medical Insurance (SMI) Trust Fund. The money in these funds comes from a variety of sources, including payroll taxes the majority of employers, employees, and the self-employed pay as well as income taxes paid on Social Security benefits, Medicare Part A premiums from those who are not eligible for premium-free Part A, and Medicare Part B premiums.

Medicare is administered by the Social Security Administration (SSA) and mostly used by people age 65 or older to pay for some or all of their medical bills, depending on whether they supplement the basic coverage Medicare offers.

In This Chapter

- What is Medicare?
- Who qualifies for the program?
- How you apply for benefits
- What Medicare insurance covers
- How much does coverage cost?

Medicare Basics

Simply put, Medicare is America's health-care insurance program for anyone 65 or older, and for younger people who have severe and specific medical conditions, such as those who need dialysis due to kidney failure or are in End Stage Renal Disease (ESRD).

Medicare is funded by taxes you pay, along with a monthly premium that is typically deducted directly from your monthly Social Security payment.

What you may not know is that you don't have to be 65 to qualify for Medicare if you have one of a number of medical conditions that qualify you as disabled by the Social Security Administration (SSA). For example, if you have kidney failure at age 45, you could qualify for Medicare if the SSA considers your condition permanent.

Due to the constant barrage of television and internet ads, most of us know by now that Medicare will not pay all medical bills. Unless you supplement basic Medicare, it will pay, on average, only 80 percent of your doctor's visits. But if you have Part A, which covers hospitalization, it should cover most of a hospital stay minus the $1,260 hospital deductible for each *benefit period*.

 **DEFINITION**

> A **benefit period** is the term applied by Original Medicare to your use of hospital and skilled nursing facility (SNF) services. The benefit period begins the day you're admitted as an inpatient in a hospital or SNF and ends when you have not received inpatient hospital care or skilled nursing care for 60 consecutive days.

After the benefit period ends, if you have to go into the hospital or an SNF again, it would count as a new benefit period and you would be responsible for another $1,260 deductible. Medicare does not impose a limit on the number of benefit periods you are allowed.

We'll get into what Medicare covers in greater detail later regarding what you should do to make up the difference between what Medicare pays for and what you're likely to be billed for depending on your medical history and health.

 WORTH NOTING

> Medicare was created on July 30, 1965, along with Medicaid, when President Lyndon B. Johnson signed amendments to the Social Security Act.

Signing Up for Medicare

Signing up for Medicare is easy, provided you qualify. Just go to socialsecurity.gov and click on the Medicare benefits application. You can complete and submit your application completely online in about 10 minutes.

If you are at least 64 years and 9 months old, you can start the process. Basically, you should sign up for Medicare three months before you turn 65 because it takes about 90 days to process your application.

You can also call SSA's toll-free number at 1-800-772-1213, or 1-800-325-0778 if you are deaf or hard of hearing. If for some reason you can't apply online or over the phone, you can go to a local Social Security field office to apply in person.

 WORTH NOTING

> If you're already signed up for Social Security benefits because you started early retirement between the ages of 62 and 64, or you are receiving benefits from the Railroad Retirement Board (RRB), you will usually automatically receive Medicare Part A and Part B commencing on the first day of the month when you turn 65. But if your birthday is on the first day of the month, Part A and Part B will begin on the first day of the previous month.

Your Medicare card should arrive through the regular mail approximately three months after you apply. If you receive Social Security benefits due to a disability, your card should be sent in the 25th month of your disability. If your card doesn't arrive automatically within a reasonable time period, contact your local Social Security office.

Defining Medicare Parts A, B, C, and D

There are four different parts to Medicare:

Part A covers hospital expenses and helps pay for inpatient care in a hospital or approved skilled nursing facility following a hospital stay, as well as for some home health care and hospice care.

Part B is medical insurance that helps pay for doctor visits and other health-care providers, outpatient care, home health care, durable medical equipment (such as wheelchairs), and some preventive services.

Part C is known as Medicare Advantage. Medicare Advantage consists of health-care plans that cover all the benefits and services under Parts A and B along with additional prescription drug coverage, which you can also receive separately under Part D. Part C plans are administered by Medicare but through approved private insurance companies and include extra benefits and services for an additional cost.

Part D is for prescription drug coverage; it helps pay the cost of your prescription drugs. These plans are available through various health-care companies with state-by-state monthly premiums, annual deductibles, and other differences.

Some of the companies offering Part D plans include Aetna, Anthem Blue Cross and Blue Shield, Cigna, Humana, Stonebridge, Unicare, and United HealthCare. It's up to you to choose the right plan by assessing your current prescription drug costs. You'll need to figure out if your monthly expenses are lesser or greater than the premium for the selected plan, as well as how much the plan will pay for the specific drugs you require.

In addition, each plan may also have an annual cap you must consider when deciding which plan is best for you and your prescription drug costs and needs.

For example, if you need only one prescription drug per month and it costs you $10 out of pocket, and the least expensive plan costs $21 per month, you'll actually spend more money for the plan than you would pay for your one drug out of pocket as long as you stay healthy and your prescription drug needs stay consistent.

However, say you have to take one or more drugs, such as one of the newer drugs to treat atrial fibrillation. This drug costs around $230 if you paid without a plan, but only $20 through a Part D plan. In that particular case, the $21 per month plan payment offers you excellent savings over paying out of pocket.

What Parts Should I Enroll In?

If you're already getting Social Security benefits, you'll automatically start receiving Part A and Part B when you turn 65. If you're under 65 and disabled, you'll also get Parts A and B after you start receiving disability benefits (which has a five-month waiting period after you become disabled). If you have amyotrophic lateral sclerosis (ALS), you'll also qualify for Medicare Parts A and B beginning the month your disability benefits start, which will be immediately because the five-month waiting period is not required.

On the other hand, if you're about to turn 65 and have not yet started to collect Social Security, you'll have to sign up for Medicare.

Most people sign up for Part A because it's free for most everyone age 65 and older. As long as you or your spouse paid Medicare taxes while you worked, and you have the required minimum of 10 years of work credits, Part A is premium-free. If not, you can buy Part A. It will cost $407 a month in 2015, reduced from $426 a month in 2014, depending on how many years, if any, you worked and paid Medicare taxes.

As for Part B, if you're already covered by health-care insurance through your own or your spouse's employer or union, you don't have to sign up for Part B, which you do have to pay for.

In any case, you should contact your employer or union benefits administrator to learn how your coverage works with Medicare.

In many cases, it would be wise to delay enrolling in Part B until you absolutely have to. You can sign up for it without a penalty any time you have health coverage from your current employer. Once that employer coverage ends, you have eight months to sign up for Part B without paying a late penalty.

> ### WORTH NOTING
>
> In 2014, most people paid $104.90 a month for Medicare Part B. (That monthly benefit amount remains the same for 2015.) However, in certain instances, if your IRS tax return was above a certain amount in 2013, in 2015 you have to pay more. See the Table below in the section entitled, "The Costs of Medicare."

Some people have what's called TRICARE, which is health insurance for active-duty military, retirees, and their families. If you have TRICARE, you must enroll in Parts A and B as soon as you're eligible in order to keep your TRICARE coverage. You're definitely going to want to do that because TRICARE will pay all Medicare deductibles and co-insurance costs for any service TRICARE covers that Medicare does not. (For more information on TRICARE, visit tricare.mil.)

To figure out the costs for either Part C or D, you can go to medicare.gov/find-a-plan, which allows you to compare various plans available to you. You'll be able to find out what each plan covers, the benefits it offers, and how much you'll have to pay monthly for that coverage. The calculator even shows you Medicare's opinion about each plan by rating its quality and performance.

You may also receive help by calling 1-800-MEDICARE and following the prompts to talk to an agent and get a representative who can provide you with more information so you can decide what's best for you.

Choosing the Correct Coverage

There are two primary paths to take regarding Medicare coverage. You can either choose Original Medicare, which includes Parts A and B and possibly also Part D and supplemental coverage; or choose a Medicare Advantage Plan or Part C, which includes Parts A and B but will cost you more because it usually covers services that Parts A and B don't. Let's take a look at what happens if you take each path.

If you choose Original Medicare, which includes Part A for Hospital Insurance and Part B for Medical Insurance, you'll be able to choose any doctor, hospital, or other provider that accepts

Medicare. All you'll have to pay is the deductible and any co-insurance along with a monthly premium for Part B, which is usually automatically deducted from your Social Security benefit. In 2015, that amount is $104.90 a month, the same amount as in 2014.

If you have Original Medicare, you'll receive a Medicare Summary notice in the mail every three months listing all the services that were billed to Medicare. This notice itemizes how much Medicare paid and how much you paid or owe to the provider.

You also need to decide if you need a prescription drug plan, for which you will pay an additional monthly premium. These plans are run by private companies approved by Medicare, and your decision over what, if any, plan to choose will depend on the drugs you're taking. In other words, you need to do a cost-benefit analysis to figure out what's beneficial for your circumstances. If you can save money by enrolling in a plan, you should do it; if you can't, don't.

Finally, you may want to consider getting Medigap insurance, which covers those gaps in your original Parts A and B. This supplemental coverage is also provided by private companies, and each plan has its own cost that rises as the benefits increase.

On the other hand, if you decide to go for a Medicare Advantage Plan, which is administered by a private insurance company, the plans are usually all inclusive in that they cover Parts A, B, and D. However, you'll have to pay a monthly premium in addition to your Part B premium and a co-payment for covered services. Also, in most plans, you have to use doctors, hospitals, and other providers in the plan or you may wind up paying for more or, in some cases, all of the costs.

Here are some things to consider when choosing which coverage path to take:

Are the doctors you'll be seeing nearby and do they have convenient hours?

What pharmacies can you use, and are they also convenient?

Can you receive prescriptions by mail and at a lower cost?

How much does the plan cost?

What are the deductibles?

Does this plan cover the kind of services you need?

Does the plan cover the drugs you need to take?

Is the quality of care satisfactory?

Is there an annual spending cap on prescription drugs? If there is, is it high enough to cover the drugs you must regularly take?

Will you be covered if you travel to other states or outside of the United States?

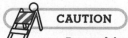 CAUTION

Be careful not to confuse the age considerations for Medicare and Social Security benefits. Full retirement age for Social Security benefits is either 66 or 67, depending on when you were born, although early retirement benefits at a reduced rate are available beginning at age 62 or, for widows, at age 60. If you want to allow your Delayed Retirement Credits to accumulate, you can begin collecting Social Security benefits as late as age 70, with the benefits increasing annually at the rate of 8 percent after reaching your FRA. Medicare, by contrast, is available for all seniors who are U.S. citizens or legal residents, beginning at age 65. But if you're receiving health insurance from your employer, you can delay or drop Medicare Part B without being penalized and start it again after your employer coverage ends.

The Cost of Medicare

The main thing to consider in making these choices is that Medicare is by and large a wonderful, cost-effective health-care plan for seniors. However, even though Medicare Part A doesn't require monthly benefit payments for most seniors who paid into the program for at least 10 years of working, Medicare is not completely free.

For example, although most will not pay a monthly premium for Part A covering hospitalization costs, there's a $1,260 deductible for each hospitalization during a benefit period.

As noted, if you didn't have a job that paid Medicare taxes, or if you did not work the required 10 years to be eligible for Social Security benefits, you may have to pay for Part A. In 2015, that monthly charge could be as high as $407 (which was reduced from the $426 a month cost in 2014).

Part B isn't free, either. For most seniors eligible for Medicare, the monthly premium is $104.90 in 2015, the same amount as for the previous year. That monthly premium is deducted from your Social Security benefits if you're already receiving Social Security, or you will be billed, if you're not. There is also an annual deductible of $147 for Part B.

If you made upwards of $85,000 or more if you're single and $170,000 or more if you're married, you may have to pay even more. That amount changes annually, depending on your income. (See the following table for a detailed listing of what Medicare Part B will cost you and your spouse in 2015 for monthly premiums, based on your 2013 tax return.)

Also, if you don't sign up for Part B when you become eligible, you may have to pay a late enrollment penalty, which is an additional 10 percent for each year you could have had Part B but failed to enroll.

Still, if you consider what private health insurance costs today, Part B is a bargain for most seniors even though it only covers up to 80 percent of doctor's visits, and there are other restrictions.

Also, if you have an income that's less than 100 percent of the federal poverty level—which amounts to around $973 a month—and minimal assets, you can probably get your Medicare deductible waived. This might also apply to the 20 percent co-insurance payments you usually have to cover since Part B usually only covers 80 percent of doctors' fees, unless you get a supplemental plan.

However, for some higher-earning seniors, Medicare Part B will cost more than the $104.90 monthly premium. The table that follows, based on information provided at Medicare.gov, the official U.S. government site for Medicare, stipulates what you will pay in 2015 based on your 2013 earnings and whether you filed an individual tax return, a joint tax return, or you filed as married but with a separate tax return.

Cost of Medicare Part B in 2015 Based on Your Yearly Income in 2013

File individual tax return	File joint tax return	File married & separate tax return	You pay in 2015
$85,000 or less	$170,000 or less	$85,000 or less	$104.90
Above $85,000 up to $107,000	Above $170,000 up to $214,000	Not applicable	$146.90
Above $107,000 up to $160,000	Above $214,000 up to $320,000	Not applicable	$209.80
Above $160,000 up to $214,000	Above $320,000 up to $428,000	Above $85,000 and up to $129,000	$272.70
Above $214,000	Above $428,000	Above $129,000	$335.70

Providers calculate their Medicare fees using the Medicare Physician Fee Schedule (MPFS), which places a value on different procedures coded by the American Medical Association. Fees are also adjusted based on what part of the country you're in.

How much will you have to pay out of pocket if you have Medicare Part B? It depends on a couple of factors. There are two types of categories a doctor can fall under. He or she can be a participating provider, which means they accept Medicare for payment, or they choose not to accept Medicare and you'll probably be responsible for the entire fee rather than just a 20 percent co-pay.

What Is Medigap?

Medigap is Medicare's version of supplemental insurance. It's sold by private Medicare-approved companies and provides coverage for some of the health-care costs not covered by Parts A and B, such as co-payments, co-insurance, and deductibles. Some Medigap plans also provide coverage for when you travel outside the United States, along with other services your original Medicare doesn't cover.

Here's what you need to know about Medigap plans:

- Before you can sign up for one, you must already be enrolled in Medicare Parts A and B.

- You'll pay a monthly premium for Medigap, in addition to the premium you already pay for Part B and, if you don't qualify for avoiding a monthly premium for Part A, that premium as well.

- Your Medigap policy will cover only one person, which means if you and your spouse both want Medigap, you'll need two separate policies.

- Medigap policies are guaranteed renewable, which means you can't be denied coverage for any medical reason as long as you pay the premiums.

- As of January 1, 2006, Medigap plans no longer cover prescription drugs.

- It's illegal for anyone to sell you a Medigap policy if you have a Medicare Medical Savings Account (MSA) plan.

 WORTH NOTING

There are currently 11 different Medigap policies to choose from. These policies go by the letters A, B, C, D, F, High-Deductible F, G, K, L, M, and N. The monthly premiums range from as low as $50 a month to as high as $698. You have to study what each policy offers to figure out which one, if any, is right for you and is within your budget. You can find detailed information about each Medigap plan at medicare. gov/find-a-plan/questions/medigap-home.aspx. Enter your zip code and just follow the instructions. Each policy for your area will pop up and you will see a checklist of what each plan covers.

Medigap vs. Part C Medicare Advantage

The most frequently asked questions regarding Medicare are "How does Medigap compare to Part C Medicare Advantage?" and the follow-up question, "Which one is better for me?"

The answer usually comes down to how much you spend on medical bills. Once you figure that out, you must look at both Medigap and Medicare Advantage to determine which one is most cost-effective and convenient for you.

The best advice we can give is to do your homework, because there are just too many variables to consider for each individual making this decision to give blanket advice.

Go to the chart listed at the website noted previously medicare.gov/find-a-plan/questions/medigap-home.aspx. You'll still have to contact the policy providers to find out exactly what the plans will cost you in monthly premiums. But this chart offers a good place to start in your comparison shopping about the various plans.

As for Medicare Advantage plans, go to medicare.gov/find-a-plan/questions/search-by-plan-name-or-plan-id.aspx and follow the instructions.

There are pros and cons to choosing either plan. For example, Medigap is usually more expensive, but it offers a larger network of doctors and significant additional coverage to Medicare Parts A, B, and D. On the other hand, Medicare Advantage plans are less expensive while offering the same additional coverage, but they're usually more restrictive in that there is a smaller network of doctors.

It all comes down to money and convenience. If you can afford Medigap that may be the best route for you, while those on more restricted budgets may want to consider a Medicare Advantage plan.

What Medigap Doesn't Cover

Although Medigap is an all-inclusive add-on to basic Medicare coverage, it doesn't cover the following:

- Prescription drugs
- Long-term care
- Vision care
- Dental care
- Hearing care
- Private duty nursing

How Medicare Works

Medicare is administered through the Centers for Medicare and Medicaid Services (cms.hhs. gov), and depending on whether you choose Original Medicare or a Medicare Advantage Plan, the plans work slightly differently.

Original Medicare is administered by the federal government, which means there are rules and regulations each step of the way. Also, as we mentioned earlier, there are costs involved, including the monthly fee as well as the annual deductible that you must pay before Medicare will pick up any medical costs.

Here's how Medicare works. First, you receive your Medicare Card in the mail. This card enables you to go to any doctor or hospital that accepts Medicare patients.

You pay the monthly premium for Part B. In 2014 the amount was $104.90 monthly, with a once-a-year deductible of $147. The monthly premium will be deducted from your Social Security monthly payment if you receive Social Security. If you don't receive Social Security, you'll get a monthly bill. Note that if your adjusted gross income exceeded a certain amount on your IRS tax return two years before, you may have to pay a higher Part B premium.

If you need to take prescription drugs, you may want to consider taking part in a Medicare Prescription Drug Plan, or Medicare Part D, since prescriptions are not covered under Parts A and B.

If you don't have any other health-care coverage, you may want to consider a supplemental or Medigap policy that pays those costs that Medicare does not cover. Only you can decide if this is something you think you'll need. Some financial advisors recommend Medigap because you never know when you'll be hospitalized or have an accident. Even though Medicare covers most of your hospital and medical costs, there's a $1,260 deductible for each benefit period.

The Donut Hole

The coverage gap in Part D drug plans is called the "donut hole," and it refers to a temporary limit on what Part D will cover for drugs.

The good news is that not everyone on Medicare has to worry about a coverage gap. This gap only occurs after you and your drug plan have spent the amount covered for drugs by your plan. In 2014, that limit was $2,850. Once the combined amount plus your deductible reaches that amount, you enter into the so-called donut hole or coverage gap.

Note that this limit could change annually. For example, in 2015 you enter the coverage gap once you spend $2,960 on covered drugs. Here's the way it works: once you reach the coverage gap in 2015, you'll pay 45 percent of the plan's cost for covered brand-name prescription drugs (down from 47.5 percent in 2014). However, you'll only get these savings if you buy your prescriptions at a pharmacy or through an accepted mail-order pharmacy. The discount will be deducted from the price your plan has negotiated with the pharmacy for that specific drug.

Most available drug plans have a website or a customer service representative who will help you figure out what pharmacies are included in their plan. They'll also help you determine how much you'll save on any of the prescription drugs you currently take, based on signing up for their particular plan. Make sure you have the correct drug name, dosage, and any other important details about every medication you regularly take so you can make the best decision about the optimum drug plan for you.

Even though you'll pay only 45 percent of the price of brand-name drugs in 2015, 97.5 percent of the price—what you pay plus the 50 percent manufacturer discount payment—will count as out-of-pocket costs, which will help you get out of the coverage gap. What the drug plan pays toward the drug cost and toward the dispensing fee isn't counted toward your out-of-pocket spending.

For example, let's say you reach the coverage gap in your Medicare drug plan. You go to your pharmacy to fill a prescription for a covered brand-name drug. The price for that drug is $60, and there's a $2 dispensing fee that is added to the cost. You'll pay 45 percent of the plan's cost for the drug or $27, plus 45 percent of the cost of the dispensing fee or 90 cents, for a total of $27.90 for that prescription.

Here's where it gets a little confusing. Because both the total amount that you paid ($27.90), plus the manufacturer's discount payment ($30.00) count as out-of-pocket spending, their total of $57.90 will be counted as out-of-pocket spending and will help you get out of the coverage gap. The remaining $2.55, which is 2.5 percent of the drug's cost and 52.5 percent of the dispensing fee paid by the drug plan, isn't counted toward your out-of-pocket spending.

Here's something else you should know. Starting in 2014, Medicare began paying 28 percent of the price for generic drugs during the coverage gap. You'll need to pay the remaining 72 percent of the price. What you pay for generic drugs during the coverage gap will decrease each year until it reaches 25 percent in 2020. So in 2015, you'll pay 65 percent of the price for generic drugs during the coverage gap.

Coverage for generic drugs works differently from brand-name drugs. For generics, only the amount you pay will count toward getting you out of the coverage gap.

Let's say you reach the coverage gap and you go to get a prescription filled for a generic drug. The price for the generic is $20, and a $2 dispensing fee is added. You'll pay 72 percent of the plan's cost for the drug and dispensing fee, which totals $15.84. That $15.84 will be counted as out-of-pocket spending to help you get out of the coverage gap.

On the other hand, if you have a drug plan that already includes coverage in the gap, you may get a discount after your plan's coverage has been applied to the generic drug's price. The discount for brand-name drugs applies to the remaining amount you owe.

Here's what counts toward the coverage gap:

- Your yearly deductible, coinsurance, and co-pays

- Discounts on brand-name drugs in the coverage gap

- What you pay in the coverage gap

Here's what does *not* count toward the coverage gap:

- The drug plan's premium

- The pharmacy's dispensing fee

- What you pay for drugs that aren't covered

If you think you've reached the coverage gap and therefore should get a discount when you paid for a brand-name prescription but didn't, review your "Explanation of Benefits" (EOB) given to you by your plan's provider. If the discount doesn't appear on the EOB, contact your drug plan to make sure that your prescription records are correct and up-to-date.

You can get your plan's contact information from a Personalized Search (under General Search), or search by plan name at the medicare.gov/part-d website.

Even if your drug plan doesn't agree that you're owed a discount, you can file an appeal.

Open Enrollment Period

There are specific times when you're allowed to sign up for or change your Medicare Plans beyond Parts A and B. These periods are known as open enrollment periods.

When you first sign up for Medicare, your first open enrollment period is seven months long. This period starts three months before the month you turn 65. It includes the month you turn 65, and ends three months later.

Your Medicare coverage will begin the first day of the month after you ask to join a plan. If you join sometime in the three months before you turn 65, your coverage will begin the first day of the month you turn 65.

Every year after that, you'll have a chance to make changes to your Medicare Advantage or Medicare prescription drug coverage for the following year. There are two separate enrollment periods each year.

The first is the Open Enrollment Period for Medicare Advantage and Medicare prescription drug coverage.

Between October 15 and December 7, you can:

Change from Original Medicare to a Medicare Advantage Plan.

Change from a Medicare Advantage Plan back to Original Medicare.

Switch from one Medicare Advantage Plan to another Medicare Advantage Plan.

Switch from a Medicare Advantage Plan that doesn't offer drug coverage to a Medicare Advantage Plan that *does* offers drug coverage.

Switch from a Medicare Advantage Plan that offers drug coverage to a Medicare Advantage Plan that does *not* offer drug coverage.

Join a Medicare Prescription Drug Plan.

Switch from one Medicare drug plan to another Medicare drug plan.

Drop your Medicare prescription drug coverage completely.

The second enrollment period is known as the Medicare Advantage Disenrollment Period. If you're in a Medicare Advantage Plan, you can leave your plan and switch to Original Medicare.

From January 1 to February 14 you can:

Switch to Original Medicare during this period, and you'll have until February 14 to also join a Medicare Prescription Drug Plan.

What you can't do during this period is:

Switch from Original Medicare to a Medicare Advantage Plan.

Switch from one Medicare Advantage Plan to another.

Switch from one Medicare Prescription Drug Plan to another.

Join, switch, or drop a Medicare Medical Savings Account (MSA) Plan.

 TIP

Figuring out what to do about Medicare can be daunting. If you feel you need outside help, don't be embarrassed to reach out to a free or fee-based service for individual consulting. Several services include the Medicare Rights Center, started 25 years ago, with offices in New York City and Washington, D.C. It's a nonprofit free consumer advocacy and education group that has a free hotline to answer questions about Medicare: 800-633-4227. The Medicare Rights Center can be found at medicarerights.org.

Conditions Covered by Basic Medicare Parts A and B

Part B covers a variety of services and medical conditions as well as a free annual wellness checkup. Here are the many other medical conditions it covers:

Abdominal aortic aneurysm: Medicare covers a one-time screening, provided you get a referral from your primary physician.

Alcohol misuse screening and counseling: Medicare covers one screening and four counseling sessions annually.

Ambulance services: Medicare will cover this service any time you need transportation to the hospital or a skilled nursing facility.

Ambulatory surgical centers: Medicare covers the facility fee.

Blood: Medicare covers the price of blood from a blood bank, but you may need to pay a co-pay for blood processing and handling.

Bone mass measurement bone density screening: Medicare covers testing once every 24 months.

Breast cancer screening: Medicare covers one mammogram annually.

Cardiac rehabilitation: Medicare covers programs that include exercise, education, and counseling for heart attack patients, as well as patients who have had coronary bypass surgery, chest pains, heart valve repair, angioplasty, or a heart or lung transplant.

Cardio disease behavioral therapy: Medicare covers an annual visit to a primary care doctor.

Cardiovascular disease screenings: Medicare covers three screenings to detect heart attack or stroke. These include tests for cholesterol, lipid, lipoprotein, and triglyceride levels.

Cervical and vaginal cancer screening: Medicare covers Pap tests and pelvic exams once every 24 months.

Chemotherapy: Medicare covers chemotherapy in a doctor's office; however, you may have to pay the 20 percent co-pay.

Chiropractic services: There is limited coverage through Medicare for chiropractic services, such as manipulation of the spine if it is deemed medically necessary. You'll still have to pay the 20 percent co-pay. Massage and x-rays are not covered.

Clinical research studies: Medicare covers some costs, such as office visits and tests, but you may have to pay a 20 percent co-pay.

Colorectal cancer screenings: Medicare covers a colonoscopy, barium enema, fecal occult blood test, and flexible sigmoidoscopy.

Defibrillator: Medicare covers most of the costs of a pacemaker, also known as an implantable automatic defibrillator. You may have to pay a co-pay.

Depression screening: Medicare covers one screening annually.

Diabetes screenings: Medicare covers up to two screenings annually.

Diabetes self-management training: Medicare covers outpatient training to teach you how to manage your diabetes.

Diabetes supplies: Medicare covers blood sugar testing monitors, control solutions, and therapeutic shoes. It also covers insulin if medically necessary. You must pay the 20 percent co-pay.

Doctor and other health-care provider services: Medicare covers necessary doctor visits and preventive services, such as physicals, but you may pay the 20 percent co-pay.

Durable medical equipment: Medicare covers such things as walkers, oxygen equipment, wheelchairs, and hospital beds for the home.

Electrocardiogram (EKG) screening: Medicare covers a one-time screening as part of your "Welcome to Medicare" preventive visit.

Emergency department services: Medicare covers emergency room visits, but you must pay the 20 percent co-pay.

Eyeglasses: Medicare covers one pair of glasses with standard frame, but you must pay the 20 percent co-pay.

Federally qualified health center services: Usually there is no deductible for such services, but you must pay the 20 percent co-pay.

Flu shots: Medicare covers one flu shot per season.

Foot exams and treatment: Medicare covers these services, but you must pay the 20 percent co-pay.

Glaucoma tests: Medicare covers one test annually.

Hearing and balance exams: Medicare covers hearing and balance exams, but you must pay the 20 percent co-pay.

Hepatitis B shots: Medicare covers shots for Hepatitis B for anyone at medium or high risk.

HIV screening: Medicare covers one test annually or 3 tests per pregnancy.

Home health services: Medicare covers medically necessary part-time or intermittent skilled nursing care, physical therapy, speech language pathology services, or anyone needing continual occupational therapy. A doctor must order this care and a certified Medicare home health agency must provide it. Medicare covers all charges and there are no co-pays.

Kidney dialysis services and supplies: Medicare covers three dialysis treatments a week. You must pay the 20 percent co-pay.

Kidney disease education services: Medicare covers six sessions of kidney education services if you have stage 4 chronic kidney disease. You must pay the 20 percent co-pay.

Laboratory services: Medicare covers most lab tests ordered by doctor. There isn't a co-pay.

Medical nutrition therapy services: These services are usually related to diabetes or kidney disease, and have no co-pay.

Mental healthcare (outpatient): Medicare covers visits to a psychologist, psychiatrist, clinical social worker, nurse practitioner, or other approved mental health-care worker. You must pay the 20 percent co-pay.

Obesity screening and counseling: If you have a body mass index of 30 or more, Medicare may cover up to 22 sessions annually with a counselor to help you lose weight.

Occupational therapy: Medicare covers treatment to help you perform activities of everyday life, such as dressing and bathing. You must pay the 20 percent co-pay.

Outpatient hospital services: Medicare covers most diagnostic and treatment services. You must pay the 20 percent co-pay.

Outpatient medical and surgical services and supplies: Medicare covers services such as x-rays, casts, stitches, etc. You must pay the 20 percent co-pay.

Physical therapy: Medicare covers evaluation and treatment for injuries, and you have to pay the 20 percent co-pay. Certain limits are often applied to the number visits you are allowed annually.

Pneumococcal shot: Medicare covers the shot to prevent pneumonia.

Prescription drugs: Medicare offers limited coverage of drugs you get in a doctor's office, such as a shot, oral anti-cancer drugs, or those that are part of a hospital treatment. You may want to buy a Part D Medicare Drug plan if you take a lot of uncovered prescriptions.

Prostate cancer screenings: Medicare covers one test annually. You must pay the 20 percent co-pay.

Prosthetic/orthotic items: Medicare covers arm, back, leg, and neck braces; artificial eyes and limbs; breast implants following a mastectomy; and replacement internal body parts. You must pay the 20 percent co-pay.

Pulmonary rehabilitation: Medicare covers rehab to deal with chronic obstructive pulmonary disease (COPD), but you must pay the 20 percent co-pay.

Rural health clinic services: You must pay the 20 percent co-pay.

Second surgical opinions: Medicare covers second and also covers third opinions in some cases, depending on the situation as each one is different. You must pay the 20 percent co-pay.

Sexually transmitted infections screening and counseling: Medicare covers one test annually. There is no co-pay.

Speech-language pathology services: Medicare covers services to help you regain speech and swallowing skills following a stroke or other illness. You must pay the 20 percent co-pay.

Surgical dressing services: You must pay 20 percent co-pay.

Tele-health services: These are services that use telecommunications to deliver health-related services. You must pay the 20 percent co-pay.

Tests (other than lab tests): Medicare covers x-rays, MRIs, CT scans, ECGs, etc. However, you must pay the 20 percent co-pay.

Tobacco-use cessation counseling: Medicare covers eight counseling visits a month. You must pay the 20 percent co-pay.

Transplants and immunosuppressive drugs: Medicare covers transplants. You must pay the 20 percent co-pay for the immune-suppressive drugs.

Travel: Medicare usually doesn't cover health care needed if you're traveling outside the United Sates. However, there are a few exceptions such as if you are on board a ship within territorial waters, or if you live in the United States but a foreign hospital is closer.

Urgently needed care: Medicare covers most urgent care and you must pay the 20 percent co-pay.

"Welcome to Medicare" preventive visit: This visit is available during the first 12 months you have Part B and if your doctor or other qualified health-care provider accepts assignment. There is no co-pay.

Yearly "wellness" visit: Medicare covers an annual assessment of your health. There is no co-pay.

Qualifying for Medicare Before Age 65 Under Disability

Warren is 42 years old and he recently learned that his back injury will prevent him from working for the next 12 to 15 months. He's married and has two children, ages 4 and 6, who are being cared for by his wife. She works part-time, but her income is insufficient to support the family. Warren has been told he should apply for SSDI Social Security Disability Insurance (SSDI), but he doesn't know how or if that will make him eligible for Medicare.

I have good news for Warren and for other disabled workers who meet certain criterion. The U.S. government has created a program that offers them financial help as well as Medicare even though they are not yet 65. In 2014, it was estimated that there are 8.8 million Americans receiving SSDI plus another 2 million family members relying on their related benefits.

There are five basic groups of disabled who may qualify for Medicare under disability before age 65 with the largest group being those who receive SSDI:

* Those who receive SSDI benefits.

* Family members of those who receive SSDI benefits.

* Those who receive Railroad Retirement Disability Board (RRDB) benefits.

* Those who receive End-Stage Renal Disease (ESRD) benefits.

* Those who receive benefits due to ALS or Lou Gehrig's disease.

Social Security Disability Insurance (SSDI) Benefits

If you're disabled and unable to work for at least a year, or if you have a disability that will lead to your death, you can apply for SSDI. If you're approved, you'll receive a monthly cash benefit in the sixth month. Twenty-four months after you are approved for SSDI, you'll automatically become enrolled in Medicare. As long as you continue receiving SSDI and you're under 65, you'll continue to receive Medicare. Once you turn 65, your Medicare will continue, but it will be paid out to you by a different fund.

The first step is to apply for and begin receiving SSDI. In order to be eligible for SSDI, you must have worked long enough to have earned the minimum required work credits based on age by paying FICA and Self-Employed Contributions Act (SECA) taxes on your paycheck.

The following table will help you see if you've earned the required minimum work credits.

Credits Earned Toward SSDI by Age and Number of Years Worked

Age You Became Disabled	Number of Required Credits	Number of Years Worked
21–24	6	1.5
24–31	6–18	1.5–4.5
31–42	20	5
44	22	5.5
46	24	6
48	26	6.5
50	28	7
52	30	7.5
54	32	8
56	34	8.5
58	36	9
60	38	9.5
62 or older	40	10

If you meet the minimum work credit requirements, see if you meet the criterion for being disabled:

- Your disability prevents you from performing typical work functions like standing, walking, or recalling information.

- You can't do the work you did before.

- You can't do any kind of work.

 WORTH NOTING

These disabling conditions may qualify you for SSDI and Medicare before age 65: Alzheimer's disease, mental illness, Multiple Sclerosis, and Parkinson's disease.

After you are approved to receive SSDI, you still have to deal with the 24-month waiting period until you receive Medicare.

What can you do for medical insurance during those two years? If your income and assets are low enough, you might qualify for Medicaid, a state-funded health-care program.

But if you do not qualify for Medicaid, there are other options. For example, if you had health insurance through your previous job, they may offer COBRA, which stands for the Consolidated Omnibus Budget Reconciliation Act of 1986. COBRA enables former employees to continue their employee-sponsored health-care program through voluntary payments. Check with human resources about the costs and regulations in your particular case.

The Affordable Care Act also provides you additional health insurance options until Medicare kicks in. Check with your state to see what they offer through their health insurance marketplace. You may also consider available private health insurance, since you can no longer be denied coverage because of your disability.

In the 25th month after your SSDI benefits began, you will automatically receive a Medicare card in the mail. If you don't want Part B, which requires a monthly premium payment, read the instructions on the card and send it back. If you keep the card, expect to pay Part B premiums, which averaged $104.90 monthly in 2014. Be sure to read all the information about how Medicare works to ensure you have the right options.

Family Members for Those Approved for SSDI

When you get Medicare, your family will also receive it if they are:

- Unmarried children who are under 18, under 19 and in elementary or secondary school full time, or 18 or older with a disability that started before age 22.

- A spouse, regardless of age, if they're taking care of a child who's under 16 or disabled.

- A spouse who is age 62 or older.

As long as your family members meet these guidelines, they will receive Medicare when you do.

Railroad Retirement Disability Board (RRDB) Benefits

The Railroad Retirement Disability Board (RRDB) is a program established by federal law for the employees, retirees, spouses, and survivors of railroad employees. It provides benefits to those workers (and their survivors) who are retired and/or disabled and qualify for Medicare before age 65. For more information, go to https://secure.rrb.gov/.

End-Stage Renal Disease (ESRD) or ALS

If you have ESRD and need either regular dialysis or a kidney transplant, Medicare will begin coverage the first day of the fourth month after dialysis starts or after your kidney transplant. To start it immediately, do the following:

1. Enroll in a Medicare-approved home dialysis training.

2. Have your physician vouch that you'll finish training.

3. Respond that you'll do your own dialysis treatments during the four months you have to wait for Medicare to begin.

Otherwise, Medicare will begin the first day of the fourth month.

For those diagnosed with ALS (or Lou Gehrig's disease), Medicare benefits begin as soon as your disability benefits begin. You'll receive Part A and Part B automatically.

The Least You Need to Know

- Medicare is a federal health insurance program for Americans age 65 and over, as well as younger disabled persons and those with ESRD or ALS.

- Medicare is funded through two different funds, which get their revenue from a variety of sources including payroll taxes from employers, employees, and the self-employed, as well as a monthly premium, an annual deductible, and the deductible for each benefit period of hospitalization or skilled nursing facility stays.

- There are four parts to Medicare: Part A (hospitalization), Part B (medical services), Part C (Medicare Advantage, a private program you have to pay for through a choice of individual carriers), and Part D (prescription program requiring an additional monthly fee).

- If you have other health insurance, you are not required to sign up for Medicare. But once that health insurance ends, you must sign up for Medicare within eight months or you'll have to pay a late signup penalty.

- In certain circumstances, those 64 and younger are eligible for Medicare if they are disabled. They will get the same Medicare benefits as if they were already a senior.

Medicaid: Medical Assistance for the Financially Challenged

Medicaid is a state and federally funded health-care program for people with limited income and resources. Along with Medicare, Medicaid was signed into law as an amendment to the Social Security Act on July 30, 1965, by President Lyndon B. Johnson.

Whereas Medicare covers full or partial hospitalization or medical coverage/assistance to Americans who are age 65 and over, Medicaid is a program for those who are financially disadvantaged or disabled that must meet certain federal guidelines, but it's administered by the state. Therefore, each state has established its own Medicaid program rules regarding who it covers and what services it provides.

In This Chapter

- The differences between Medicaid and Medicare
- Who qualifies for Medicaid?
- Where to apply for benefits
- How different states deal with Medicaid

What Does Medicaid Cover?

In general, Medicaid offers a wide spectrum of services from physician services and inpatient hospital services for children, pregnant women, the elderly, and seniors who meet certain low-income or poverty-level criteria, and for the disabled. It not only covers medical expenses, but nursing home care as well.

According to Medicaid.gov, Medicaid and its sister program, Children's Health Insurance Program (CHIP), provide health coverage to 60 million Americans. Approximately 4.6 million low-income seniors receive Medicaid benefits, and most are also enrolled in Medicare.

How to Apply for Medicaid

Where you live influences how you apply for Medicaid. Currently, 32 states and the District of Columbia provide Medicaid to anyone eligible for Supplemental Security Income (SSI) benefits. In fact, if you live in one of those states, your SSI application is also your Medicaid application.

However, if you live in Alaska, Idaho, Kansas, Nebraska, Nevada, Oregon, Utah, or the Northern Mariana Islands, you must file for Medicaid separately, even though they use the same eligibility rules for both SSI and Medicaid.

And if you live in Connecticut, Hawaii, Illinois, Indiana, Minnesota, Missouri, New Hampshire, North Dakota, Ohio, Oklahoma, or Virginia, those states use a separate application for Medicaid and also have their own eligibility rules for Medicaid that are different from SSI.

One of the easiest ways to apply for Medicaid is to go to medicaid.gov and select your state's website. Click on the link to that website and apply under your state's rules governing Medicaid.

Medicaid Requirements

Although what is covered may vary from state to state, there are three general requirements you must meet in order to qualify for Medicaid. First, you must be a citizen or a legal resident of the United States.

Second, there are income limits. Since January 2014, because of the Affordable Care Act (ACA), eligibility for Medicaid for an individual was changed to include anyone earning below 133 percent of the federal poverty level. For a single individual, that means anyone earning less than $15,521.10 is eligible for Medicaid. The amounts are higher for the states of Alaska and Hawaii, respectively: $19,391.40 and $17,848.60.

For a family of four, earnings below $31,720.50 would make someone eligible for Medicaid. In Alaska, for a family of four, the maximum amount is $39,660.60; for Hawaii, the maximum is $36,481.90.

Since Medicaid is administered through each state, check with the state where you reside and where you will be applying for Medicaid about their income eligibility requirements. The amounts given here are the general income limits for a single person or a family of four. You'll be able to find the income limits for families of two, three, five, or more persons for your state.

The third requirement for consideration is the amount of assets you are allowed to have. In 2014, the asset requirements for Medicaid included the following:

- An individual cannot have countable or liquid assets totaling more than $2,000. However, if your income is less than $844 per month, you can have up to $5,000 in assets.

- As part of the Spousal Impoverishment Prevention Coverage, your spouse can keep up to $117,240 in individual or joint assets (in addition to noncountable assets), if only one spouse needs to get nursing care services in either a facility or at home. (To qualify for health-care coverage under Medicaid, the limit for a couple is $6,000; under the Medicare Savings Programs, states govern the limits.

- Your home is not counted as an asset if you or your spouse lives in it. If the home is used for income, however, it is counted.

- You are allowed one vehicle of any age and a second vehicle over 7 years old, with some notable exceptions. For example, neither car can be a luxury, antique, or custom vehicle.

- Personal items in the home, such as furnishings, are not counted as assets. Other items, such as jewelry or art, may be countable if they're considered collectibles.

- Retirement Accounts—IRAs, 401(k)s, 403(b)s—are not counted as long as those accounts are properly structured and you're taking regular and periodic income distributions. Keep in mind that the minimum distribution requirements for Medicaid are different than those for the IRS.

- Burial funds and prepaid funeral contracts are not counted as assets if irrevocable. If the plan or funds are revocable, Medicaid will not count up to $2,500.

- If you have income from rental property that contributes to the cost of patient care, it is counted toward monthly income.

- Term life insurance policies with no cash value are excluded, but whole life or other forms of life insurance that have a cash value of more than $2,500 may be counted as assets.

- Annuities are countable unless they're part of a retirement plan. However, assets placed in a properly structured immediate annuity may not be countable, provided the contract meets strict Medicaid guidelines.

How Does Medicaid Compare to Medicare?

Medicaid and Medicare are often confused because the names of the programs are so similar and both deal with benefits related to health care. There are, however, major differences between these two programs.

For starters, Medicare is a federally run health insurance program for people 65 and older and those under 65 who are disabled and can't work because of their impairment. Medicaid, on the other hand, is a program that is jointly run by both the federal government and the individual states; it provides health-care benefits for people with limited income and resources.

Like Medicare, Medicaid provides hospital, medical, and in most cases, drug coverage—although prescription drug coverage is an optional benefit, so check with your particular state to see if that's covered.

To qualify for Medicare, you have to be 65 years old or older, or disabled. You also have to have paid into Medicare through funds that were withheld from your salary or, if self-employed, through the Medicare tax you pay.

By contrast, to qualify for Medicaid, the only requirement is that you earn less than a certain amount and have limited financial assets. With Medicaid, each state has its own rules and regulations regarding eligibility.

People who are eligible for both Medicare and Medicaid are known as "dual eligible." For example, if you're over 65 and are living on a fixed income, such as Social Security, you could still qualify for Medicaid based on your income level. (Let's say you're single and your only income is your monthly Social Security benefit of $1,200 a month. Since that amounts to an annual income of $14,400, and eligibility for Medicaid in most states except Alaska and Hawaii is by earning below $15,521.10, you would be eligible for Medicaid on the basis of income.)

WORTH NOTING

If you have Medicare and qualify for Medicaid, any services that are covered by both programs will first be paid by Medicare. Medicaid will then pay the remaining costs up to the limit allowed by the state where the senior's Medicaid is being administered.

Medicaid Benefits

As previously noted, Medicaid is a federally supervised program that requires certain benefits to be offered to recipients. However, the individual states do have some leverage over what additional benefits they will cover for qualified enrollees. The only way to know what your state offers its Medicaid recipients is to go to the website for your own state's Medicaid program.

The following table highlights the mandatory benefits you should expect to receive no matter what state you live in, in addition to the optional benefits you will need to find more about on a state-by-state basis.

Mandatory Medicaid Benefits

Mandatory Benefits	Optional Benefits
Inpatient hospital services	Prescription drugs
Outpatient hospital services	Clinic services
Early and Periodic Screening, Diagnostic, and Treatment Services (EPSDT) and nursing facility services	Physical therapy
Home health services	Speech, hearing, and language disorders
Physician services	Respiratory care services
Rural health clinic services	Other diagnostic, screening, and preventive care services
Federally qualified health center services	Podiatry services
Laboratory and x-ray services	Dental services
Family planning services	Dentures
Nurse midwife services	Prosthetics
Certified pediatric and family and nurse practitioner services	Eyeglasses
Freestanding birth center services (when licensed or otherwise recognized by the state)	Chiropractic services
Transportation to medical care	Other practitioner services
Tobacco cessation programs	Private duty nursing services
	Personal care
	Hospice
	Case management
	Services for individuals age 65 and older institutionalized for mental disease

continues

Mandatory Medicaid Benefits   (continued)

Mandatory Benefits	Optional Benefits
	Services in an intermediate care facility for the mentally handicapped
	State plan home- and community-based services
	Self-directed personal assistance services
	Community First Choice
	TB-related services
	Inpatient psychiatric services for individuals who are 21 or over
	Other services approved by the secretary of state
	Health homes for enrollees with chronic conditions

Source: "Medicaid Benefits" at Medicaid.gov.

Financial Help for Medicare Part D

If you meet certain low-income criteria, you could be eligible for financial aid from Medicaid to pay for the costs associated with Medicare Part D, which provides prescription drug coverage.

If your monthly income is below the Medicaid limit, you could be eligible for full drug coverage from Medicaid. If you have both Medicare and Medicaid, you first have to enroll in the Medicare Part D drug program, and if you qualify, you would automatically receive help from a federal program called Extra Help, which offers extra financial assistance. If you receive Supplemental Security Income (SSI), you automatically qualify for Extra Help.

The Social Security Administration (SSA) has put together an entire booklet to help you figure out if you're eligible for the Extra Help program. It's titled "Apply Online for Extra Help with Medicare Prescription Drug Costs" and you can read it at ssa.gov/pubs/EN-05-10525.pdf.

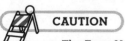 **CAUTION**

The Extra Help program is not available in Puerto Rico, the U.S. Virgin Islands, Guam, the Northern Mariana Islands, and American Samoa.

To qualify for Extra Help in 2014, you had to earn less than $23,595 annually for couples or $17,505 annually for single people. Your assets had to be less than $13,440 for a single person or $26,860 for a married couple living together.

Additional Help with Prescription Drug Costs

If your income is too high to qualify for Medicaid, there are other programs that may help with paying for Medicare Part D, which covers prescription drug costs. One is called the Medicare Savings Program (MSP). This is a program, administered through each state, that will pay for several parts of Medicare for those who qualify by meeting certain monthly income levels and are already getting Medicare Part A, which usually does not have a monthly fee. It will also provide a Low Income Subsidy (LIS) to those who meet those qualifications if they are paying for Medicare Part D by covering the Medicare Part D monthly premium and helping with the yearly deductibles. For more information, go to medicare.gov/contacts/staticpages/msps.aspx and click on your state. You will go to the website for your state where you can find more information about its Medicare Savings Program, as well as how it can help with the costs associated with Medicare Part D for prescription drugs.

You can also search for a low-cost drug program. During your annual open enrollment period, you can change your Medicare Part D drug plan to a lower-cost plan than the one you've been using. The premiums on these plans vary greatly, so study each one to make sure it's the most cost-effective plan for you. One plan, for example, through Humana, is affiliated with Walmart stores for fulfillment of your prescription drugs. But the monthly premium is only $15.70 a month. (Go to humana.com for more information on what the plan covers and how it works.)

There are also a number of discount programs you can use, such as the National Prescription Savings Network. The only stipulation is that you can't use their discount card if you're also using a Part D program.

There are a number of ways to lower the costs of the medicine you have to take. You can:

- Use generics instead of more expensive brand-name drugs. Just check with your doctor to make sure the generic will work as well as the brand before you switch.

- Use a mail-order pharmacy for your prescription needs.

- Select a different plan that charges a lower premium but provides coverage for the drugs you use.

- Find a pharmaceutical company assistance program to help you pay for their drugs. You can find out if your particular drug is among those for which assistance is offered. Just go to medicare.gov/pharmaceutical-assistance-program to see if the drug's manufacturer provides assistance.

- Use a state pharmaceutical assistance program if your state has one. Again you can find out by going to medicare.gov/pharmaceutical-assistance-program/state-programs.aspx and searching for a program in your state.

- Apply for Extra Help, the Medicare program for anyone with limited income or resources.

- Check out national and local charitable groups such as the National Patient Advocate Foundation or the National Organization of Rare Disorders. They may have assistance programs that help people in need with their drug costs.

WORTH NOTING

Finding out if you qualify for a drug company assistance program can be a daunting task. Fortunately, there is a group called the Partnership for Prescription Assistance that will help you learn if you qualify for a particular program. Go to pparx.org to see if you qualify for free.

State-Run Financial Assistance

The Affordable Care Act enables states to create a Basic Health Program (BHP) for people with low incomes as a way to ensure everyone has access to some kind of health insurance.

It also gives states the ability to offer more affordable coverage to those whose incomes sometimes rise above the federal qualifying level for Medicaid or the Children's Health Insurance Program (CHIP). States then can provide health-care coverage to residents who may not be eligible for Medicaid because they earn too much. Each state controls the levels to qualify for a Basic Health Program, but they run between 133 and 200 percent of the federal poverty level.

For more information on the eligibility requirements, you can go to medicare.gov.

Paying for Part A and Part B Medicare Premiums

There are four kinds of Medicare Savings Programs (MSPs):

Qualified Medicare Beneficiary (QMB) program: A program that helps pay for Part A and Part B premiums as well as any related deductibles, co-insurance, or co-payments. To qualify for this program, you must earn less than $993 per month as a single person or $1,331 as a married couple.

Specified Low-Income Medicare Beneficiary (SLMB) program: A program that helps pay for Part B premiums. To qualify, you must earn less than $1,187 per month as a single person or $1,593 for married couples.

Qualified Disabled and Working Individuals (QDWI) program: This program pays for Part A premiums for disabled singles earning less than $3,975 or disabled married couples earning less than $5,329 per month.

Qualifying Individual (QI) program: This program pays for Part B premiums for single and married couples living in Alaska or Hawaii who earn less than $1,333 a month as a single person or $1,790 as a married couple.

Covering Other Costs

If you qualify for Medicaid, you may find that some health-care costs Medicare does not take care of are covered by Medicaid. These include eyeglasses, hearing aids, prescription drugs, and nursing facility care beyond Medicare's 100-day maximum.

The four Medicare Savings Programs may also cover most out-of-pocket costs for Medicare, such as deductibles and co-payments for doctor or hospital visits.

Check out the monthly income limits for each of these programs at medicaid.gov/Medicaid-CHIP-Program-Information/By-Population/Medicare-Medicaid-Enrollees-Dual-Eligibles/Seniors-and-Medicare-and-Medicaid-Enrollees.html to see if you are eligible to apply for additional aid. Remember, Medicaid eligibility includes not just a limit on monthly income, but also a total asset limit of $2,000 for an individual and between $23,000 and $117,000 for a couple depending on the state they live in.

The Least You Need to Know

- An estimated 4.6 million low-income seniors receive health coverage through Medicaid; most are also enrolled in Medicare.
- Eligibility for Medicaid requires that you are a citizen of the United States or a legal resident. It's also based on your income being below a certain level and the amount of countable assets you own also not exceeding specific amounts.
- If you qualify for Medicaid, you can use it to pay the costs Medicare does not cover. In cases where both Medicare and Medicaid cover the same services, Medicare pays first.
- There are services that Medicaid is required to cover, such as hospitalization. Each state decides which optional services it will offer as part of its individualized Medicaid plan.

PART 4

Living with Social Security

Now that you're on Social Security, here's what you need to know about taxes and how to maximize your benefits. We'll also show you how to determine whether your benefits are taxable and the best states to live in to pay the least amount of taxes.

Beyond taxes, you'll learn some easy strategies to help you live on your Social Security benefits, the best cities for living on a fixed income, and why it may be financially beneficial to live in a warmer climate. We'll also show you what to do if you want to return to the workforce.

We'll explain how returning to work could affect your benefits and what you should do to notify the Social Security Administration. You'll also learn the pros and cons of suspending benefits and different strategies you can use to increase your monthly benefits if you do go back to work.

Taxes and Social Security

Social Security benefits were not taxed by the federal government from 1938 until after the Social Security Act was amended in 1983. Beginning in 1984, part of Social Security benefits became subject to federal income taxes. Additional changes were made to Social Security taxation in 1993 as part of the Omnibus Budget Reconciliation Act.

According to "Taxation of Social Security Benefits," Larry DeWitt from SSA Historian's Office states, " … under present law, almost all Social Security beneficiaries still enjoy more favorable tax treatment of their benefits than is the case for recipients of private pensions."

In this chapter, we discuss whether it's likely your benefits will be taxed by the federal government or by the state you live in. As usual, when it comes to taxes, it all depends on how much you earn.

In This Chapter

- Are your Social Security benefits taxable?
- How to figure your adjusted gross income
- Deductions you can claim to reduce income taxes
- Reasons to withhold part of your benefits for taxes

Determining If Your Benefits Are Taxable

There are two key factors that determine how much of your Social Security benefits are taxable: your total income and your marital status.

Usually, if your Social Security benefits were your only income for the year, they will not be taxable. You may not even have to file a federal income tax return as long as you don't have additional income from a job; from a pension; or from stocks, bonds, or dividend income from savings and other accounts.

However, if you worked full or part time and received income from those other sources, your benefits can be taxed depending on how much additional income you had that year.

One way to determine whether your benefits are taxable is to calculate your modified adjusted gross income (MAGI). If it's more than the base amount for your filing status, your benefits will be taxed. If it's not, it won't.

Here's a fast way to figure it out. If your total income is:

- Between $25,000 and $34,000, you may have to pay income tax on up to 50 percent of your benefits.

- More than $34,000, up to 85 percent of your benefits may be taxable.

If you file a joint return, and you and your spouse have a combined income that is:

- Between $32,000 and $44,000, you may have to pay income tax on up to 50 percent of your benefits.

- More than $44,000, you may have to pay income tax on 85 percent of your benefits.

 WORTH NOTING

According to IRS rules, no one pays federal income tax on more than 85 percent of their Social Security benefits.

It All Depends on Your Total Income

Chances are, the more money you earn, the more taxes you'll pay. This includes income from other sources besides a job, such as dividends from stocks, bonds, savings, investment accounts, pensions, or other dividends.

According to the SSA, in 2013 the average monthly benefit for a retiree was around $1,294, or $15,528 a year. If that's all the income you received, you won't pay any taxes on it because it falls below the maximum of $25,000 per year for single people or $32,000 for married couples.

For additional information regarding federal taxes on your Social Security benefits, read Publication 915, "Social Security and Equivalent Railroad Retirement Benefits," at irs.gov/pub/irs-pdf/p915.pdf.

TIP

You don't have to worry about federal taxes if you're receiving Supplemental Security Income (SSI) payments, because SSI is not taxed.

Calculating Your Adjusted Gross Income

To figure out if you will have to pay taxes on your benefits, especially if you have income from other sources, you'll need to calculate your adjusted gross income, which is your income minus any deductions.

To compute that amount, add up all your wages from the current year's W-2 forms, 1099s, any tips, taxable interest, ordinary dividends, capital gains (or losses), taxable IRA distributions, and taxable pension and annuity payouts.

From that you can deduct any IRA contributions; student loan interest; moving expenses; 50 percent of self-employment tax; self-employment insurance premiums; contributions to SEP, SIMPLE, or any other qualified plans for yourself; and other expenses such as alimony and legal fees. You can also claim some deductions tied to your Social Security benefits, such as:

- Disability repayments you had to make to your employer or insurance company.

- Legal expenses you had to pay in order to collect your benefits.

- Medicare premiums deducted from your monthly benefits.

- Any workers' compensation offset if your benefits were reduced.

- Child care or money paid to caregivers for another family member.

Once you have your adjusted gross income figured out, add it to 50 percent of your Social Security benefits. The total is your combined income. The IRS also provides a worksheet at irs.gov/pub/irs-pdf/p915.pdf to help you figure your adjusted gross income.

When Your Combined Income Isn't Taxed

If your combined income is less than $25,000 for singles or $32,000 for couples, your Social Security benefits are not taxable. If that combined income is more than those levels, some of your benefits may be taxable.

Also, if you're living outside the United States in any of the following countries, your benefits are exempt from federal tax:

- Canada

- Egypt

- Germany

- Ireland

- Israel

- Italy (You must also be a citizen of Italy to receive the exemption.)

- Romania

- United Kingdom

If you're living in India and a citizen of both India and the United States, you're exempt from U.S. tax if the benefits are for services or work performed in the states.

If you're a resident of Switzerland, all of your Social Security benefits are taxed at 15 percent.

If you also received a Lump Sum Death Benefit (LSDB), which has been capped at $255 since 1954, it's not considered taxable income.

Do You Want Voluntary Withholding?

You can ask to have federal taxes withheld from your Social Security when you apply for benefits. Why would you want to do that? One reason is that you already know you'll owe taxes because your income puts you in the taxable bracket.

A quick way to determine if any of your benefits are taxable is to add one half of your benefits to all your other income, including any tax-exempt interest. If the total is more than one of the following base amounts, you could owe taxes come April 15th:

- $25,000 for single, head of household, qualifying widow or widower with a dependent child, or married individuals filing separately who didn't live with their spouses during the year.

- $32,000 for married couples filing jointly.

For married persons filing separately who lived together at any time during the year, there is no limit.

What If You Earned Nontaxed 1099 Income?

If you earned money as a freelancer, consultant, vendor, or contractor, and you received a 1099 form reporting this income, it will be counted as any other income when calculating whether you owe taxes on your Social Security Benefits.

If you're self-employed and you use an accountant to file your annual tax return, discuss your situation with him or her before you start receiving Social Security benefits. Your accountant can help you determine if you should have taxes withheld or if you will have to pay taxes by April 15th.

Withholding Taxes

You might want to have a portion of your benefits withheld for taxes so you won't be hit with a larger tax bill that has to be paid on or before April 15th. By having a smaller amount withheld each month, you can reduce or even eliminate what you owe.

If you have a nice nest egg to draw from for any unanticipated expenses, such as paying federal income tax on your benefits, monthly withholding may not be an option you want to pursue. However, if you don't have any extra funds, or you simply don't like surprises, withholding smaller amounts on a monthly basis may be the right route for you to help reduce what you owe in taxes.

If you decide you want to have taxes withheld monthly, SSA will ask you to advise them what percentage you prefer to have withheld: 7, 10, 15, or 25 percent.

You can't request that a specific dollar amount be withheld, only a consistent percentage. You can, of course, use a calculator to figure out just how much money will be withheld monthly for each of the four percentages, as long as you know the amount you will be or are receiving.

If you're unsure what percentage to suggest SSA withholds, and you have an accountant who regularly handles your annual tax return, make a quick phone call to find out what he or she recommends. On the average monthly benefit of $1,200, for example, asking to have 15 percent withheld for federal taxes means you will get approximately $180 less each month.

Requesting the Withholding of Federal Taxes

If you want to have taxes withheld from your benefits, call Social Security at 1-800-772-1213 and ask for IRS Form W-4V. You can also get this form online at irs.gov/pub/irs-pdf/fw4v.pdf.

After you fill out the form and indicate what percentage of your monthly benefit you want withheld regularly, sign the form and return it to your local Social Security office in person or by mail.

 WORTH NOTING

You use the same "Voluntary Withholding Request" form to either start or stop voluntary withholding.

State Taxes

Some states allow full tax exemption for your Social Security benefits, while others tax that income the same way the federal government does.

In the following states, plus the District of Columbia, Social Security benefits are exempt from state income taxes:

Alabama	Massachusetts
Arizona	Michigan
Arkansas	Mississippi
California	New Jersey
Delaware	New York
District of Columbia	North Carolina
Georgia	Ohio
Hawaii	Oklahoma
Idaho	Oregon
Illinois	Pennsylvania
Indiana	South Carolina
Iowa	Virginia
Kentucky	Wisconsin
Louisiana	Wyoming
Maine	

The following states have no state tax on any income, so Social Security benefits are therefore not subject to taxation:

> Alaska
>
> Florida
>
> Nevada
>
> New Hampshire (only taxes dividend and interest income)
>
> South Dakota
>
> Tennessee (only taxes dividend and interest income)
>
> Texas
>
> Washington
>
> Wyoming

These states tax the Social Security benefits in the same way as the federal government; namely, up to 85 percent of benefits would be taken into consideration on the state tax return:

> North Dakota
>
> Minnesota
>
> Nebraska
>
> West Virginia
>
> Vermont
>
> Rhode Island

Other states set income levels higher than the federal level does before taxing your Social Security benefits. If your income is at that level or higher, your benefits will be taxed.

The following states do not tax Social Security benefits if the recipient is earning less than a certain amount, as noted:

> Connecticut: Exempt if income is less than $60,000 for joint filers
>
> Kansas: Exempt if federal adjusted gross income is $75,000 or less
>
> Missouri: Exempt if adjusted gross income is less than $100,000 for joint filers
>
> Montana: Exempt if total income for joint filers is $32,000 or less

The following states have other considerations that impact how much state tax, if any, you may have to pay on your Social Security benefits:

Colorado: There's a $24,000 retirement income exclusion.

Utah: There's a retirement income tax credit for up to $450.

New Mexico: According to Rachel L. Sheedy's article "Retiree Tax Burden Differs by State" published in October 2012 and posted at Kiplinger.com, "Social Security benefits may qualify for the state's $8,000 exclusion."

CAUTION

Sit down with your financial advisor, financial planner, or accountant and discuss the state or federal tax situation related to Social Security benefits for you and your spouse, especially if you are new to Social Security. You don't want any unpleasant surprises when April 15th is looming on the horizon, turning what should have been a positive additional source of revenue into a tax obligation nightmare.

The Least You Need to Know

- Social Security benefits may be taxable by the federal government based on earnings and marital status.
- The maximum you can be taxed federally is 85 percent of the Social Security benefits you receive.
- You can ask the SSA to withhold income taxes at 7, 10, 15, or 25 percent of the amount of benefits you are due.
- Whether or not you have to pay state taxes on your Social Security benefits is determined on a state-by-state basis.
- Thirty-seven states either don't tax Social Security benefits or don't tax income at all.

Making the Most of Social Security

According to the Social Security Administration (SSA), approximately one out of every five of the nearly 60 million Americans currently receiving Social Security benefits are living on those monthly benefits without any other source of income. That amounts to around 12 million people who are living their lives on *only* the Social Security benefits they receive each month. Another 22 percent of married seniors and 47 percent of single seniors are relying on Social Security for 90 percent of their income.

If you're wondering how so many people ended up in that situation, consider this: according to the SSA, over half of all working Americans have no pensions and over one third have no savings.

What's really troublesome is that it's only going to get worse. According to Bankrate.com, more than 36 percent of Americans still working have not saved a single penny for their retirement. Meanwhile, another Bankrate.com survey found that over 68 percent of all Americans are not saving enough to retire.

In This Chapter

- How to survive on retirement benefits
- Where to find financial assistance
- How to stretch those Social Security dollars
- The best places to live on Social Security

How can anyone live on only Social Security benefits? That question has many answers. It *is* possible to survive on Social Security, but it may take some scrimping and saving. This chapter addresses ways to live on just your benefits, or, if you're fortunate enough to have some savings or even a small pension, ways to stretch your resources so they go farther.

When That's All There Is

If you truly have to live on just your Social Security benefits, you need to create a budget and stick to it. In your case, the term "fixed income" is all too real. You need to be clear as to what your fixed monthly income is being spent on.

There are lots of software programs you could use, and books you could read, to help you create a budget. But you don't need anything more than a piece of paper and a pencil.

Start with the amount you receive for your Social Security benefits. That's your income. If it's between $25,000 and $34,000, you may have to pay federal income tax on up to 50 percent of your benefits. If your income is more than $34,000, you may have to pay tax on up to 85 percent of your benefits.

If you file a joint return and you and your spouse have a combined income between $32,000 and $44,000, you may have to pay federal income tax on up to 50 percent of your benefits. If it's more than $44,000, you might have to pay tax on 85 percent of your benefits.

On your own, or with the help of an accountant, take your monthly Social Security benefit and figure out what your federal income tax responsibility is, then multiply that by 12 for your yearly income tax responsibility. If you're receiving the average benefit of $1,328 monthly ($15,936 annually), you probably won't have to pay federal income tax on your benefits. But if your benefit is the maximum of $2,663 ($31,956 annually), if you took it at full retirement age, you will have to pay federal income tax. (If you let your benefit accrue delayed retirement credits and didn't start your benefits till age 70, since your benefit will be 32% higher, or as much as $3,500 a month, you will also have to pay federal income tax on your benefits according to the rates based on annual income noted above.)

Now that you're clear on your net income—your Social Security benefits minus federal taxes— the next step is to create a worksheet to record your expenses. Note the amount of federal taxes you will probably have to pay on the right side, which is the expenses side of your worksheet.

Another fixed expense might be state taxes on your Social Security benefits. But this depends on what state you live in. If you live in one of the 38 states, or the District of Columbia, where Social Security benefits are not taxed, you can ignore that as a possible expense. (The states that tax Social Security benefits were listed in Chapter 15.) So if your state does tax benefits, you may have to consider it as an anticipated expense.

After you've noted what state taxes you might have to pay on your Social Security benefits, if any, now write down the category of expenses that are consistent, and the amount you typically spend. Here's an example:

Rent or mortgage: _____

Weekly gas costs: _____

Utilities (gas or oil): _____

Electricity: _____

Phone (including cell phone and/or landline): _____

Cable bill: _____

Internet provider (if separate): _____

Food:

Groceries: _____

Dining out and/or takeout: _____

Total: _____

Now consider any additional monthly payments you have to cover, such as any loans you need to repay (including student or car loans), homeowners, apartment, or car insurance, and credit card payments. If anything does not apply to you, just leave it blank.

Student loan repayment: _____

Car loan payment: _____

Credit card payment: _____

Homeowners or renters insurance: _____

Car insurance: _____

Total: _____

Now consider your miscellaneous expenses, such as entertainment and clothing purchases. List those expenses below.

Misc. expenses:

_____ _____

_____ _____

Add up all these expenses. Put the total here: _____

Now reenter your individual or combined Social Security benefits with your partner (after estimated federal and/or state taxes): _____

Subtract your expenses from your net income, and that's what you have left if your fixed Social Security benefit is your sole source of income.

Is your balance in the red or in the black? If you have any money left over after deducting your expenses, that's terrific! But if you're at 0 or in the negative, let's explore some ways to supplement your Social Security benefits even though you lack any savings, investment income, a pension, or a rich uncle who left you his million-dollar estate in his will.

There Is Help out There for You!

Because you were working and probably earning more than the monthly Social Security benefits you're now receiving, or you had a savings account that's now depleted that you could tap into if you needed additional funds, many of you may be unaware that you're eligible to receive help from the government. That assistance is for such things as Supplemental Security Income (SSI) or from the Department of Housing and Urban Development (HUD), which provides low-cost housing to about 1 million seniors through public housing programs, multi-family subsidized housing, and vouchers. There are also public housing agencies that offer rental assistance for the private housing market.

How to Save on Food

The best-known and most used service to help defray the cost of food is the Supplemental Nutrition Assistance Program (SNAP). However, you probably know it as the place to go for food stamps.

 WORTH NOTING

Eligibility for food stamps is based on income, resources, deductions, employment requirements, special rules for the elderly and disabled, and immigrant status. Generally, your gross monthly income before any deductions has to be below $1,265 for an individual or $2,584 for a family of four. If you're single and living on just your Social Security benefits, it's quite possible your monthly benefit is below that minimum requirement.

According to SSA, approximately 48 million Americans use food stamps. What's interesting is that only 9 percent of those who use food stamps are seniors. In fact, only about one third of all seniors eligible for food stamps are using them, and the reasons they aren't may surprise you.

According to the Food Research and Action Center (FRAC), 76 percent said there was a stigma attached to receiving food stamps. Meanwhile, others mistakenly believed that food stamps are not worth enough to bother with going through the application process. In reality, FRAC found the average monthly food stamp benefit for people 60 and older in 2009 was $102. (In 2014, the maximum for a family of one was $194 and $357 for a family of two, which are the two most common sizes for senior families without children living at home.)

So don't deny yourself this life-affirming benefit if you qualify for it. To find out if you are eligible just go to SNAP's website, www.fns.usda.gov/snap, and use their prescreening tool.

There are also other state-sponsored programs for food assistance that are not as well known. To find out what's available in your state, go to benefitscheckup.org, which is run by the National Council on Aging. It has information on 1,650 public and private food benefit programs around the country.

For example, many states have their own version of the well-known Meals on Wheels program. Meals on Wheels, a volunteer organization that delivers meals to one million seniors in America, dates back to 1940 when nurses delivered meals to British servicemen in World War II. According to the Meals on Wheels website, the first program in America to deliver meals to homebound seniors was in Philadelphia in 1954. Currently, there are 5,000 Meals on Wheels programs throughout the 50 states. To find out more about this effort to combat senior hunger, go to mowaa. org/ and click on the special "Senior Hunger" section at the top of the home page.

If you live in California, check out the CalFresh program, which helps financially strapped families buy food at grocery stores and senior centers. (CalFresh is the California version of Supplemental Nutrition Assistance Program.) For more information, go to http://www.calfresh. ca.gov/.

Check with your local senior center to find out what food assistance they offer. For example, in Seattle, Washington, Senior Services offers a Community Dining Program. Through the five local senior centers that participate, a lower-cost lunch is available; the suggested donation is $3. For more information, go to seniorservices.org/foodassistance/CommunityDining.aspx.

Whether it's through your town or city, the Department of Aging, or a religious institution, such as a church or synagogue, there may be breakfasts or lunches offered for free, for as little as $1.00 a meal, or on a suggested donation basis so you give as much as you can.

Some communities have come up with innovative ways to offer low-cost meals to seniors including for dinner. For example, in San Francisco, the San Francisco Department of Aging and Adult Services (DAAS) offers a dining program for seniors called CHAMPSS, which stands for Choosing Healthy and Appetizing Meal Plan Solutions for Seniors. Through this program, seniors can go to a participating restaurant and have a complete meal. Although the cost of a meal is between $8 and $9, the suggested donation is just $3.50. To find out more about the program, or to enroll in Self-Help for the Elderly, which administers the program, go to selfhelpelderly.org/.

> **WORTH NOTING**
>
> In 2011, the U.S. Administration on Aging (AoA) entered into an agreement with the Meals on Wheels Association of America to create the National Resource Center on Nutrition and Aging. For more information, go to nutritionandaging.org.

There's also a Senior Farmers' Market Nutrition Program (SFMNP) that provides food coupons for use at farmer's markets, roadside stands, and community programs that grow fruits and vegetables. Find more information at fns.usda.gov/sfmnp/senior-farmers-market-nutrition-program-sfmnp..

As for other food assistance programs, there's the Commodity Supplemental Food Program (CSFP), which provides seniors a monthly food package. Call 1-866-348-6479 to find out if your state participates and if you qualify.

Another federal program is the Emergency Food Assistance Program, which provides low-income seniors free food and nutrition assistance through local food pantries and soup kitchens. Learn more at www.dss.cahwnet.gov/efap.

For those who are really hungry and unable to pay for food, there's help available through the National Hunger Hotline at 1-866-348-6479. They'll help you find food options near where you live. They also have a search tool online (www.whyhunger.org/findfood) to help you find food in your area. There is absolutely no reason for any senior in America to go hungry.

Transportation

If you're no longer able to drive, or can't afford to keep a car because of the cost of insurance, car payments, maintenance, and fuel, consider other transportation options.

If your health permits it, you might consider a bicycle a good low-cost way to get around. Of course many seniors have to be concerned about mobility and balance issues, so keep that in mind if you're thinking about riding a bicycle. Although the initial investment may be as much as $2,000, consider an electric bicycle with additional battery power. Or you also could consider a motor scooter or motorcycle, instead of a more costly car. Of course, in all these situations, always wear a helmet, obey all traffic rules, and ride only where you're confident of your safety!

If bike or scooter riding is not for you, find out what local travel assistance is offered in your community. Many suburban and urban communities fund vans for seniors or the disabled that are either free or very low cost, such as $1.50 a ride. Some of the vans make stops on a schedule, like a more traditional bus. Others may require that you give the van service a specific pick up and return time. There also are volunteer transportation programs provided by local residents who team up to help seniors to be able to stay in their own homes.

In addition, low-cost local transportation is available through Eldercare, a public service of the U.S. Department of Aging, which helps seniors find local amenities. Go to eldercare.gov and type in your zip code. That will take you to the local services nearest you. One of the categories you can search is "Transportation." Another good resource is the American Public Transportation Association at apta.com.

Most public transportation organizations offer senior discounts on tickets for trains, subways, and buses. For example, Metro-North, which provides train service to and from Grand Central Station in New York throughout Connecticut and New York State, offers a substantially discounted senior ticket for anyone age 65 and over; it has to be used during off-peak hours. Even most airlines offer a discount to seniors, although some start at 62 and some at 65.

Additional Ways to Reduce Expenses

If you're living on a tight fixed income, you need to be very strict with yourself about where every penny you spend is going. We already discussed putting together a simple budget so you have a good idea about your expenses. If you need help with budgeting and other financial management tasks, there are a number of Daily Money Management (DMM) programs that provide financial assistance to seniors. At nolo.com, a popular legal website, they can connect you to DMMs who offer help with paying bills, budgeting, negotiating with creditors, balancing a checkbook, and avoiding scams and fraud.

If you decide to work with a DMM, nolo.com cautions that they are not financial advisors or lawyers. But a good DMM can help with referrals to professionals who could provide the help you need, such as an accountant. You may be able to find a DMM who is a volunteer at an eldercare law firm. Nolo.com also mentions the AARP Money Management Program, which uses volunteers to provide bill paying, budgeting, and other practical financial services for low-income seniors.

Do you need a phone? You may qualify for low-cost home or mobile phone service through the Lifeline Program. For more information, go to lifelinesupport.org.

There are a number of other areas where assistance is offered, such as legal services and tax preparation. There's even a program that provides financial assistance to cover some of your utility expenses. It's called the Low Income Home Energy Assistance Program (LIHEAP), and it's designed to help pay for heating and cooling costs. According to the SSA, more than five million households take advantage of this program every year.

Property Tax Relief for Seniors

As a senior, you may also be entitled to a reduction or exemption of your property taxes. However, this varies by state and in some communities there may be an income limit you have to fall under. In Colorado, anyone 65 and older can exempt 50 percent of the first $200,000 of their home's value. Colorado also has property tax deferment, which enables seniors to defer property taxes until the property is sold or the owner dies. In Connecticut, what property tax relief is offered, and what the eligibility requirements are, varies by community. Check with your state or community to find out what might be available for you.

Health-Care Cost Help

For help with health care, there's Medicaid, which helps low-income Americans cover those costs that Medicare doesn't, along with Extra Help, which helps pay monthly premiums, deductibles, and co-pays. (For more on this, please refer to Chapter 14.)

You can even receive free or low-cost dental care from agencies like Dentistry from the Heart, a nonprofit organization that provides free care to those who need but can't afford it, or the Dental Lifeline Network, which provides access to dental services to people with disabilities.

Programs of All-Inclusive Care for the Elderly (PACE) offers medical, social, and rehabilitation services for eligible seniors in nursing homes.

Most pharmaceutical companies also offer patient assistance programs (PAPs) providing low-income people access to prescriptions drugs.

For additional information on a number of government benefits, grants, and financial aid programs, go to usa.gov/Citizen/Topics/Benefits.shtml.

> **WORTH NOTING**
>
> If you have a sick pet but can't afford a vet, there are organizations that will help. Each state usually has its own, so you'll have to search around. One such group is called The Pet Fund, and you can call them at 1-916-443-6007.

Housing Help

The idea of living on $1,000 to $2,000 per month may be daunting to many, but if you do your homework and make use of everything that's available to you, you won't have to live somewhere unsuitable.

The federal government also provides housing to people living on low income, such as anyone living totally on Social Security benefits. The U.S. Department of Housing and Urban Development (HUD) provides grants to Public Housing Agencies (PHAs) to pay for the construction, rehabilitation, and acquisition of housing to be made available to the public at a low rent.

In 1933, the National Industrial Recovery Act initiated the first series of projects across the country to provide shelter for people who couldn't afford to pay much rent. Four years later, the Housing Act of 1937 created the first of many Federal housing programs to meet the growing demand of people in financial need brought on by the Great Depression. Other housing acts were passed in 1949 and 1954 that resulted in giant urban renewal programs as well as what became known as Section 8 Housing, which put roofs over the heads of hundreds of thousands of people living in poverty.

WORTH NOTING

To qualify for HUD's housing assistance for elderly citizens, at least one member of the household must be 62 years old and meet HUD's income limits for very low income families, which is 50 percent of the median income in that area.

Meanwhile, in rural communities, the Department of Agriculture was setting up assistance programs for low-income families who needed help repairing or improving their homes or paying their rent.

Today, the federal government provides three kinds of financial assistance for anyone on a low income. Here's what you need to qualify for each one:

Public Housing. A program for low-income families and individuals that provides homes based on income levels determined by the Public Housing Agency. This income level varies from community to community based on a number of factors, so you may be eligible at one address but not at another. Usually those income levels are tied to the median income for the county or metropolitan area in which the residence is located, and they use the same formula HUD uses. For example, HUD sets the lower income limits at 80 percent of the median income for that area, and very low income limits at 50 percent of the median income. Rent is then based on a family or individual's annual income less deductions, which means some people will be paying different rents for similar apartments in the same building.

Section 8. This program uses rental vouchers, which enable renters to live in privately owned apartment residences, provided they meet certain requirements set by the federal government. This offers families a greater choice of where to live. According to the SSA, most families under the voucher system end up paying more than 30 percent of their adjusted gross income for rent. Eligibility is similar to that for public housing. Your income can't exceed 50 percent of the median income for the county or metropolitan area where the residence is located. For more information on *Section 8* housing in your area, go to section8search.org.

Privately owned subsidized housing. In this program, the government provides subsidies to the owner, who in turn applies those subsidies to the rent he or she charges low-income tenants. These tend to be multi-family private homes and apartment buildings.

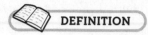 **DEFINITION**

> The term **Section 8** comes from Section 8 of the Housing Act of 1937, authorizing the payment of rental housing assistance to private landlords. Currently, the program provides subsidized housing for 3.1 million low-income households.

Far too many seniors are just one or two huge unpaid medical bills or other unexpected expenses away from defaulting on their mortgage or being unable to make the next month's rent. For those who don't have anywhere to live, there are Special Needs Assistance programs that provide housing for the homeless. These range from shelters to permanent housing for people who are disabled and fall into one of three categories:

The Shelter Plus Care Program. This is aimed at providing housing and support services on a long-term basis for homeless people with disabilities (including mental illness, alcohol or drug dependencies, and AIDS). The program offers a variety of housing choices.

Section 8 Single Room Occupancy. Known also as SRO housing assistance, this is usually in a rundown hotel, old school, or abandoned home that has been rehabilitated. Rental assistance for SROs lasts 10 years and owners are compensated for the cost of rehabilitation.

Military Base Redevelopment Planning. For the past 30 years, the Department of Defense has been closing down military bases around the country, leaving those bases in the hands of the communities where they're located. In 1994, the Base Closure Community Redevelopment and Homeless Assistance Act was passed to help communities meet the needs of their homeless. This act superseded the 1987 McKinney Homeless Assistance Act, which made serving the homeless the first priority for use of surplus military bases.

Strategies to Stretch Your Social Security Benefits

Some people are fortunate enough to have more than just Social Security benefits to live on, and that's great. But for millions of retired Americans, Social Security may still be the biggest, and most dependable, part of their monthly retirement income. So how do you stretch that amount, whether you're single and receiving $1,200 a month, or married and receiving two benefit checks or direct deposits equaling $3,500 a month?

In previous chapters, we discussed delaying your benefits, in addition to certain strategies such as file and suspend or spousal or ex-spousal benefits. In this section, we focus instead on ways to stretch the Social Security benefits you are currently receiving through such cost-saving strategies as downsizing where you live (but staying in the same community or state); relocating to another state, climate, or country; and living more frugally, as well as exploring what free goods, services, or discounts are available to seniors that can make a huge difference to your bottom line.

Downsizing Within Your Community

You can move to another country where the cost of living is lower and housing is much more affordable, but there are relationship and emotional consequences to such drastic moves. Before you sell your house in suburban California and move to a rental in Lithuania, consider downsizing within your own community. If you own your home, you can sell it, placing the sale's profits in a bank account or in investments, and then rent a home in the same community.

Before you do this or make any other major life change involving real estate or investment strategies, consult with your financial planner, real estate agent, and of course, your spouse and other immediate family members. But before you even talk with them, you might want to do some preliminary research on your own and do the math about what you might earn and what it would cost you, since even downsizing within your community will require an investment of time and money to move.

WORTH NOTING

When downsizing, you'll have to decide whether the next, smaller residence is one you'll own or rent. Just keep in mind that finances are just one factor, and that you also need to determine how long you intend to stay in that community, and what your plans for the future hold. Many times you can rent with an option to buy, which could be the best choice.

You must determine if your benefits will cover the cost of everything, including a house, or if you can use the income from any annuities, pensions, or investment money you have to pay for utilities, food, and incidentals.

Downsizing can mean everything from going from a large house to a smaller house; from a medium-size house to renting an apartment; to selling everything, including your home; and buying or renting an RV in which you'll live and travel for at least a couple of years.

The possibilities are endless, but it all starts with a decision about whether you want to stay in the community you're now in, where you may have roots and relationships and even family members, including grandchildren. Or whether you want to move away because it's going to be cheaper and easier to actually make your Social Security benefits last.

Relocating to Another State

While you may have to pay federal taxes on your Social Security benefits depending on your income, there are 28 states (plus the District of Columbia) where you would not have to pay state taxes on your benefits and 9 where you would not have to pay state income tax at all. (Refer again to the list of tax-exempt states in Chapter 15.)

If you live in a state where there's cold weather, you could relocate to a state with a warmer climate, saving heating costs and the cost of owning two wardrobes. States with warmer climates are experiencing a boom in population growth.

 WORTH NOTING

According to Penske Truck Rental, the top 10 cities where Americans moved in 2012 were, in reverse order: Sarasota, Charlotte, Seattle, Denver, Houston, Chicago, Orlando, Phoenix, Dallas-Fort Worth, and Atlanta. Only half could be considered warmer-climate cities.

Having two homes, if it's affordable, is a solution for some seniors who want to maintain ties with their family and friends in the colder climate. Most rent or buy in the warmer climate for the winter months.

What's new is that so many more seem to be doing it today, but also that there are so many more choices. Besides the obvious ones of Florida, Nevada, Arizona, and California, according to Richard Barrington writing for Moneyrates.com and cited by AARP, here are the top states they recommend for retirement. (Note, we've regrouped by weather and high life expectancy, with a couple of states also listed due to the low crime rate or economy.)

Best states because of weather and/or secondary reason:

- Hawaii (also high life expectancy)
- Arizona (also high life expectancy)
- Florida
- New Mexico
- California (also high life expectancy)
- Texas (also solid economy)

Good economy:

- Idaho (also low crime rate)

- Virginia

- South Dakota (also low crime rate/high life expectancy)

- Colorado (also high life expectancy)

Relocating to Another Country

Real estate property taxes are another factor to consider when choosing where to live in retirement. Property taxes will be a lot lower in many places around the world compared to some areas in the United States—for example, a suburb close to New York City. Although some find this too dramatic a move even if it's much easier to live on a fixed income, for others moving to another country has worked out just fine.

 WORTH NOTING

According to seniorplanet.org, the five best countries to grow old in are France, the Netherlands, Japan, Nicaragua, and Mexico. France has the best health-care system according to the World Health Organization; the Netherlands has the best pension plans; and Japan offers a better chance for employment if you're over 65. Nicaragua has the lowest cost for housing, where you can rent a nice two-bedroom house for $250 a month. Mexico has been declared by *Foreign Policy* magazine as one of the best places for seniors looking for an active social life, plus the cost of living is a lot less than north of the border.

Kathleen Peddicord is an expert on retiring overseas. In addition to relocating internationally herself three times—first to Ireland, then to Paris, and finally to Panama City where she lives with her husband and two children—Peddicord is the author of *How to Retire Overseas* and founder of LiveandInvestOverseas.com. She shared her suggestions for places where you can retire and live comfortably on two different Social Security benefit incomes:

On $1,200 or less (to as little as $700/month), check out:

- Cuenca, Ecuador (a colonial town in the highlands)

- Granada, Nicaragua (another colonial town on a lake)

- Pedasi, Panama

- Chiang Mai, Thailand (an historic city in the hills)

Peddicord says that if your budget is $2,400 a month or less, you can live comfortably in these additional international locations:

- Ambergris Caye, Belize (an island off the coast in the Caribbean)

- Abruzzo, Italy (Peddicord notes that this region is similar to Tuscany in its weather, history, and atmosphere, but it's not yet as popular as Tuscany, so it's still more affordable)

- Pau in Southwestern France (a rural country town)

On a budget of $3,600 or less of monthly benefits, Peddicord states, "You could retire almost anywhere. You couldn't afford Paris or Florence, but anywhere in the world outside of a big city, you could live comfortably." She named a few of her favorite places for retirees:

- Barcelona, Spain

- Buenos Aires, Argentina (you can take a ferry between Buenos Aires and Montevideo)

- Montevideo, Paraguay (quiet, charming, old world)

Finally, for a high-earning couple whose combined monthly benefits are $7,200, Peddicord says, "Honestly, with that much income, you could live anywhere." She adds that it depends on what kind of lifestyle you want. For places that are closer to the United States and where English is the main language, she suggests:

- Cayman Islands

- British Virgin Islands

- St. John's

In Puerto Vallarta, Mexico, Peddicord states, "You could live a 'jet set' lifestyle with a beachfront condo, right over the Pacific, with country clubs and five-star restaurants and a really interesting local culture."

If you're reluctant to learn another language, such as Spanish, French, or Portuguese, Peddicord recommends picking an international place to relocate that already has a large expatriate population who speak English. Cuenca in Ecuador, Granada, and Panama City are all places with lots of foreign retirees.

Why is relocating to another country being embraced by so many Baby Boomers? "The Baby Boomer generation has traveled more than any other generation before them," says Peddicord. "It's less of an outside-the-box idea today since Baby Boomers have traveled. They've spent time in other places."

It's also easier than ever to get your Social Security benefits if you relocate to another country, since so many today receive their benefits via direct deposit into a bank account. Peddicord points out you can keep your American bank account and access the funds through local ATM machines. However, sending Social Security payments to the countries of Cuba and North Korea is strictly prohibited.

 TIP

Check out the SSA's booklet covering this topic titled, "Your Payments While You Are Outside the United States." It's available for free at ssa.gov/pubs/EN-05-10137.pdf.

If necessary, you might even be able to pick up your check in person monthly at the American Embassy in certain countries!

Living Frugally

Co-author Jan Yager remembers her first trip to India when she was 23 years old and doing research for her first book. During her week in Delhi, she stayed at the Gandhi Peace Foundation for $1 a night. Co-author Fred Yager remembers the trend when he was in his 20s of finding furniture put out on the streets of the nice neighborhoods in Manhattan. That's how you furnished your apartment when you were trying to survive on less!

And when Fred was in the Navy, his sister Becky sent him a birthday card with $1.25 in it. He went to the Goodwill store on the base and bought a corduroy jacket, a belt, and a red Frisbee.

If you want to stretch your Social Security benefits, now is the time to remember and implement some of these strategies. Jan was thrilled when she and Fred were living temporarily in Nashville, Tennessee, when they discovered a Sears outlet store. For just $2, she bought a black winter sweater that helped shelter her from the Nashville winter.

Exploring Available Discounts and Free Goods or Services

You can choose free goods or services as a way to stretch your Social Security benefits. Turning 65—and for some goods and services as young as 62 or even 50—can lead to a discount that could range from just a dollar or two off to as much as a 50 percent discount, or even for free. Here are just some of the examples I've personally discovered:

- Metro North, which has train service between Connecticut and New York, offers a substantial discount for seniors over 65. However, the senior (or disabled) ticket must be used during off-peak hours. For more information, go to mta.info/mnr.

- The New York City subway system passenger fare card, known as the MetroCard, offers a 50 percent discount to seniors. You have to apply online, and that enables you to get a refillable discounted card. Technically you're only supposed to use it during non-rush hours. You will need to attach a photograph as well as a copy of your driver's license with your application. For the online application, go to web.mta.info/nyct/fare/pdf/seniors.pdf.

- Check out retiredbrains.com/products-services/discounts-for-seniors for an extensive list of discounts for seniors in these categories: retail and apparel, travel, grocery, activities and entertainment discounts, and other discounts. Most of these discounts are for 10 percent off, but some go as high as 30 to 50 percent.

- Many of your current associations offer as much as a 50 percent discount if you've been a member for a certain number of years and you are a senior over a certain age.

- Certain associations, such as AARP, focus on helping seniors and have lots of free or discounted services that they're affiliated with if you're a member. (Currently the membership fee is $16/year.) Check out aarp.org to find out more about membership as well as what discounts membership will entitle you to.

- Most movie theaters offer a senior discount, although you might have to use it during certain days of the week or hours on the weekend. Check with your local theaters for details for those specific chain or independent theaters.

If you're used to entertaining and spending lots of money on food, next time you want to have guests, ask everyone to make it a pot-luck event. Each person brings a main dish or dessert, and some may even bring wine, beer, or beverages for their contribution. Finally, make eating out a special treat. Cook at home more often, so you save on food expenses.

Do you have gifts that are not your favorites but you can't return them? Could you re-gift to someone, or maybe sell them? Many seniors have their own eBay stores, selling unwanted gifts and items they run across in their daily lives.

Schedule your trips, including even your nearby traveling, during nonpeak travel times so you can get the best deals on airline tickets as well as the lowest cost for your hotel accommodations.

The Least You Need to Know

- You can live on just your Social Security, but for most it's quite a challenge. Fortunately, there are government and private programs that can help with everything from free food to discounted transportation.

- If you're trying to stay in your home, your community or state might offer eligible seniors a reduction in property taxes. There are federal and state programs to help you find more affordable housing if moving would help you live on Social Security.

- You can downsize to a smaller home in your community, or relocate to another state or country that has economic advantages over where you currently live.

- You may be eligible for a free cell phone as well as reductions in the cost of your utilities.

Remaining in, or Returning to, the Workforce

Whether they're working for the fun of it or due to economic necessity, many people are going to continue working or will have to return to work. Of course, there are some who are able to completely retire. We've all seen the commercials promising that if you manage your finances, nest egg, or pension funds wisely, a blissful retirement is possible. If you're in that elite group, that's great. But even if you can afford to retire, you still might want to keep working, whether it's for just a few more years or for as long as you're physically able.

If you're still working, want to return to work, or want to start your own business due to economic necessity or just to keep busy, this chapter offers you guidance about how working may impact your Social Security benefits.

In This Chapter

- Why more Americans are working in retirement
- How continuing to work impacts your Social Security
- How the Windfall Elimination Provision works
- Pros and cons of suspending or paying back benefits

The Aging of the American Workforce

If you're 64 and still working, you're not alone. A 2014 Merrill Lynch/Age Wave survey of 7,000 people found that nearly half (47 percent) of all current retirees are still working or plan to return to work.

Moreover, the study found that three out of four Americans over 50 expect to work in retirement, either because they want to or because they have to just to pay their bills.

Ironically, the term *retirement* is falling out of favor. Even the well-known organization AARP, which is 37 million members strong, no longer refers to itself as the American Association of Retired People, but just as AARP.

The Merrill Lynch/Age Wave study, titled "The New Retirement Workscape," also exposed these four myths about retirement:

Myth #1: Retirement equals the end of work.

Reality: According to the study, 80 percent of working retirees are working because they simply want to.

Myth #2: Retirement is a time of decline.

Reality: Of the retirees still working, 83 percent see work as an antidote to aging because it helps them stay more youthful. In fact, 66 percent said when they didn't work, their physical and mental abilities deteriorated more rapidly.

Myth #3: People work in retirement because they need the money.

Reality: Only 20 percent of retirees said they were working because they had to; the rest were working for nonfinancial reasons.

Myth #4: New career ambitions are for the young.

Reality: Nearly three out of five (58 percent) working retirees changed careers and are three times more likely than younger workers to be entrepreneurs.

This chapter discusses the impact of working on your Social Security benefits and also covers some important work-related issues.

How Does Continuing to Work Affect Your Benefits?

Here's the good news: you *can* claim Social Security benefits and go right on working. The bad news is that if you haven't reached your full retirement age (FRA), your benefits could be reduced. However, the SSA says your benefits will be *increased* when you reach your FRA to account for those reductions and the added income to your total amount of earnings because you continue working and earning.

We discussed the income caps on your Social Security benefits in previous chapters. Now we'll address income considerations for all three types of Social Security benefits—retirement, disability, or survivors—depending on the age at which you file and other factors.

The Impact of Working on Retirement Benefits

If you began receiving Social Security benefits before reaching your FRA, there will probably be an income cap, meaning there's a limit on how much you can earn and still receive full benefits. For example, if you were born between January 2, 1943, and January 1, 1955, your FRA is 66. If you were younger than 66 during all of 2014, your income cap was $15,480. If you earned more than that in 2014, the SSA deducted $1 from your benefits for each $2 you earned above $15,480.

 **CAUTION**

Spouses and survivors who receive benefits because they have minor or disabled children in their care *do not* receive increased benefits when they reach full retirement age if their benefits were reduced because of income from work.

If you reached your FRA during 2014, the income cap is much higher. During that year, the SSA would deduct $1 for each $3 you earned above $41,400 until the month you reached your FRA.

Beginning at your FRA and beyond, there's no income cap on earnings. That means if you earn $75,000 a year, you still receive *all* of your Social Security benefits, no matter the amount you're entitled to each month. Remember, as noted in Chapter 15, you may also have to pay federal taxes or even state taxes on your Social Security retirement benefits. Although 38 states and the District of Columbia do not tax Social Security benefits, the other states do.

The following table helps you see how much you received in 2014 based on your estimated earnings and the amount of your monthly benefit.

For People Younger Than FRA During the Whole Year

If your monthly Social Security benefit is ...	And you earn ...	You'll receive yearly benefits of ...
$700	$15,480 or less	$8,400
$700	$16,000	$8,140
$700	$20,000	$6,140
$900	$15,480 or less	$10,800
$900	$16,000	$10,540
$900	$20,000	$8,540
$1,100	$15,480 or less	$13,200
$1,100	$16,000	$12,940
$1,110	$20,000	$10,940

Source: "How Work Affects Your Benefits," Social Security Administration, January 2014, SSA Publication No. 05-10069.

Here are a few scenarios to help you understand how this works:

Scenario 1. According to John F. Wasik, who wrote The *New York Times* article "Social Security at 62? Let's Run the Numbers," many people file for Social Security as soon as they're eligible (46 percent of women and 41 percent of men). Let's say your monthly benefit is $600 a month, which amounts to $7,200 in Social Security benefits for the year. But although you're still working, since you only earn $12,000, you fall below the income cap of $15,480, so none of your benefits have to be withheld or returned.

Scenario 2. Let's say you're a 63-year-old claimant and you worked and earned $20,800 during 2014. Since you're below your FRA, your income cap is $15,480. Because you earned $5,520 above that income cap, the SSA withheld $1 for every $2 or $2,660. To do that, the SSA withheld all of your monthly $600 benefit payments from January 2014 through May 2014. Then, starting in June, you started to receive your $600 benefit and kept receiving that amount for each month for the rest of the year. In 2015, the SSA would pay you the additional $340 that was withheld in May 2014.

Scenario 3. Let's look at someone who reached their FRA in 2014, but not until November. They managed to earn $42,900 during the first 10 months of 2014. For that period, the SSA withheld $1 for every $3 above the special $41,400 earnings cap during the year you reach your full retirement age or $500. (As noted previously, that's the increased income cap for someone who reached their full retirement age during that year.) To do that, the SSA withheld their first check of the year and then started giving them their $600 benefit in February and for each remaining month of the year. Then, in 2015, they would pay the $100 they withheld in January 2014.

Scenario 4. A man has been living on his retirement savings and his additional Social Security benefits for the last year. But now, at age 68, one year after reaching his FRA, he feels somewhat bored. He also realizes that at the rate he and his wife are spending their retirement savings, he may be out of additional funds within five years. He finds a job that pays $65,000 per year. Since he's past his FRA, there's no income cap on his earnings. He can work and receive the same Social Security benefits he's been collecting all along.

However, remember he will have to pay federal taxes on both his job income and his Social Security benefits. And, depending on what state he lives in, he may also have to pay state taxes on his Social Security benefits. He must take those taxes into consideration so he can avoid dipping into his retirement savings account.

Disability Benefits and Work

If you're receiving Social Security disability benefits when you return to work, you must report what you earn to the SSA, but that doesn't mean your benefits will be affected. First, there's a nine-month trial period that lets you test your ability to go back to work. This is known as the Ticket to Work program, and during the nine-month period you'll continue to receive disability benefits no matter how much you earn as long as you have a disability. Once this trial period is up, you still have another 36 months when you can work and still receive benefits, as long as you don't earn above a certain amount. What are those caps? In 2014, the earnings cap was $1,070 a month or $1,800 if you're blind.

WORTH NOTING

Different rules apply for receiving disability benefits or Supplemental Security Income if you return to work. Refer back to Chapter 9 for further details. There are also special rules if you work outside the United States. You should contact the SSA if you're working or plan to work outside the states. For more information on how working outside the United States affects your Social Security benefits, go to ssa.gov/retire2/international.htm.

For more information on how work impacts your disability benefits, you can refer back to Chapter 9. You can also refer to the SSA publication "Working While Disabled—How We Can Help" at ssa.gov/pubs/EN-05-10095.pdf.

Survivors Benefits and Work

As discussed in Chapter 11, full survivors benefits are available to a surviving spouse at their FRA or at a reduced level as early as age 60. However, if a widow or widower is taking care of dependent or disabled children, survivors benefits are available at any age.

However, if you're below FRA and receiving survivors benefits, your Social Security benefits may be reduced if you exceed the limits set on earnings as noted previously. Similar to the way benefits are impacted if you receive benefits between age 62 and your FRA, survivors benefits have an income cap of $15,720 on earnings until the year you reach you FRA, when (in 2015) the cap rises to $41,880 for the year that you reach your FRA. There is no income cap after you reach your FRA.

However, the reduction in survivors benefits because of working before reaching your FRA applies only to the survivor who is working, not to any survivors benefits being paid to other family members, including children or dependent parents.

To find out more about survivors benefits, including how work impacts survivors benefits, check out the SSA's booklet "Survivors Benefits" at ssa.gov/pubs/EN-05-10084.pdf.

TIP

The SSA publishes a booklet titled "How Work Affects Your Benefits" at ssa.gov/pubs/EN-05-10069.pdf.

How Increased Earnings May Impact Your Retirement Benefits

Keep in mind that other family members who may be receiving benefits based on your work record will have their benefits adjusted as well. On the other hand, if your spouse and children receive benefits based on their own work records, then only earnings from their work records will impact their benefits.

Also, as we've mentioned, if your benefits are reduced due to your earnings, your monthly benefit will increase when you reach your FRA to make up for all the months your benefits were reduced or withheld.

For example, let's say you began taking retirement benefits at 62 and you receive $750 a month in benefits. But then you return to work and make so much that you have 12 months of benefits withheld. In that case, the SSA would adjust your monthly benefit at your FRA (which would be 66) and give you $800 a month. If you earned the same for each year between 62 and 66 and all your benefits were withheld, then the SSA would increase your monthly benefit to $1,000 a month starting at age 66.

WORTH NOTING

There's a special rule for the first year of your retirement. If you retire mid-year and have already earned more than the annual earnings limit, you can still receive a full Social Security monthly benefit for any whole month you're retired regardless of earnings.

Each year the SSA reviews the records for everyone who works and receives Social Security benefits. If your latest year of earnings is among your highest years, they will recalculate your monthly benefit and give you any increases you have coming. This is done automatically and any increase is reflected in December of the following year. So, for example, if you deserved an increase from your 2014 earnings, you should see it in your December 2015 payment. That increase is also retroactive to January 2015.

Understanding that this is an automatic process, you may still want to check to ensure it actually happened. If it didn't, contact the SSA and let them know.

CAUTION

The Social Security Administration goes by the information you give them when they figure the amount of your benefit. If you're receiving benefits while still working and have given SSA an estimated income but then learned your earnings are going to be different than what you reported, get in touch with your local office immediately so they can make the adjustment.

What If You're Self-Employed?

If you own a business or are self-employed, the SSA counts only your net earnings. Also, the net income counts when you receive it, not necessarily when you earn it—unless it's paid in a year after you became entitled to Social Security but you earned it before you became entitled.

Net earnings are your gross earnings minus your allowable business deductions and depreciation.

Some income doesn't apply to Social Security and doesn't have to be counted when determining your net earnings, such as:

- Dividends from stock or interest on bonds, unless you receive it as a securities dealer.

- Interest from loans, unless you're in the money-lending business.

- Rent from real estate, unless you're a real estate dealer or provide services mostly for the convenience of the occupant.

- Income received from a limited partnership.

Does It Matter Whether You Work Full-Time?

It doesn't matter to the SSA whether you work full-time or part-time. If you work for someone else and earn income, it counts whether it is done on a full-time or part-time basis. And it counts when it is earned, not necessarily when it's paid. For example, if you earned income in one year but didn't receive the actual payment until the following year, it will be counted in the year you earned it and not the year you actually received the payment.

Other Factors and Strategies That Affect Your Benefits

There are several considerations and strategies to know about that can affect the Social Security retirement benefits you receive. These include the Windfall Elimination Provision, suspending benefits, or repaying benefits and restarting when you claim your benefits at an older age. These considerations have been mentioned previously in this book but we thought we should restate these factors here since it could be tied to continuing to work, or deciding to return to work, in terms of making new or different decisions because your financial situation has changed.

The Windfall Elimination Provision

Some people work for an employer who doesn't withhold Social Security taxes from their salary. This could be a government agency or a company that's based in another country. If this describes your situation, any pension you receive based on that work could reduce your Social Security benefits under the Windfall Elimination Provision.

This provision affects how much the amount of your retirement or disability benefit is adjusted if you receive a pension from work where you paid no Social Security taxes. The SSA uses a formula to determine how much to reduce your monthly benefits.

There are some exceptions to the provision. For example, if you have 30 or more years of what are considered "substantial" earnings in a job where you paid Social Security taxes, then your benefits will not be reduced. If you have between 21 and 29 years of substantial earnings on which you paid taxes, the reduction would be less. How much less would depend on a number of factors. If you have to deal with any of these scenarios, it's best to consult your local Social Security office or a financial advisor for a detailed explanation of what benefits you can expect to receive.

There are some other exceptions to the Windfall Elimination Provision, including:

- If you were a federal employee who was hired after December 31, 1983.

- If you were employed by a nonprofit organization on December 31, 1983, that did not withhold Social Security taxes at first, but started to later.

- If your only pension is based on working for the railroad.

- If the only work you did in which you didn't pay Social Security taxes was before 1957.

- If you receive a relatively low pension.

Suspending Your Benefits

If you took your Social Security benefits early, you may be thinking you made a mistake that could cost you thousands of dollars over the years because of the reduction in benefits. If you can afford to, you can still suspend those benefits and re-apply at a later age. For example, let's say you took Social Security at age 62, which meant your monthly benefits would be 25 percent less than if you had waited until you reached full retirement age at 66. Now you're about to turn 66 and can afford to suspend Social Security until age 70. If you do that, your benefits would grow 8 percent per year, so when you reapply at 70, you'll get pretty much what you would have received if you had waited until your full retirement age to collect.

There are a few pros and cons associated with doing this. On the pro side, your life benefits will be higher. On the con side, you could die at 71 and you would have sacrificed four years' worth of reduced Social Security benefits, which would have equaled about $60,000.

On the other hand, if you're married your spouse would benefit from the suspension even if you die early, because in her spousal survivors benefit, she would receive 100 percent of your increased payment.

Paying Back Benefits

Suspending and then paying back benefits is a radical option, but something you should know about. Of course, you never know what can happen to you once you begin receiving your Social Security benefits. You could win the lottery, inherit money from a long-lost relative, or get a job that pays enough you don't need to collect Social Security any more.

If that happens, or if you simply change your mind about when you should start receiving benefits, you can withdraw your claim and re-apply later, provided you do so within 12 months of your original claim. But you can only suspend and delay your benefits once. And if you do decide to do this, you have to repay all the benefits you and your family received up to that point.

The pros of doing this are obvious. As you know, the longer you put off taking your Social Security benefits, the larger the monthly benefit is going to be. If you live to 80, 90, or 100, getting an extra $1,000 or more a month can add up to literally hundreds of thousands of dollars. For example, if by delaying when you start benefits your monthly benefit is increased by $1,000 per month, that amounts to $12,000 per year. If you live 30 additional years, you'll collect $360,000 more than if you had received just $1,000 per month.

The con is that you might need the money now, or you could die before taking the delayed payment that seemed to make financial sense at the time.

If you want to pay back your benefits and refile later on, you have to contact the SSA and fill out Form SSA-521, which you can download from the website. Once you submit the form, the SSA will let you know how much you need to repay.

The Least You Need to Know

- Your age should not stop you from working. The current trend is toward more older men and women continuing to work or returning to work.
- You can receive Social Security benefits while you're still working but, depending on your age, it may impact the amount of your benefits.
- Once you reach full retirement age, there are no income caps if you wish to return to work while receiving Social Security Benefits.
- If you're receiving disability benefits, for the first nine months after you return to work your benefits will not be reduced.

Safeguarding Your Future

None of us can know what the future holds, but the more you can do now to prepare for it financially, the better. It's no secret that most Americans nearing retirement age don't have enough money saved, which means many of us will be working a lot longer, or we'll have to learn how to live on a lot less.

This part is designed to help you prepare for your financial future as much as you can. This may mean you'll have to lower your expectations about the lifestyle you'll be able to afford. Financial advisors recommend you take inventory by writing down your goals and objectives. We'll provide a number of financial planning tips to help you navigate the last chapters of your life. We'll show you how to create a budget, cut expenses, and make suggestions for paying down credit card debt. We'll also recommend what to look for in a financial advisor.

Finally, we'll discuss the future of Social Security and how we can all work together to keep this vital program alive and thriving for generations to come.

How Will You Spend the Rest of Your Life?

There's a good chance you'll live almost as long in your senior retired years as you did in your working years. With medical advances continuing to prolong the average life span, one of the fastest-growing segments of our population is men and women over the age of 100.

The key question is, how are you going to spend the next 20, 30, or even 40 additional years? Do you plan on traveling the world, visiting places you've only read about in books or seen in movies? Does the golf course beckon? Or will you create that novel, screenplay, or sculpture that you never had the time to develop because of your job or family obligations? What about acting in the community theatre or taking singing lessons? Some of these pursuits, such as travel, may be more costly than others, such as writing a screenplay. So one thing you may want to consider before taking any action is how much a particular activity will cost and whether you can afford it.

In This Chapter

* Deciding how to live this next stage in your life
* Taking inventory of your assets
* Comparing what's coming in with how much you spend
* Calculating your medical expenses
* How will you cover the shortfall?

Taking Stock

Before entering our Social Security years, many of us were identified by the work we did, or by our profession, which may be why so many of us want to continue working as long as we can. But what if you can't work anymore? While ageism is supposed to be against the law, many corporations are hesitant to hire workers 60 and over because they wonder just how long such an employee is going to stick around to justify the hiring and training costs associated with a new worker. Or they question whether those who are older are able to connect to the younger workforce, or are keeping up with the technological trends.

Yes, some corporations are going out of their way to hire people over 65 who offer unique skills that make the age consideration negligible. But since those sought-after jobs are few and far between, it makes it much more difficult for the unemployed seniors to find jobs for which they are qualified and that pay much more than the minimum hourly wage.

 QUOTATION

> "I started taking Social Security at age 66, my full retirement age. I have 10 percent deducted for taxes, and then the monthly Medicare premium is also deducted, so I get $1,800 a month. It basically pays my rent. But it [Social Security] definitely helps since I'm not working full time anymore, just doing some freelance, and making very little. It's ridiculous how little I'm making."
>
> —A 69-year-old semi-retired divorced educator

A question that usually follows, when newly minted seniors think about the gift of those added decades their parents could not count on, is, "Will I outlive my money?"

Use this opportunity to take stock of what you hope to accomplish in your senior years as well as how you're going to finance those years.

Creating Your Bucket List

We suggest you start by writing down what you want to achieve—namely, your goals and objectives. Some people call this their *bucket list* of things they would like to do before it's too late. But it's actually much more important than that.

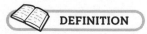 **DEFINITION**

The term **bucket list** stems from the phrase "kick the bucket," and refers to the list of things you want to do before you die.

Your bucket list should include your goals, objectives, and, most importantly, the purpose that you see in what you do over the next couple of decades. Some people get depressed by living a life without structure or purpose. Co-author Fred once asked his 78-year-old father-in-law, who had retired from dentistry at the age of 65, how life in retirement was. His answer: "It's death."

But others, like so many of the seniors co-author Jan asked how they were enjoying retirement, responded in these or similar words: "I'm so busy now, how did I ever find the time to work before?"

Creating your own bucket list could include your dreams, goals, and objectives. A bucket list is a great way to avoid a retirement that is unsatisfying. Instead, with some planning and thoughtfulness, you just might find these years are far more rewarding than you ever thought they could be.

For example, Jan remembers listening to the brief biographies shared at a breakfast organized by one of the associations she belongs to, the Dramatists Guild. As they went around the table of 20 or so members, the older ones would introduce themselves by giving their name, the "day job" they had before retirement, and how they're now writing plays and getting their work produced.

Rodney Brooks confirms this trend in his article "Boomers turn to encore careers after retiring," sharing the example of then 74-year-old Yuval Zaliouk, who retired as conductor of the Toledo Symphony and then began his second dream career: selling cookies based on his grandmother's recipe. Another example Brooks cites is David Roll, who, a decade before at age 62, concluded his Washington, D.C. law career to become a historian and author and to start a global nonprofit organization called Lex Mundi, which locates pro bono lawyers for social entrepreneurs.

What is your dream for your senior years? It helps to start with a plan. It might be just a general goal, or it might be something very detailed, like how you will spend your time each day. Of course, you may not want your plan to look as structured and pressured as when you had your 9-to-5 job. But you might not want all your time totally open-ended, either.

As you write down all the things you want to do, you may want to set aside a special section for volunteer work. It not only makes you feel good to help those in need, but you get to interact with like-minded people and maybe even make new friends. Jan recently learned that a married retired radio host, upon her arrival in Florida for her second winter as a retiree, shared on social media how thrilled she was to have just signed up to be a volunteer at a local animal shelter.

Your bucket list could include visiting places, like the 2011 1,200 page bestseller *1,000 Places to See Before You Die* by Patricia Schultz. But it could also include people you want to reconnect with, or even meet for the first time, and maybe projects you've wanted to do your whole life, but you've been putting off until now. Maybe it's starting a new company or volunteering in another part of the world. Perhaps you have a bucket list of must-read books you always hoped to get to read "someday." Or maybe it includes traveling with your family or some of your friends to someplace exotic or far away, or writing a play or a book.

Make your personal bucket list as short or as long as you want it to be. Put it in order of priorities or chronologically, by what you plan to do first, second, third, and so on. Put it on your computer, or in a journal, and make it flexible so you can revise it, or make it hard and fast so that you'll go right down your list, sticking to every single entry in order.

If you're married or you have a significant other, include him or her in your choices and selections. Will you do everything together? On your own? With others?

Are You Going to Outlive Your Money?

We've talked to a lot of people in their 60s and learned something interesting: in addition to many of them preferring to avoid using the word "retire," discussions about money are even less popular. Certainly there are some individuals with ample pensions, impressive savings set aside for retirement that they do not have to dip into yet, or even sufficient Social Security benefits, who are able to live a comfortable life without having to earn additional income to survive.

But for many Americans, total retirement is still just a goal. The recession of 2008 diminished or wiped out retirement savings. The bursting of the real estate bubble left many either underwater on their homes or forced to sell and live in rentals that are just as high or even higher than their previous mortgages. Because of those and other related economic downturns, including short- or long-term periods of unemployment, the number of American retirees in their late 50s or 60s appears to be dwindling each year.

Fewer and fewer workers are receiving the kinds of pensions our parents received. Today, it's either a 401(k) or similar employee-funded retirement savings account, or an IRA. Self-managing one lump sum has proven a lot harder to do well than receiving the monthly pension benefit that at least has some economic checks and balances on spending built in.

QUOTATION

"You have to put money aside. People need to have a reality check. 'What have I done? Am I on the right path?' Regardless of what their resources are, they need to sit down with an advisor and learn the numbers. To me, that's a wake-up call. 'I have to save $500 a month.' 'I have to start saving somewhere.' It might mean a change in lifestyle, one less vacation a year, or working a second job for that purpose. It just really comes down to proper planning."

—Dan Fisher, Financial Advisor and Founder, Fisher Financial

Most of us want to live in a financially independent way. So it's time to ask ourselves some difficult questions, such as "How much money will I need to continue to pay my bills, take an occasional vacation, and not have to turn to anyone else for help as I enter these final decades of my life?"

According to the Social Security Administration, a man reaching age 65 today can expect on average to live until 84.3. A woman turning 65 can expect to live to 86.6. It's not uncommon to find men and women living into their 90s and 100 and beyond. This means you can expect to live for another 20 to 40 years after becoming eligible for Social Security benefits.

How widespread a concern is it to wonder if you will outlive your money? According to Bankrate. com, 40 percent of retirees say they fear outliving their money. More women have this fear than men. Moreover, three out of four workers in America expect to keep working as long as they can.

For too many in America, unfortunately, there is the reality of poverty—those who truly are poor, are trying to live on just their Social Security in retirement, and are in need of government or private aid to get by. With the average Social Security retirement benefit in 2014 at $1,294 and the maximum, if you retire at full retirement age, at $2,642, trying to live on just your Social Security benefits can be a struggle—especially if you're single, it's your only source of revenue, you have little or no savings or investment income, and you live in a high cost of living area.

 WORTH NOTING

According to the U.S. Department of Health and Human Services, a person was considered living below the poverty level in 2014 if he or she earned less than $11,670 a year as a single person. For a family of four, the poverty level in 2014 was $23,850.

Then there's the elite group who have a fixed income that is much higher than the poverty level, possibly even over $100,000 per year, from pension income as well as earnings from dividends and investments. However, those in this group may still see themselves as potentially outliving their money because they're earning less in retirement than they earned when they were working. Because of that, they'll probably have to start dipping into their savings. Unless their dividends and investments keep growing to make up that shortfall, they'll feel that as their nest egg shrinks, so does their security that they'll have enough money to enjoy a comfortable retirement.

Taking Inventory of Assets, Savings, and Investments

When you write down your goals, be clear about the expenses you'll have to cover each year going forward. Make a list of your assets, savings, and investments, including any real estate holdings such as your apartment or house if you own it.

This list of your assets should also include all of your bank accounts, brokerage accounts, Individual Retirement Accounts, 401(k)s, deferred compensation, life insurance, safety deposit boxes, automobiles, home furnishings, collectibles, antiques, jewelry, and any other items that have value.

You'll also want to record your debts, including all credit card debts, first and second mortgages, student loans, car payments, and so on.

When Catherine Kitcho, a business consultant, started to worry about whether or not she and her husband would outlive their money, she began a research project that turned into a book titled *Happy About® Being a Baby Boomer: Facing Our Newfound Longevity.* Unlike those who do an income projection analysis of their retirement years, Catherine focused on what expenses she needed to cover. That way she could see her estimated expenses and compare them to her income from Social Security and any other sources she could count on, such as a pension, as well as any savings she had amassed. In *Happy About® Being a Baby Boomer,* published in 2007 right before the crash of 2008, Kitcho wisely suggests that everyone create a Longevity Plan and shares examples and guidelines on how to make one.

WORTH NOTING

When it comes to long-term care, where you live matters. Most people want to stay in their own home for as long as possible. Whether that's even feasible depends on the condition of your home; whether it can be modified to accommodate a wheelchair or other health aid devices; whether there are long-term care services in your area; and whether your community is "age friendly" and offers services that aid the elderly, such as free or low-cost van services for those with mobility issues.

As hard as it is to think about being 85 when you're only in your 50s or 60s, you really do need to take into consideration some of the age-related costs you may incur down the road. If you have an aging parent, you may be watching them spend much or all of their money on such expenses as an assisted living residence, which can cost as much as $6,000 a month in some places; part- or full-time private care, including live-in care; and nursing assistance.

Other age-related costs include the following:

- Supplemental insurance to pay health-care costs not covered by Medicare. Or, if you don't opt for a supplemental plan, the 20 percent of costs Medicare does not cover.

- Lifestyle change costs: if you wish to downsize your home, the cost of moving to another location.

- If you can no longer drive yourself, the cost of hiring a driver, calling a taxi, or using an alternative car service on a regular basis.

- Legal services for preparing wills, trusts, health-care directives, and any other specialized documents related to your estate.

- If you downsize, and do not donate or give away your extra possessions, the cost of storing the furniture, clothing, or other items you want to keep.

Developing a Budget

Even if until now budgeting was not something you did on a regular basis, now is the time to commit to developing a budget. Start by keeping track of your expenses.

How Much Money Is Going Out?

It all comes back to planning and being prepared. The better you are prepared for retirement, whatever your age, the better the outcome when that day occurs. Hopefully, because of your plans, you won't run out of money.

You start by either creating a budget or revising the budget you already have. You need to know what your fixed expenses are each month. (See Chapter 16 on a more detailed discussion about how to create a budget.)

That includes everything you spend money on each month including such essentials as: mortgage or rent, utilities such as water, heat, and electricity, telephone (cell phone and/or landline), and groceries.

Next figure out any nonessential expenses such as your cable TV bill, eating out, and vacations. Financial advisors recommend cutting these nonessential expenses to less than 30 percent of your income.

Determining How Much Is Coming In

The second part of a budget is figuring out how much money you can count on each month. As long as you keep working and you postpone taking Social Security for as long as possible so you get a bigger payout, you should have more funds to work with than you will when you can no longer work. You may want to continue working the same job you're in now because you already know the ropes, and they have a loyalty to you, despite your older age. You might not want to take on the challenge of a new job situation, if you could even find one that suits your skills.

 WORTH NOTING

The AARP keeps track of those companies that hire and reward workers over 50. Each year it publishes the top 50 companies for older people to work for. In 2013, the top 10 places were the National Institutes of Health (NIH), Scripps Health, Atlantic Health System, University of Texas MD Anderson Cancer Center, Mercy Health System, YMCA of Rochester, West Virginia University, Bon Secours Virginia, National Rural Electric Cooperative Association, and WellStar Health System. To see the full list, go to aarp.org.

Of course you might be able to switch to another job. But the key is to keep one or more income streams coming in so you're not trying to live off only your pension, if you have one, or off your savings or investment dividends.

If you're already living on a fixed income, which means the amount of money you get from various sources, such as Social Security, pensions, and any other regular income, add this up and that's what you have to spend each month.

Projecting Future Health-Care Costs

If we live long enough, at some time in our lives most of us are almost certain to require some kind of long-term health care. According to the SSA, 70 percent of people who live to 65 can expect to need long-term care during their lives. This percentage increases the older we get. Long-term care encompasses a wide range of services and support you might need help with, such as:

- Bathing

- Dressing

- Eating

- Using the lavatory

- Transferring from chair to bed

- Caring for incontinence

- Being transported, if you lose the ability to walk or you need to get around in a wheelchair

Evaluating Health and Medical Costs

If you're 65 or older, Medicare Part B provides a free "wellness consultation" with your doctor. This would be a perfect place to start evaluating your health as you enter this next chapter of your life.

One thing your doctor will probably go over is your medical history up to this point, as well as your family's medical history. Like it or not, research has found that we inherit much of our propensity to certain illnesses. For example, if your father and every one of your uncles developed heart disease, you have a greater risk of suffering that same fate than someone whose relatives never had the disease.

Next examine your lifestyle, which includes what you eat and drink, whether you smoke, and how physically active you are.

You may want to consider getting a Medicare Part C or Medigap insurance plan just in case, especially if you fall into a high-risk category based on your family's history of disease.

The good news is, as you know, we're all living longer. The bad news is that as we age, our medical costs often go up. What can you do to keep your medical expenses from getting out of hand? One thing is to stay as healthy as possible.

Consider any conditions that may impact your health that you can proactively prevent by changing your behavior, such as giving up smoking, losing excess weight that makes you prone to diabetes or heart conditions, eating a healthier diet to keep your cholesterol lower, or increasing physical exercise to help reduce your risk of heart disease.

Consider Long-Term Care Insurance

If you or your spouse requires *long-term care,* it can quickly eat up your savings, even if you're eligible for Medicare or Medicaid. As we've noted, if certain financial conditions are met, nursing home care is usually covered by Medicaid. Assisted living, however, is not covered by Medicaid. Therefore, one option to consider is long-term care insurance.

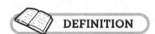 **DEFINITION**

> **Long-term care** insurance is designed to cover long-term services such as personal and custodial care in a variety of settings including your home or apartment, specialized continuing care retirement communities and other residential situations such as public housing and assisted living.

Every long-term care policy is different in regards to what's offered. The monthly premium will vary according to the age at which you get the policy, your overall health, where you expect to live, and what health care services you want it to cover.

The first consideration is getting realistic about what long-term care might end up costing you. If you had any family member go through this, you might know that it can cost between $10,000 and $20,000 a month for long-term care that is not covered by health insurance. If you have not had any first-hand experience with long-term care, do research to find out what the costs might be if, for example, you need to have a nurse from 9 to 5, for two shifts, or even a live-in care provider.

Then find out what the premiums will be for a long-term care insurance policy. For example, for a 50-year-old in good health, the premium would probably run between $4,000 and $8,000 a year; for a 60-year-old in good health, $6,000 to $10,000 a year. The cost goes up quite a bit as you age, with a healthy 75-year-old having to pay $8,000 to $15,000 for a year of long-term health-care insurance.

Now that's a lot of money per year for practically anyone, unless you're super wealthy. But if you consider that by paying those annual premiums you may get as much as $200,000 to $300,000 in coverage for long-term care when you need it, it's a relative bargain.

Make sure that if you go this route the cap on the policy is realistic. You don't want to pay those kinds of premiums for all those years only to find out that when you need to rely on the policy, the maximum benefit is $100,000. If you've been paying for the policy for 20 years at $10,000 a year, you've already paid double the value of the policy in benefits.

So do your homework on whatever policy you're considering to understand what its maximum benefits are. Then do a cost-benefit analysis of what your premiums would be and what you would have to pay out of pocket if you had to pick up all the costs of long-term care on your own.

For more information on long-term care insurance, go to the AARP website, aarp.org, and type "long term care" in the search box.

Will You Have Enough to Live On?

The key is to be able to live on your new or reduced income stream, which may now or in the future include your Social Security benefits; part- or full-time work, if you plan to keep working; a pension if you're lucky enough to have one; and any retirement savings you have in the bank or through 401(k)s or IRAs.

Is this amount going to be enough to finance your goals and objectives? The answer will of course be that it depends on your monthly income compared to how much you're spending. If you're spending more than you're taking in, you may have to revise or at least postpone some of the goals on your bucket list until you can afford them.

Once you're on a fixed income, everything changes. You now have to live within your means, because you can't afford to take on any more debt.

How Will You Cover the Shortfall?

Social Security was never designed to be anyone's only source of income during the senior years. In fact, according to SSA projections, it only replaces about 40 percent of an average person's income. So how will you make up the rest? If you're like most Americans, you'll have to keep working. That will help, but only up to a point.

Continuing to work in your 60s and 70s may seem exciting and even preferable to retiring, especially if you don't yet have the money to retire to the lifestyle you would like to live. But working in your 80s or 90s might not be all that appealing a thought. And, if statistics are at all reliable, it will be a lot less feasible as even the healthiest of Americans start to suffer from motor issues, macular degeneration, heart disease, Alzheimer's, Parkinson's, and any number of ailments associated with aging.

We don't want to depress our readers, but the reality is that certain diseases and ailments are age-related. As a National Institutes of Health (NIH) study of 642 persons age 65 and older concluded in "Age-Specific Incidence of Alzheimer's Disease in a Community Population," published in the *Journal of the American Medical Association (JAMA),* people of age 85 and older are 14 times more likely to get *Alzheimer's* than those in the 65 to 69 age group.

 **DEFINITION**

> **Alzheimer's** is a disease that wreaks havoc with memory, thinking, and behavior. Its symptoms include memory loss and changes in personality, and it usually starts slowly and gets worse over time until you can no longer perform daily tasks.

So if you haven't saved enough for retirement, and most of us haven't, the only way to maintain the lifestyle you're accustomed to is to continue to work and earn income during your 60s and 70s, and as long as possible into your 80s. Otherwise, dramatic changes in lifestyle will have to be made.

Fortunately, as we learned in Chapter 16, changes are possible, such as moving to another state or even another country where the cost of living is lower. But that's not for everyone, and we all want such a decision to be based on such concerns as climate or proximity to family and friends, or a culture or lifestyle we're curious about, rather than desperation or economic necessity.

Fortunately, some of us are still able to look toward our home, condominium, or retirement getaway as the way to generate the retirement savings we need. That might work if you have enough equity in your home and the price is high enough that when you sell it you see a profit.

There are some dire statistics floating around that highlight how urgent it is for you and your loved ones to really take these issues seriously. For example, one statistic we found is that it's predicted that by 2020, one in every three Americans 65 and older are going to be living in poverty.

We're talking about Americans who were considered upper lower class and middle to upper middle class when they were working and bringing in a paycheck. But, because they were too often living from paycheck to paycheck without any real savings, and with mounting credit card debt and escalating unreimbursed health-care costs, many are finding themselves part of "The New Poor."

This is a huge retirement crisis on the horizon and, unfortunately, not enough is being done to address it. However, you can start addressing it yourself by making sure you at least start taking stock of how much longer you can work, what spending habits you can change so you keep more of what you do earn, and how to reverse the American trend of having a resistance to saving that, sadly, characterized so many of the Baby Boomers.

Maybe this was because they were raised by parents who, having lived through the Depression era were dedicated to saving, so deep was their fear of the poverty they had witnessed firsthand. Or maybe it was a reaction to the boom years of the 1990s up to 2008 that lulled many people into a false state of confidence that the money would always be there. Whatever the reason for past spending habits, it's now time to get your own financial house in order. It is, after all, the only house you can really do something about.

You also want to be aware of trends that have the goal of helping more Americans remain in their home or apartment and as financially independent as possible, without having to rely on public assistance, the community, friends, or family. One such movement is known as "virtual villages," a nonprofit organization with annual dues paid by members. These villages are sprouting up throughout the United States, providing services for their members, from cleaning up the yard to driving members to the airport.

The services are provided through volunteers who devote their time to these associations, as noted by Constance Gustke in her *New York Times* article, "Retirees Turn to Virtual Villages for Mutual Support." Some experts, including Andrew Scharlach, Kleiner professor of aging at the University of California, Berkeley, who studied nine retirement villages in California, predict that virtual villages are going to grow in popularity, especially as the Baby Boomers continue to age.

The Least You Need to Know

- It's important that you know what your true financial situation is right now and going forward into your retirement years.
- Create a budget with your retirement in mind. Determine how much you spend each month and how much you have coming in from any earnings, savings interest, investments, and your Social Security benefits.
- Consider the state of your health and whether you'll need long-term care down the road, as well as how you'll pay for it.
- If you have to continue working, be aware of how it will impact your Social Security benefits if you've taken them before reaching full retirement age.

What the Future Holds for Social Security

Anyone facing a life dependent on receiving Social Security benefits, whether for retirement income, survivor's benefits, or disability benefits, is worried about the future of this vital program.

As Drew DeSilver, writing for the think tank Pew Research, points out, Social Security touches the lives of a huge number of Americans. At the end of 2012, that was to the tune of 57 million Americans receiving retirement, disability, or survivor benefits, amounting to $786 billion—that's billion with a "b"—close to a trillion dollars!

The number of people paying into Social Security is even greater. By the end of 2012, according to DeSilver, 161 million Americans paid payroll taxes into the system.

So, yes, Social Security matters to a great many Americans, and not just seniors or retirees. What happens to Social Security is on the minds of those 57 million+ who are already receiving benefits, as well as younger workers who wonder if there will be any money for them when it's time for them to retire. And workers who fear if they become disabled down the road, the funds for them and their dependents will have dried up by then.

In This Chapter

- The debate over whether Social Security can survive
- Pros and cons of raising the full retirement age
- Considering whether raising the earnings base would help
- Is privatization a sensible solution?

Will Social Security Survive?

The concern about Social Security's survival is well justified in that sometime during the next decade, there will be more people taking money out of the fund than those who are contributing to it. It's known as the worker to beneficiary ratio, and it's about to experience its greatest drop in history as more Baby Boomers leave the workforce.

According to the SSA, when Social Security was created, the worker to beneficiary ratio was 15 to 1. Today the ratio is 3 to 1. It will continue to shrink until the balance shifts to more money taken out than is coming in through payroll taxes.

The future of Social Security is actually in the hands of Congress. It was Congress that passed the law that created it in the first place, and it's Congress that votes on a budget each year containing funds to repay the money it borrowed from the Social Security trust funds to pay out benefits. But it doesn't have to do that.

WORTH NOTING

The trust fund for Social Security Disability Insurance will become insolvent in 2016. According to the trustees, if Congress doesn't act by then, people receiving disability benefits will see a 19 percent cut in SSDI payments.

Congress has the authority to default on its debt to Social Security. There is no legal obligation for the government to pay Social Security benefits. In fact, there's a section of the 1935 Social Security Act that states that Congress has the right to alter, amend, or repeal any provision in that act. That means Congress could do whatever it wants with Social Security, including getting rid of it.

While doing away with Social Security is a highly unlikely scenario—it's been a much-loved program for almost 80 years—there will have to be changes made for it to survive, such as raising the retirement age or increasing the taxes collected to fund it.

At the current rate, it's predicted that the Social Security retirement trust fund will run out of money by 2037. Does that mean the end of Social Security? According to the SSA, if nothing is done, retirees will see a reduction in monthly benefits to along the lines of 75 percent of their scheduled payment. Basically, the SSA is saying it can only pay out benefits based on what's coming into the system from taxes.

Does this mean current retirees or those who are about to retire will see their benefits cut 25 percent if they're still alive in 2037? The SSA says no and that it only intends to reduce benefits for those who are 25 to 30 years away from reaching retirement age. Okay, so that means the seniors may be appeased, but what about those who are 20, 30, or 40 years old now? What are they supposed to do if the Social Security benefits they were told to look forward to are either diminished or disappear when they reach retirement age?

WORTH NOTING

The U.S. population is aging. Today, 12 percent of the total population is age 65 or older. By 2080, it will be 23 percent. At the same time, our working-age population is shrinking from 60 percent today to a predicted 54 percent in 2080. By 2040, there will be twice as many people receiving Social Security than workers paying into the system.

For starters, let's look at two ways Congress can enact laws to change Social Security so it will survive and continue in basically the same way we know it now.

Raising the Retirement Age

With the fate of Social Security in the hands of Congress, there are currently proposals in both the House and Senate to gradually raise the full retirement age to 70 or 72. That might sound somewhat extreme compared to the current typical retirement age of someone born in 1937, which is just 65, or between 1943 and 1954, which is 66. But for someone born in 1960 or later, it's already up to 67. Going from 67 to 70 isn't as big a leap as 65 to 70. And with life expectancy up to 84.3 for men and 86.6 for women, it's not so farfetched. (Compare those life expectancies to the numbers in 1935, when Social Security was started: 59.9 years for men and 61.6 years for women.)

WORTH NOTING

Low-income people would be adversely affected by an increase in the retirement age because many of them are not able to extend their working lives—the work they do is too physically demanding. By the time they reach their 60s, their bodies are already worn out. Therefore, raising the age of retirement could cause severe hardship for many people already leading financially challenged lives.

Similar steps to raise the retirement age are already being proposed elsewhere in the world. According to Ariana Eunjung Cha, writing in the *Washington Post*, 14 countries, including Germany, Spain, Italy, Greece, and Ireland, are planning to increase their retirement ages to between 67 and 69 by 2050.

The proposals to raise the full retirement age to 70 or 72 leave the earliest date you can claim benefits at 62. However, because of the increase in the full retirement age, early benefits would be reduced by 43 to 45 percent. Currently, if you take benefits at age 62, your benefit is generally reduced by 25 percent.

Those supporting the age increase cite the actuarial tables showing that people are living longer and healthier, and therefore can work longer. There also are studies that show a correlation between income and longevity, with those having a higher income tending to live longer.

For this plan to succeed, however, there will need to be changes in the way corporations treat older workers. It's a simple fact that corporations that are willing to hire people in their late 60s or early 70s are in the minority. And if they do hire older workers, they're usually paid a considerably lower salary than they were earning during their younger, peak years.

The trend today among corporations is to offer buyouts to older employees, who are usually seen as more expensive to employ than younger workers for a variety of reasons, from their higher salaries to higher health insurance costs.

Another foe to the older worker is ever-changing technology. Unless older workers keep up with the latest generation of technology products and software, they make themselves obsolete. Unfortunately, too few companies invest in training older workers because they can more easily snap up seemingly more knowledgeable younger workers at a lower salary.

Raising Funds by Increasing the Earnings Base

Another proposed way to save Social Security is to increase the pool of money used to fund it. Many experts have suggested one way to raise money and narrow the gap between money coming in and money going out is to increase the maximum level of earnings subject to the Social Security payroll tax. Between 1937 and 2014, that maximum grew from $3,000 to $117,000 in earnings.

 WORTH NOTING

> Removing the earnings cap on Social Security taxes and having a 12.4 percent tax on all earnings would add an estimated $100 billion a year to the Social Security trust fund.

One proposal now before Congress would gradually phase out the maximum between now and 2018. Social Security actuaries say eliminating the cap would reduce the deficit by 86 percent over 75 years. On the other hand, if the cap was raised from the current 82 percent of the payroll to 90 percent, it would only reduce the deficit by 28 percent.

Will the Government Ever Cut Benefits?

Yes, there are even a number of proposals in Congress to cut Social Security benefits. (If you're getting $1,400 a month as a Social Security benefit, which is the average amount, you're probably wondering, "Cut benefits? Could they really be considering that?") The best known is the

Bowles-Simpson Plan, introduced by Republican Senator Alan Simpson of Wyoming and Erskine Bowles, a former Morgan Stanley CEO and former Chief of Staff to President Clinton.

The Bowles-Simpson Plan would ...

- Cut future Social Security benefits between 19 percent and 42 percent for anyone just now entering the workforce.

- Reduce the annual Cost of Living Adjustment (COLA) for current and future Social Security recipients; benefits would decline by 3.7 percent at age 75, 6.5 percent at age 85, and 9.2 percent at age 95.

- Raise the full retirement age to 69 and earliest eligibility to age 64.

Meanwhile, President Obama's 2014 budget included a plan that would make small annual increases in Social Security benefits for the poor and elderly, while middle-income workers would see an increase in taxes. There would also be a cut in Social Security benefits of about $1,000 per year (*not* per month) for someone 85 years old. Younger retirees would also see smaller reductions. However, this plan received no support from Republicans and little from Democrats. It was defeated 413 to 2.

The president's 2015 budget includes ways to raise more tax revenue to fund Social Security, but there was no language about any cuts. This bill appears to be receiving broad support.

Debates over Privatizing Social Security

The debates over privatizing Social Security have been going on for decades, and, according to the Brookings Institute, there is a growing interest among the public about replacing Social Security with privately run Individual Retirement Accounts (IRAs).

Those in favor of *privatization* say it would ...

- Increase the rate of return you would get on your retirement contributions.

- Raise the rate of national savings and spur future economic growth.

- Be smarter politically than raising payroll taxes or reducing benefits.

 **DEFINITION**

> **Privatization,** as used here, is defined as the transfer of a government-run system or organization to a privately owned entity. The argument for doing this stems from the notion that a privately run operation primarily concerned with turning a profit would be more efficient than a government-run organization that isn't as concerned about making money.

This all sounds good until it comes to transitioning from the current system to a private one. Consider this: according to the Brookings Institute, Social Security has trillions of dollars in liabilities that need to be paid each month to millions of retirees, along with a huge number of Baby Boomers getting ready to retire.

Before we can shift to a new private system, we have to find the money to keep up with the current benefit payments, while allowing younger workers enough money to deposit into those private retirement accounts.

One way to do this would be to reduce current benefits or raise payroll taxes to cover the transition. Brookings says most privatization plans also would require additional federal borrowing.

Those arguing against privatization say it would …

- Result in greater risk on the part of every American because they would be investing in stocks and other securities instead of Treasury bonds.

- Require cuts in benefits.

- Require a huge increase in a federal debt that is already excessive.

But the notion that we may not be able to depend on Social Security is reflected in a new study sponsored by Bank of America/Merrill Lynch and Age Wave. The study found that an overwhelming majority (72 percent) of Americans age 50 and over plan to continue working after they reach full retirement age. The study adds that working past FRA will become even more the norm for Generation X and Millennials who say they expect to rely more on their own personal savings and income from working than on Social Security benefits to fund their retirement.

Rethinking the Third Rail of Politics

We began this book by noting that, for years, Social Security (along with Medicare) has been considered the "third rail" of politics, in that you don't touch it if you ever want to get re-elected. However, that perspective may be coming to an end.

Each day, more and more politicians, most of them Republicans, are taking shots at Social Security, a once untouchable program, and reform is now seen as a necessary evil if there's any hope of preserving it.

A number of Social Security reform plans are wending their way through Congress. For example, Republican Representative Paul Ryan of Wisconsin, who ran as Mitt Romney's running mate in 2012, has introduced his so-called "Roadmap to Prosperity" plan. In his plan, the age for Medicare to kick in would rise from 65 to 67. He also suggests giving vouchers with various values that would reduce the cost of premiums. However, Democrats are opposed to the plan and are stalling its progress. Another plan would distribute Social Security and Medicare benefits on a sliding scale according to income.

One bipartisan group is calling on states to set up retirement insurance programs to supplement Social Security. States that are in solid shape economically seem to be for it, but states already burdened by deficits don't find the plan quite as appealing.

The bottom line is, it seems that Social Security is no longer the third rail it once was. In fact, if something isn't done to change the current system, Social Security could die under the weight of its own debilitating deficit. It becomes a simple situation of more money going out than coming in, until there's no more money left to pay out.

According to the SSA's Trustee Report, unless Congress takes action, there only will be enough money in Social Security to pay out benefits at their current rate until 2033. After that, taxes on income would cover benefits at a reduced rate of 75 percent until 2088.

Funds for Medicare are expected to be depleted by 2030. After that, Medicare benefits will be reduced to 85 percent at first and then to 75 percent until 2047.

One thing is crystal clear: Social Security in its present state needs to be reformed. When it was originally created, at the tail end of the Depression, it was designed to help motivate older workers to get out of the workplace and retire to make room for younger workers, as well as to help people who were too old or physically unable to work. But back then, as noted before, life expectancy for American men and women was 59.9 and 61.6, respectively, compared to 84.3 and 86.6 today.

Keeping the original goals of Social Security in mind, the most sensible solution might be to raise the age of full retirement to the more realistic age of 70, to move the early retirement option at a reduced benefit rate from 62 to 65. Other options might be to move Delayed Retirement Credits from 70 to 75, to motivate delaying claiming benefits, to remove the income cap on taxes, and to pass laws that would protect older people from being pushed out of the workforce too soon so seniors can continue to work until 70 or even later if they want to.

The Least You Need to Know

- Social Security needs to be reformed, or by 2033 there will only be enough money to pay about 75 percent of scheduled benefits until 2088.

- Some of the less dramatic and more popular proposals to save Social Security involve raising the full retirement age from 66 or 67, where it is now, to as late as 69 or 70.

- Although raising the full retirement age may seem like a radical step, if you consider the longer life expectancy of Americans today, higher age limits to start benefits make sense. However, it might be unrealistic for those working in jobs dependent on physical labor to work after a certain age.

- You can be confident that Social Security and Medicare will still exist in some form or another. However, the privatization route doesn't look likely any time soon.

Taking Control of Your Financial Future

Here's the good news: it's never too late to take control of your financial future. Whether you have $1,000 in the bank or $500,000, if you're still breathing and able to think, there are things you can do to help yourself right now but especially during your later years. Obviously, the sooner you begin to take control of your finances, the more you'll be able to save. The key message here is that it's up to you to do whatever it takes to improve your financial situation.

In this chapter, we'll explore some of your options. For example, who says you have to retire at a certain age? You might live to be 100; do you really want to stop working when you're in your 60s or even in your 50s? One important strategy you may want to consider is to keep working as long as you can and continue saving part of the income for those years when you can no longer work.

In an interview on the PBS show "Frontline" on February 6, 2006, Professor Alica Munnell, who is also Director of the Center for Retirement Research at Boston College's Carroll School of Management, pointed out that continuing to work in their 60s is one of the key ways seniors can help themselves financially.

In This Chapter

- The best ways to save for retirement
- The differences between an IRA and a 401(k)
- How to find a financial advisor
- Ways to reduce expenses and downsize
- Taking advantage of time and the miracle of compounding

Ironically, now Professor Munnell's suggestion that seniors keep working "until 63, 64, 65, or even 66" seems like she was aiming too low! With what's been happening in the financial and housing markets in the ensuing years, we think it's more likely that should now be "until even 76." (Indeed, in her brief for the Center for Retirement Research, published in October 2013, Professor Munnell's updated and revised view of retirement age is highlighted by the title of her brief: "Social Security's *Real* Retirement Age Is 70.")

Start Saving *Now*, Whatever Your Age

While you're still working, start saving. If you're like most Americans, you haven't put much money away for retirement. According to Bankrate.com, one in three working Americans haven't saved anything at all. A 2013 Retirement Confidence Survey sponsored by the Employee Benefit Research Institute, as reported by Philip Moeller in his article "Challenges of an Aging American Workforce," found that 36 percent of the 1,254 individuals surveyed, including 251 retirees, had saved less than $10,000.

WORTH NOTING

According to a study sponsored by Merrill Lynch, Millennials—workers currently in their 20s and 30s—appear to be better savers than Baby Boomers or Generation Xers. The same study found Millennials expect to get 32 percent of their retirement income from personal savings and investments, while Boomers expected only 12 percent from these sources.

So start saving now. It's never too late, whatever your age. The more you save now, the better you'll feel later when you need the money because you can't work any longer. Of course, becoming a saver after living most of your life as a spender isn't going to be an easy adjustment. Following are a few tips to help you transition to this new saver lifestyle.

Start saving *today*. Don't wait until it's convenient. Pick a number you can live with and decide this is how much you're going to put away every single week for your future. It may not sound like all that much, but let's say you pick a conservative amount, $50. You make a commitment to save $50 every week. That's $200 a month. Now if you multiply $200 a month by 12, that equals $2,400 for the year.

Let's say you're 60 now and you think you can easily keep working until age 70. If all you do is leave that $2,400 a year in the bank, even at 0 or .80 percent interest, that $2,400 will grow to at least $24,000, or even more, in 10 years.

After 5 years, when you have $12,000 put aside, you'll probably be able to find a financial advisor who can direct you to a secure and safe investment option, where the minimum is $10,000 but the interest yield is at least 3 to 5 percent.

There might be some who are thinking that $24,000 is not a whole lot to get you through your retirement years. But of course, hopefully that savings account will keep growing, and it's a lot more than the zero in savings that one in three Americans now have.

If you don't think you can do this because you need every cent you make, take a hard look at what you're spending your money on. Put what you spend into two categories, things you need and things you want. It's in giving up some of those things you want but don't need that you'll find that money for savings. Eating out more than for just special occasions and buying things you don't absolutely need are habits to start reversing.

If you don't have a weekly or monthly budget, create one and then stick to it. Include the amount you decide to save so it becomes part of your weekly and monthly budgeting habit.

Pay off your high-interest credit cards, starting with the highest-interest card first, and working your way down through the lower-interest loans, such as student loans. You'll at least get rid of debt and the interest that keeps accumulating, and you'll become more of a "cash only" operation.

Become a comparison shopper for everything from food and gasoline to bank accounts to make sure you're getting the most out of your money. Clip coupons and check out sale days, especially for seniors, because those savings can really add up.

Savings Options

Now that you're finally saving, or now that you want to grow the savings you already have, consider these seven ways people in your situation save money for retirement:

1. Individual Retirement Accounts (IRAs) are accounts in which your earnings grow tax deferred. That means your contributions are tax deductible.

2. A Roth IRA is an account that also grows tax free, but your withdrawals are tax free as well because you've already paid taxes on your contributions.

3. A 401(k) or 403(b) is a retirement plan set up with your employer, either a company or an organization, who then deducts pre-tax contributions that grow tax deferred.

4. Keogh or profit sharing plans are for the self-employed and grow tax deferred. Your annual contributions are based on your income.

5. Tax-deferred annuities are usually sold by insurance companies and involve after-tax contributions, but annuities also grow tax deferred.

6. A life insurance policy that has a cash value can be a source of income. (This is known as whole life insurance, as opposed to term life.) You can borrow against your policy as tax-free income. (Some refer to whole life policies as "forced" savings.)

7. If you own your apartment or home, especially since the housing slump has been reversing, it's probably continuing to build value. If you've accumulated enough equity in it, usually at least 50 percent of its current market value, you might be able to qualify for a reverse mortgage when you reach age 62.

Living in Retirement Longer Than You Work

The notion of living longer is usually comforting to most people, until they start thinking about how much it's going to cost. Then they start thinking about what would happen if they outlive their money. Since so many Americans don't have a very big nest egg, it won't be that hard to outlive their money once they stop working.

The reality is that even the maximum Social Security benefits are not that huge. You may have to do something radical, like move to a place where the cost of living is dramatically lower, if continuing to work isn't an option, or it's an unpleasant one to consider. Doing things differently now could at least offer you some better retirement scenarios.

WORTH NOTING

When Social Security was created, the life expectancy for the American worker was 58 for men and 62 for women. People were never expected to live very long in retirement, whereas today you could live in retirement for as long as you worked.

Fortunately, as long as you and your spouse or eligible partner qualify for Social Security benefits, you probably will never outlive *all* your money. You can at least depend on something coming in every month.

But let's say you make it into your 90s and are still in good health. If you retired at age 66, you've been living in retirement almost as long as you worked. You could easily live into your 100s, and longer in retirement than in your working years.

How are you going to fund those years, especially the later years when you can no longer work? Social Security benefits, although they could possibly let you get by, might not allow you to live the lifestyle you had dreamed of, especially when it comes to traveling to visit family members who are spread out or going on an occasional fun excursion.

Following are some options to consider to help you do things now that will give you more revenue during those nonworking retirement years. This will make it easier to pay for not just the extras in life, but even some of the necessities.

Contribute to Employer 401(k) Plans

If you're working for a company or organization that offers a 401(k) or 403(b) retirement plan, sign up for it. In fact, don't just sign up—make sure you're contributing the maximum amount allowed each month. Your employer will probably contribute a certain percentage to the plan, too; but even if they don't, you should.

Your contributions are taken out of your payroll check *before* taxes are calculated. The money you contribute will go into a mutual fund, company stock, or whatever securities are deemed acceptable to the plan. (This varies from plan to plan.) Then this money will grow tax deferred, which means you don't pay any taxes on it until you withdraw the money. If you're already in retirement when this happens, chances are you'll be in a lower tax bracket so you even save on taxes.

 WORTH NOTING

> The 1978 IRS code that led to 401(k) plans was originally intended to give taxpayers a break on deferred income. In 1980, a benefits consultant named Ted Benna used the new code to create a tax-advantaged method of saving for retirement. He installed the first 401(k) plan for his employer, the Johnson Companies. For most companies today, 401(k)s have replaced pension plans.

If you're over 50, you can contribute even more through "catch up" provisions. These also vary from plan to plan, so check with your employer on what their plan offers.

In most cases, your contributions are made pre-tax, meaning they're deducted before taxes are taken out and continue to grow tax deferred. You don't pay taxes until you take money out. The exception is if you use a Roth 401(k) account, which deducts the contributions after taxes are taken out. That means you don't have to pay taxes when you take the money out later, because you've already paid them.

The IRS has a few restrictions on when you can withdraw this money. For example, if you use the 401(k) before turning $59\frac{1}{2}$, you'll pay a 10 percent excise tax on top of the regular tax you have to pay. There are a few exceptions, such as if you needed the money for paying unreimbursed medical expenses, buying a home, paying for college tuition, preventing foreclosure, paying funeral expenses, or repairing damage to a home.

There's a required minimum distribution (RMD) starting on April 1st of the year you turn $70\frac{1}{2}$. How much you'll receive will be determined by your life expectancy based on actuarial tables used by the IRS. Of course, there are exceptions. One is if you're still working, the RMD goes into effect on April 1st of the year *after* you retire. The other is if you contributed to a Roth 401(k), which doesn't have an RMD.

If you change jobs or go to work for yourself, you can do a "rollover" whereby you roll the funds you've accumulated in one 401(k) plan into either another 401(k) or an Individual Retirement Account (IRA). When you do this, your retirement plan continues to grow tax deferred. Typically, there's a time limit imposed, usually 60 days, for a rollover to have occurred. If you miss the deadline, the money will be taxed as ordinary income. If this happens before you're $59\frac{1}{2}$, the 10 percent additional tax will also apply.

For most employees, these plans have a maximum limit on how much you can contribute each year. For 2015, it's $15,000, except for the catch-up contribution, which is another $6,000 for 2015. Roth 401(k)s have no limits.

After you've signed up for a 401(k), you have to decide where you want your money to go. Each plan will have a list of choices. This is an important decision to make because whatever you choose will determine how your retirement savings account will grow. This decision will determine how much you'll have in the future. A typical plan will offer somewhere between 8 and 12 choices, although some plans give you a lot more choices and a few offer a lot less. Some plans offer only mutual funds, while others offer company stocks, or annuities and exchange traded funds (ETFs).

This is where having a financial advisor can really make a difference. (We discuss how to find a reliable financial advisor later.) He or she will be able to recommend an investment choice suitable to you that matches your risk tolerance. For example, if you're risk averse, you may want to stay away from the stock market and stick to more stable investments that provide regular safe returns, such as government bonds.

Usually a 401(k) plan will have advisors available to help you make a choice based on a number of variables, including your age and how many years you have until retirement. The closer you get to retirement you should start to shift more of your 401(k) into so-called safer, less risky investments. For example, if you had most of your portfolio in the stock market in 2008 and 2009, you may have lost over half of your retirement savings. On the other hand, the problem with investments that protect your principal is they don't grow at a very rapid pace.

Some plans offer variable annuities, which typically combine a group of funds that look like mutual funds but have protection guarantees or insurance that gives your survivors your principal if you die before you collect the benefits.

If your plan offers a brokerage account, you can invest in anything the brokerage firm has access to, such as stocks, bonds, mutual funds, and commodities like oil and gold. The positive side to this is you have even more choices, which is also the downside because it can become even harder to decide what to do. You could also buy and sell at a frequent pace that could, over time, erode your retirement savings.

Putting Money into an IRA

If you don't have access to a 401(k), the next best alternative is an Individual Retirement Account, or IRA. An IRA allows you to save money and make investments that will grow tax deferred just like a 401(k). The main difference is your 401(k) is through an employer, while an IRA is an account you open and control on your own.

IRAs come in a few flavors: the traditional IRA, Roth IRA, SEP IRA, and SIMPLE IRA. Their rules and restrictions are, in a nutshell, as follows:

- **Traditional IRA:** You pay taxes when you take money out, which in retirement may be at a lower tax rate. Your money grows tax free. You must start withdrawing the money when you reach age 70½. There's also a $5,000 per year contribution limit if you're under 50.

- **Roth IRA:** You pay the taxes on your contributions so there will be no tax when you take the money out. The money grows tax free. You can leave your money in as long as you want, and you can withdraw money at any time with no penalty.

- **SEP and SIMPLE IRAs:** These are for the self-employed and small business owners. To set up a SIMPLE IRA, you have to have fewer than 100 employees who earn more than $5,000 each. A SEP, which stands for Simplified Employee Pension, is for small business owners and the self-employed who have no employees. For employees to be eligible for a SEP, they must be 21 years old, have worked for at least three of the last five years, and receive at least $550 for the tax year.

Finding a Financial Advisor for Your Investments

There's a misconception that you have to be wealthy to be able to afford a financial advisor. This myth is perpetuated by the fact that some of the larger financial services institutions, such as Morgan Stanley, UBS, and Merrill Lynch, have Wealth Management Divisions with financial advisors serving the higher- and ultra-high-income segments of the country. While that's true, there are still a number of banks and brokerage houses, such as Fidelity and Charles Schwab, that offer financial advice to almost anyone who asks.

Darrin Courtney, a Boston-area certified financial planner, recommends you work with a professional. He suggests finding "someone you trust to do the research and to find the best diversified mix of investment products and solutions about how to best meet your goals, knowing it might not be possible to meet all of them."

Courtney points out most financial planners will offer a free consultation to help you decide if working with an expert is right for you.

TIP

The AARP has a relationship with Charles Schwab that offers members a free financial consultation without any obligation. Then if you want to open a Schwab account, to continue receiving advice all you need is a minimum of $10,000 you can invest.

If you can't afford the services of a financial planner, Courtney says most local chapters of the Financial Planners Association (FPA) may offer pro bono assistance.

A new cottage industry of online financial advisors has also developed in recent years. They tend to offer services at reduced fees. For example, LearnVest has a one-time set-up fee that ranges from $89 to $399 and then charges a $19 per month fee that includes access to a Certified Financial Planner (CFP).

When looking for a financial advisor, you should try to find someone who has his or her CFP designation. That means they've passed a personal finance test so they should have at least enough knowledge to understand the basics.

If you want to limit your search to fee-only advisors, you can check with the National Association of Personal Financial Advisors (NAPFA), who are all fee-only. It's probably wise to run a background check on whomever you choose, just to see if they've ever been convicted of a crime, or had a regulator investigate them. Then ask for references from current clients to find out if a particular advisor is right for you.

TIP

You can go to socialsecuritytiming.com for a free Social Security Calculator, as well as a list of Social Security advisors based on the zip code you enter into the website. Please note that this free site is not associated with the Social Security Administration. The National Association of Personal Financial Advisors also has a free database at their website to locate a financial advisor, based on the zip code you enter. Go to www.napfa.org.

D. Drummond Osborn is a fee-only financial advisor. He's been helping people manage their money for over 20 years. Most of his clients have assets ranging from $100,000 to many million dollars. But, as Osborn notes, "The zeros in front of the decimal may differ, but the fear of running out of money is often the same."

Osborn says that while a healthy relationship with money needs to be a balance of intellect and emotion, he's found that most individuals address the issue from one perspective or the other. "The intellect has them eyeing an imaginary number that the retirement planning industry tells them will make them happy," says Osborn, "while the emotional side either has the sky falling or a *c'est la vie* attitude."

Osborn wants his clients to create a balance—beginning the process of how they want to live and the legacy they wish to leave behind—and then start talking about the numbers.

"While this approach doesn't negate the possibility of running out of money," he adds, "it does empower people to address the reality of their financial life. There are almost always ways to avoid running out of money; unfortunately the majority of people are unwilling to face the right/hard choices."

The significance of choosing the right financial advisor cannot be emphasized enough. Think of the thousands of investors who were cheated by Bernie Madoff, whose Ponzi scheme lost money into the billions for individual investors who lost their life savings, and companies and institutions that lost millions of dollars that were supposed to fund pensions and other funds.

However, you have to be careful that being afraid of picking an unscrupulous financial advisor justifies you making all these financial decisions on your own. Unless you take the time to really learn about the various financial options available to you, as well as to monitor your investments so that your savings can grow at a reasonable rate, trying to do it all yourself might lead you to make poor financial decisions.

An eldercare attorney might also be able to advise you on an asset protection plan that makes the most sense for you and your family. No two situations are the same, so if possible, seek help and work with someone who has the expertise to guide you to make the best financial decisions in your older years and avoid outliving your money.

Ways to Cut Expenses

Co-author Jan Yager originally became aware of frugality expert Judy Woodward Bates for Jan's "Boomers: Don't Outlive Your Money" article for the online column "Boomerific." Bates, who coined the term *bargainomics*, has a weekly show on how to save money on Fox-6 News TV in Birmingham, Alabama, is seen the first Thursday of each month on *Good Day Alabama!*, and is the author of *Bargainomics: Money Management by the Book*. She credits her grandmother who showed her by example how to be thrifty and also her own parents who, when Judy decided to get married at the age of 17, announced to her that if she was going to do that, she and her husband would also have to make it on their own financially. And they did.

Judy prides herself on the fact that they have never had a large income and "never needed one" because "we've learned to live and live well within our income." Judy is dedicated to spreading the word that it's possible to live happily within your means.

Here are some of her tips:

- She doesn't eat out unless it's a two-for-one deal or an early-bird special. She uses discount coupons to help offset the cost of eating out through Groupon, restaurant.com, or currentcodes.com. She goes to currentcodes.com first, gets a code, and then goes to restaurant.com so she'll pay just $3 for a $25-off certificate that would have cost her $10 without the code.

- She uses a local entertainment.com book and if she's going to any major city for even a couple of days, she'll get one of those books because it helps her save a lot of money. She especially likes the certificates for movie ticket admissions.

Do You Really Need 1,000 Cable Channels?

Being more frugal is an approach to spending that you can embrace if you really want to, although it takes some work, just like learning to eat healthier and exercise. Of course, you don't have to go to the extreme of one couple we know who sold almost all their possessions to live in an RV for a couple of years before relocating to Florida. But you can start with little changes, such as comparison shopping for the best cable provider for the money, if you even need cable service, depending on your viewing habits. If you mostly watch network TV anyway, maybe it's time to rely on just basic cable if you need it for TV reception in your area.

Buy yourself a little notebook, or use your smartphone, to keep track of every single penny you're spending, and what you're spending it on. You'll be amazed just how much you can save when you see your spending patterns.

If you have a problem with overspending, consider joining a local chapter of Debtors Anonymous (DA), a program founded on the Twelve Step principles of Alcoholics Anonymous. It will teach you how to track, and better control, your spending; it may also help you get to the root causes of your overspending.

For optional purchases, rather than buying something the first time you see it in the store, make a mental note about your selection, give yourself 24 to 48 hours to reconsider it, and buy it only upon returning to the store after you've reassured yourself that the purchase is truly necessary.

Use a no-interest layaway plan to purchase gifts or holiday items, getting out of the habit of putting things on a credit card unless you're that rare individual who is disciplined enough to use a credit card but completely pay off the balance when the bill is due.

Consider an Electric or Hybrid Car

If you use your car only for short trips, an electric car could save you thousands of dollars a year by not having to fill up at the pump every week. If you drive a bit farther, you can consider a plug-in hybrid that also uses gasoline, which extends your mileage range. You also save money on maintenance. There are no more oil changes, and wear and tear on other parts is typically less than gas-powered cars.

Then there are the tax credits to think about. The Federal government gives you a $7,500 federal income tax credit, and several states offer their own tax credits. That way you could get an electric car like the Nissan Leaf or a Ford Fusion hybrid that typically sell for $30,000 for less than $20,000 when you figure in the tax breaks. And if you decide to lease one of these cars, leasing companies will often take the tax credits and lower your monthly lease payments.

Pay Off Credit Card Debt

You've heard it before. Getting out of credit card debt as you head into your potential retirement years is more important than ever before. Make it one of your top financial priorities. You might even be able to stop using credit cards altogether.

Study your credit card statements, whether online or paper, and put them in this order: the highest-interest rate card is first, followed by the second highest, and so on. Then focus on paying off the highest-interest card first by doubling the minimum payment each month. Continue to make the minimum payments on the rest until the highest one is paid off, and then do the same thing with the next highest-rate card.

If you can, transfer balances on higher-rate cards to lower-rate cards. Just make sure you don't use these cards to incur more debt. Be careful with those 0 percent come-ons. They usually include transfer fees that often cost you more in the end. Also, even if it's 0 percent for a certain period of time, it will go to an APR, as high as 13 to 19 percent or higher, and if you don't pay off the balance that interest will start to add up fast.

 **CAUTION**

> Another reason to pay off your credit card debt is that any travel plans you have may impact your ability to get your credit card statements. These must be paid on time or you get charged a late fee, as much as $35, and can have your APR increased to the maximum delinquency rate allowed—as high as 29 percent. If you're traveling and have credit card payments due, pay them online or call the customer service number on your card and pay by phone. You can also sign up to have the minimum payment due automatically deducted from your checking account each month.

Grow Your Own Vegetables

Growing your own vegetables is actually becoming more popular, especially among the Baby Boomer generation. It's also a lot easier than you can imagine. And as money savers go, you can't beat it. Vegetables are becoming the most expensive item in the supermarket. Even if you shop at farmer's markets, you can spend as much as four dollars on two large, choice tomatoes.

Guess what? Tomatoes are one of the easiest vegetables to grow. The most important thing is to grow only those vegetables you like to eat. Plus, you don't need a lot of land. You can grow most vegetables in any containers that will hold soil, water, and seeds.

Growing your own vegetables will not only cut your food bill by as much as 50 percent, but the vegetables will be fresher and taste better.

Downsize by Moving to a Smaller House

Do you really need a five-bedroom house now that the kids have moved out? Companies downsize all the time to bring expenses in line. Why can't you?

Think of the money you could save by selling your current home and moving into a smaller house or renting an apartment. But be careful that you really will save money by doing this. There are costs related to moving that have to be considered. Also, if you bought at a time when houses were a lot less expensive, it might be hard to find something in the area you want to live that's as cost-effective as your mortgage.

With a smaller home or apartment, you might save on the cost of the upkeep of your home, including lower property taxes and heating and electric bills.

You might also consider renting instead of buying a new home, and invest or save any profits you get from the sale of your original home.

Where you live can be one of the biggest cost issues you'll need to address. In addition to moving to a smaller home, you can also consider relocating to a less expensive community, another state, or even another country where your dollars will go farther.

Manage Your Credit Rating

You may not know it, but the better your credit rating, the cheaper your credit. Your credit rating will impact the interest rate you'll pay for a car loan or a mortgage. That's why it's important to keep your credit score as high as possible.

Even if you pay your credit card bills on time, how much you charge to your credit card will impact your score. And you may think it's a good idea to cancel those credit cards you rarely use, but it's not. Canceling credit cards could hurt your credit score.

It's also important to check your credit report once every few months just to make sure your credit history is up to date and accurate, and there is no fraudulent activity. To do this, you can go to freecreditscore.com or creditkarma.com.

Credit scores range from 300 to 850 and you should at least maintain a score over 680. To do this, make sure you pay your credit card bills on time because payment history counts for 31 percent of your score. One late payment could give you a black mark on your credit history, so if you're late on a payment, call the card company and explain why. Most lenders will give you a break if you've been a good customer with a strong payment history.

Another factor determining your score (30 percent) is how much you owe on each card. If it's more than 50 percent of your total available credit, it can lower your score. If you're close to 50 percent, you may want to postpone putting any large purchases on your card until you've paid down your balance.

The Miracle of Compounding

If time is still on your side, meaning you're in your late 40s or 50s or even younger, you have an opportunity to take advantage of what's called "the miracle of compounding." You can save a lot of money with fairly little effort when you add any interest or capital gains you get to the principal of your savings or investment. That added amount also earns interest and capital gains, and this process is called "compounding."

Here's how it becomes a miracle. Let's say you were able to put $10,000 into an IRA when you were 40 and that IRA earned an average of 10 percent per year. By the time you turn 70, that $10,000 would be worth $174,494. Moreover, $134,494 of that would have come from the miracle of compounding. Without compounding, your $10,000 would only have grown to $40,000 earning 10 percent per year.

What's the message here? If time is still on your side, take advantage of it. Even if you didn't start saving that $10,000 until you were 50, at age 70, it would be worth $67,275. Even if you're in your 60s or beyond and this advice is no longer going to reap the benefits for you that it would have if you were younger, if you have children or grandchildren, give them a huge gift of this approach to saving. At least you'll have the satisfaction of knowing you inspired the next generation or two to do better at handling their money.

Turning Around Your Reversals of Fortune

Now that we've shared with you the gift you can give your younger children or grandchildren, let's turn back to those of you who are in your late 50s, 60s, or beyond. What can you do to make your Social Security, disability, or survivors benefits last longer? Through your hard work of at least 40 work credits, and meeting other eligibility requirements, you have earned those monthly benefits. So how can you make that income last whether it's the average of $1,180 or the maximum amount of $2,366 for someone retiring at full retirement age?

Here are some suggestions:

- Stop living beyond your means. That's a lot easier said than done, but it's possible to prune down your spending. Consider selecting products on the basis of price, if everything else is equal.

- Pare down to the necessities. This is a time in your life when less really is more.

- Consider changing your eating habits so that you get high-quality protein sources that are less expensive. Although co-author Jan is a vegetarian again after a hiatus from vegetarianism for many decades, she's finding the meatless lifestyle very nutritious, easier than it used to be due to all the products now available, and also less expensive. Even if you just have one day a week that's meatless, you can save money that way.

- Pay off your credit card debt so you don't continue to incur more debt from the interest. Allow yourself only one credit card and pick one with a low APR that also suits your spending habits. Go to creditcards.com or to the websites for individual companies that offer cards, such as citicard.com, capitalone.com, or Americanexpress.com. Compare what the cards offer, as well as any fees. Pick that one card wisely so you have it for emergencies or for travel.

- Spend wisely, especially for gifts and around the holidays. Create a firm budget for your spending. "I won't spend more than $20 for a birthday present" or "I will get all the gifts for the holidays this year for $250 or less." If you receive a gift you don't like or need, don't be shy about exchanging it for something you do need or even for a gift for someone else.

- If you're in your 50s or 60s and you haven't taken your Social Security benefits yet, see if you can hold out until age 70. It's so hard to resist taking the money as soon as you're eligible, whether that's 62 or full retirement age at 66 or 67. But, as we've seen throughout this book, if you can possibly hang in there until 70, whether or not you continue working, your benefits grow 8 percent each year until age 70. With the possibility that you'll live until you're 90, 100, or beyond, the increased monthly benefits will be substantial. Yes, it's a guessing game, and a huge challenge to make the right guess. Is it better to have that bird in the hand at 66 on the chance you might not live until 70?

- It's never too late to create a retirement plan. Maybe you and your spouse have not had the talk before. For whatever reason you put that talk off, have it now. What are your hopes, goals, and dreams for retirement? Can you see yourself moving to a smaller home, or to another community that's less expensive? Do you need as many cars as when you both worked full time? Is it time to reconsider your cell phone carrier or cable TV service provider?

The Least You Need to Know

- No matter what your age, it's never too late to start saving. Don't wait until tomorrow. Even if you save only $50 a week, you'll have $24,000 in 10 years!

- If you're still working and your employer offers a 401(k), sign up for it. There are many tax and savings advantages to participating in a 401(k) that will help your retirement portfolio.

- To make your Social Security benefits last, whatever amount you're receiving, start living within your means. Curb your spending and become more frugal in your lifestyle.

- Pay off any high-interest credit cards, and allow yourself only one credit card for emergencies and travel expenses. Pick a card with a low APR, or, even better, a 0 APR for a period of time, followed by a low APR, and without an annual fee attached to it.

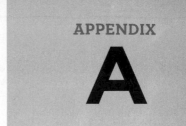
Glossary

administrative law judge (ALJ)   The judge who presides over an appeal about a decision related to Social Security benefits.

amyotrophic lateral sclerosis (ALS)   Also known as Lou Gehrig's disease, ALS is a progressive neurodegenerative disease that affects the brain and the spinal cord.

appeal   If you disagree with a decision by the Social Security Administration (SSA), you have the right to file an appeal of the decision. You have a right to have representation for your appeal. You must have the Notice of Decision on your benefits before you begin the appeals process.

Appeals Council Review   This is the third step in the appeal process, after reconsideration and the hearing. The Appeals Council is a panel of three administrative law judges (ALJs).

applicant   Someone who is applying for Social Security benefits. Also known as a *claimant*.

assisted living   Facilities offering assistance to seniors or the disabled, ranging from meals in shared dining halls to assistance going to and from activities for those with physical or mental limitations.

auxiliary benefits   Social Security benefits that go to family members, based on the eligible worker's earnings record. Also known as *family benefits*.

average indexed monthly earnings (AIME)   The SSA takes an eligible worker's earnings for 35 years and divides it by 12 to calculate their AIME. This amount is used when the SSA decides what an eligible claimant's monthly benefit should be.

bend points   The dollar amounts in the formula for the AIME or primary insurance amount (PIA). These are referred to as bend points because when you graph the formula, it looks like a series of line segments connecting at certain amounts.

beneficiary   A recipient of Social Security benefits.

benefit period   This term is applied by Original Medicare to the use of hospital and skilled nursing facility (SNF) services. The day one is admitted into a hospital or SNF as an inpatient is considered the beginning of a benefit period. It ends when no inpatient care has been received for 60 consecutive days.

break-even point   A break-even point is the specific age at which you will have received the same amount of benefits no matter whether you choose to retire at 62, your full retirement age, or age 70.

child   Refers to a dependent biological, adopted, or stepchild, as well as a dependent grandchild, who is eligible to receive benefits based on a worker's work credits.

claimant   Someone who files for Social Security benefits. Also known as an *applicant*.

co-payment   The amount of a medical service you're responsible for after Medicare or any other health-care insurance has paid for what it will cover.

Cost of Living Adjustment (COLA)   An annual increase in benefits tied to increase in inflation.

deductible   The amount you have to pay before Medicare or any other insurance program starts to cover some or all of the costs.

delayed retirement credit   This refers to the 8 percent (on average) that Social Security benefits grow annually from the amount you would have received at your full retirement age if you instead delay starting benefits until age 70.

dependent   A child, spouse, ex-spouse, or parent who is dependent on the eligible worker and who may be entitled to retirement or disability benefits from Social Security.

direct deposit   The ability to deposit funds electronically into a personal bank account. Social Security benefits are deposited directly into a bank account instead of mailing a check.

disability benefits   If you meet the criteria for being disabled that the Social Security Administration (SSA) follows, you're eligible for monthly disability benefits.

Disability Determination Services (DDS)   A state agency, which is funded by the federal government or the residing state, that determines if someone meets the criteria to be considered disabled or blind under the law and possibly eligible for benefits.

disabled   You are considered disabled if you're unable to engage in any substantial gainful activity due to a medically determinable physical or mental impairment that lasts for at least 12 months or is expected to cause death.

donut (or doughnut) hole   The term used to describe the gap in Medicare prescription drug coverage. This coverage gap highlights the situation in which once you and your prescription drug plan have spent a certain amount of money for covered drugs, you may find yourself having to pay more for your prescription drugs up to a certain limit.

earliest eligibility age (EEA)   The age when you can apply for Social Security benefits based on your own or someone else's work record.

early retirement age   The earliest age you can start taking your own benefits on your work history, which is age 62.

earnings caps   See *wage caps*.

earnings record   Also known as your earnings history, this is a list of all your earnings since you began working and your employer-paid Social Security benefits on your behalf. This record is the basis upon which the SSA will determine what your monthly benefits should be when you apply to start collecting Social Security.

eligible   A designation that you have met all the legal requirements to receive a benefit. However, eligibility is only one step in the process of receiving benefits.

end stage renal disease (ESRD)   A kidney disease that requires a transplant or dialysis. An ESRD diagnosis qualifies you for Social Security benefits or SSI disability benefits, and the waiting period is waived.

ex-spousal benefits   If you were married for at least 10 years, you have been divorced for at least 2 years, you haven't remarried, and your ex-spouse is eligible for Social Security benefits and has reached full retirement age, you can file for benefits on your ex-spouse's record.

family benefits   Benefits from the Social Security Administration that go to family members, such as a spouse, ex-spouse, or dependent child or parent, based on the eligible worker's earnings record. Also referred to as auxiliary benefits.

family maximum   The total benefits amount that can be paid to family members based on a worker's earnings record.

Federal Insurance Contributions Act (FICA) tax   The payroll tax for Social Security and Medicare.

file and suspend strategy   When a worker files for Social Security at full retirement age, but then suspends benefits for him- or herself, which enables the spouse to file for spousal benefits. The spouse, however, continues to work and grow his or her potential benefit due to delayed retired credits, finally taking his or her benefits at the age of 70, when the benefits reach their maximum monthly amount.

financial advisor (FA)   Someone trained to give financial advice. Also referred to as a financial planner or benefits consultant. The Financial Industry Regulatory Authority (FINRA) oversees the activities of brokerage houses in the United States as well as their registered representatives.

full retirement age (FRA)   The age the SSA has determined at which you can receive 100 percent of your Social Security retirement benefits.

Government Pension Offset (GPO)   If a worker spent some or all of his or her career working in a government job that didn't pay Social Security, the Social Security survivors or spousal benefits may be reduced.

hearing   This is the second level in the appeal process, after reconsideration (or Request for Reconsideration) and before the Appeals Council Review.

hospital insurance   See *Medicare Part A*.

identity theft   When someone takes on someone else's identity illegally for the purpose of opening up bank accounts or credit cards and making purchases in the other person's name.

life expectancy   How long you can be expected to live, based on actuarial tables, with the key factors being gender and date of birth.

life expectancy calculator   A calculator that helps you determine what your life expectancy might be.

long-term care insurance   Also known as long-term life insurance, this is insurance you can purchase privately to help cover the costs of long-term care.

Lump Sum Death Benefit (LSDB)   A one-time benefit of $255 available to a child or spouse of a worker who is eligible for Social Security benefits.

maximum family benefit   See *family maximum*.

Medicaid   A program coordinated by the U.S. government but run through individual state Medicaid programs for those who are eligible for health care and other basic needs such as food and housing.

Medicare   A federally financed and administered program of health-care coverage for seniors age 65 and up and others who qualify due to disability. Medicare is commonly divided into four parts: Part A (hospitalization), Part B (medical services including doctor's visits), Part C (additional programs you can buy privately), and Part D (prescription drugs).

Medicare Advantage   See *Medicare Part C*.

Medicare Part A   The part of the Medicare program that provides insurance covering hospitalization.

Medicare Part B   The part of the Medicare program that covers physician services and visits and other medical bills.

Medicare Part C   Also known as Medicare Advantage, this is a privately run part of Medicare that enables recipients to pay additional coverage for anything not covered by Original Medicare, including prescription drugs and costs that Medicare Part B does not cover.

Medicare Part D   This part adds prescription drug coverage to your Original Medicare plan since drug coverage is not included. There is a wide variety in what each plan offers, including what the monthly premium will be as well as what drugs are covered and any annual caps on coverage.

Notice of Decision   The formal communication from the SSA regarding their decision about what benefits, if any, you will be receiving, as well as when the first benefit payment will be issued.

Old-Age, Survivors, and Disability Insurance (OASDI)   Insurance covering benefits for retirees, widows and widowers, disabled workers, and dependent family members.

primary insurance amount (PIA)   The benefit amount you would receive if you begin receiving retirement benefits at your FRA. At this age, the benefit is neither reduced for early retirement nor increased for delayed retirement.

quarter of coverage (QC)   The number of work credits you receive in a year, which is used to determine eligibility for Social Security benefits. You can only receive four QCs in a year.

Railroad Retirement Board (RRB)   Started in 1935, this is an independent agency and part of the executive branch of the U.S. government that administers the retirement benefits available to the country's railroad workers.

Request for Reconsideration   The first step in the appeal process where you put in writing why you're appealing the SSA's decision. Reconsideration occurs before a hearing is set.

retirement age   See *full retirement age (FRA)* and *early retirement age.*

Self-Employment Contribution Act (SECA) tax   The payroll tax that those who are self-employed must pay.

Social Security   A retirement benefits program started in 1935 by President Franklin D. Roosevelt that provides monthly benefits to those who qualify by being a U.S. citizen and having the minimum number of work credits. A series of compromise laws in 1952 and 1954 regarding disability benefits paved the way for the final passage of Social Security Disability Insurance in 1956. Social Security is funded through contributions from employers and employees as well as from the self-employed.

Social Security card   The card you're issued from the Social Security Administration (SSA) with your unique Social Security number on it.

Social Security number   The unique nine-digit number you're given by Social Security that will be used throughout your life to track all the earnings you've made in addition to your payments into Social Security through payroll taxes.

Social Security statement   This statement summarizes your earnings during the previous year, in addition to your earnings from your first job forward. You should check it at least once annually, especially right before you apply for Social Security benefits the first time.

spousal benefits   When you file for retirement benefits, your spouse may be eligible for a benefit based on your earnings, which can be as much as half of your primary insurance amount, depending on the spouse's age at retirement.

Supplemental Security Income (SSI)   A program administered by the SSA providing Medicaid as well as other benefits to those who are financially needy and who qualify because they're disabled, blind, or old.

survivors benefits   Benefits paid by the SSA to the surviving spouse, eligible ex-spouse, child, or dependent parent of a worker who has died.

third rail   A term often used in reference to Social Security or Medicare that suggests radically reducing or eliminating either one is politically disadvantageous for any legislators or business leaders making such a recommendation.

Ticket to Work   The term for the nine-month trial period you're allowed in order to see if you're able to return to work without having your disability benefits cancelled.

wage caps   These are the caps on earnings that those receiving Social Security benefits before their full retirement age must consider or they will have to return part of the benefits. Also known as *earnings caps*.

widow's or widower's benefits   See *survivors benefits*.

Windfall Elimination Provision   If you received a pension for government work for which Social Security was not paid, your benefits may be reduced.

work credits   The unit the SSA uses to determine benefit eligibility. Forty credits are the minimum number required for eligibility, and you can receive up to four annually.

Social Security Decision Tree

At what age should I take my Social Security benefits?

The decision about when to start taking your Social Security retirement benefits is a very important individual and personal one, based on many factors such as your health, life expectancy, whether or not you need the money right away, spending and saving styles, etc. This decision tree is just a general overview of considerations.

Current life expectancy for men and women who reach age 65 is 84.3 for males and 86.6 for females.

At what age should I take my Social Security benefits?

Age 62

The earliest you can begin taking your retirement benefits

- Your benefits are permanently reduced by 25%. ($1K monthly benefit would be reduced to $750.)
- There's an income cap of $15,720 on earnings until the year you reach FRA, and then it rises to $41,880.
- Do you need the money? You'll get your benefits sooner and for more years even though the amount will be reduced.
- You may have to pay federal or state taxes on benefits.
- How's your health? What's your life expectancy? If your life expectancy is low, you might want to take your benefits sooner.

Full Retirement Age (FRA)

Age 66 or 67, depending on your birth year

- Your monthly benefit is 100%. ($1K = $1K)
- There's no income cap on your earnings.
- You should start (or switch over to) spousal benefits at 50% of your spouse's earnings record if their benefits are greater than yours.
- You may have to pay federal and possibly state taxes on your benefits.

Age 70

There are financial advantages to delaying benefits until age 70

- If you're in good health, meet the average life expectancy, and have enough money to live on, you might want to delay receiving benefits.
- $1,000 of your FRA amount will have accrued to as much as $1,320. Your monthly benefit will have increased 8% per year from your FRA.
- You will receive your monthly benefit for fewer years, but it will be a higher amount—which will be especially important if your spouse ever needs survivors benefits.
- You may have to pay federal and possibly state taxes on your benefits.

Resources

Further Reading

AARP. "How to Maximize Your Social Security Benefits" (Part of the "Ready for Retirement?" Initiative). Washington, D.C.: AARP, 2012. Posted online at aarp.org/content/dam/aarp/money/budgeting_savings/2012-02/How-to-Maximize-Your-Social-Security-Benefits-AARP.pdf.

Associated Press. "Baby Boomers Fueling Wave of Entrepreneurship," *Houston Chronicle*, October 13, 2013. Posted at chron.com/business/article/Baby-boomers-fueling-wave-of-entrepreneurship-4892937.php.

Astor, Bart. *AARP Roadmap for the Rest of Your Life*. Hoboken, NJ: Wiley, 2013.

Bates, Judy Woodward. *Bargainomics*. Bargainomic Publications, 2009.

Begley, Sharon and David Morgan (reporting). Editing by Amanda Kwan. "6.3 million eligible for Medicaid since Obamacare launch: U.S. Agency," *Reuters*, January 22, 2014. Posted at reuters.com/article/2014/01/22/us-usa-healthcare-medicaid-idUSBREA0L27N20140122.

Blahous, Charles P. III. *Reforming Social Security: for Ourselves and Our Posterity*. In cooperation with the Center for Strategic and International Studies, Washington, D.C. Westport, CT: Praeger, 2000.

Borchard, David, with Patricia A. Donahue. *The Joy of Retirement*. New York: AMACOM, 2008.

Brooks, Rodney. "Boomers Turn to Encore Careers After Retiring," *USA Today*, October 21, 2013.

Cha, Ariana Eunjung. "Europe Looks to Pension Changes to Ease Economic Crisis," *The Washington Post*, July 10, 2012.

Chimsky, Mark. *65 Things to Do When You Retire*. Sellers Publishing, 2013.

Cox, Mike. "Consumer Alert: Your Social Security Number." (no date) Posted at aaa1c.org/docs/whatsnew/091905wn.pdf.

Deppe, John D. CMFC, and Angela S. Deppe CPA. *It's Your Money! Simple Strategies to Maximize Your Social Security Income.* Second City Books, 2012.

DeSilver, Drew. "5 facts about Social Security," *Pew Research,* October 16, 2013. Posted at pewresearch.org/fact-tank/2013/10/16/5-facts-about-social-security.

Franklin, Mary Beth. "Social Security Resumes Mailing Statements," *Investmentnews.com,* September 17, 2014. Posted at investmentnews.com/article/20140917/BLOG05/140919930/social-security-resumes-mailing-statements.

Gustke, Constance. "Retirees Turn to Virtual Villages for Mutual Support," *The New York Times,* November 28, 2014. Posted at nytimes.com/2014/11/29/your-money/retirees-turn-to-virtual-villages-for-mutual-support.html.

Hebert, L.E., P. A Scherr, L. A. Beckett, M.S. Albert, et al. "Age-Specific Incidence of Alzheimer's Disease in a Community Population," *JAMA* 273, no. 17 (1995): 1354-1359. Posted at ncbi.nlm.nih.gov/pubmed/7715060.

Hosier, Fred. "Top 10 Jobs with High Death Rates," *Safety and OSHA News.* Posted at safetynewsalert.com.

Infoplease.com. "Life Expectancy at Birth by Race and Sex, 1930–2010." Posted at infoplease.com/ipa/A0005148.html.

Jason, Julie. *The AARP Retirement Survival Guide.* New York: Sterling, 2009.

Kotikoff, Laurence. "44 Social Security 'Secrets' All Baby Boomers and Millions of Current Recipients Need to Know—Revised!" *Forbes.com,* July 30, 2012. Posted at forbes.com/sites/kotlikoff/2012/07/03/44-social-security-secrets-all-baby-boomers-and-millions-of-current-recipients-need-to-know.

Landis, Andy. *Social Security: The Inside Story, 2014 Edition.* North Charleston, D.C.: CreateSpace, 2014.

Laursen, Eric. *The People's Pension: The Struggle to Defend Social Security Since Reagan.* Edinburgh, Scotland: AK Press, 2012.

Levin, Adam. "Five Places Where You Should Never Give Your Social Security Number," *The Huffington Post,* March 28, 2013. Posted at huffingtonpost.com/adam-levin/identity-theft_b_2967679.html.

MacDonald, Jay. "3 Financial Do-Overs with Social Security," *Bankrate.com,* January 23, 2009. Posted at bankrate.com/finance/retirement/3-financial-do-overs-with-social-security-1.aspx.

Maxwell, John. "Social Security: What Percent of Americans Claim Benefits at Age 62?" *The Motley Fool,* June 7, 2014.

Mercadante, Kevin. "How to Protect Your Social Security Number and When Not to Give It Out," *MoneyCrashers.com*. Posted at moneycrashers.com/protect-give-out-social-security-number/.

Merrill Edge. "Time Is Money: How Waiting to Collect Social Security Can Boost Your Benefit," *Bank of America Corporation*, June, 2013. Posted at merrilledge.com/publish/content/application/pdf/gwmol/me_timeismoney_topic_paper.pdf

Moeller, Philip. "Challenges of an Aging American Workforce," *U.S. News & World Report*, June 19, 2013. Posted at money.usnews.com/money/blogs/the-best-life/2013/06/19/challenges-of-an-aging-american-workforce.

Morton, David A. III. *Nolo's Guide to Social Security Disability: Getting and Keeping Your Disability Benefits, Seventh Edition*. NOLO, 2014.

Muldoon, Dan, and Richard Kopcke. "Are People Claiming Social Security Benefits Later?" *Center for Retirement Research at Boston College*, May, 2008, Number 8-7.

Munnell, Alicia H. "Social Security's *Real* Retirement Age Is 70," *Center for Retirement Research at Boston College*, October, 2013.

———. Transcript of interview conducted on PBS's "Frontline" on February 6, 2006 and posted at pbs.org/wgbh/pages/frontline/retirement/etc/script.html. Part of the show "Can You Afford to Retire?" Produced and Directed by Rick Young. Written by Hedrick Smith and Rick Young.

O'Connell, Brian. "Why 80 Percent of Women Take Social Security Too Early," *MainStreet.com*, September 23, 2014. Posted at mainstreet.com/article/why-80-of-women-take-social-security-too-early-for-full-benefits

Orr, Mark J. *Social Security Income Planning, Second Edition*. North Charleston, D.C.: CreateSpace, 2013.

Peddicord, Kathleen. *How to Retire Overseas*. New York: Plume, 2011.

Piper, Mike. *Can I Retire?* Simple Solutions. 2013.

Reichenstein, William, and William Meyer. *Social Security Strategies*. 2011.

Savage, Terry. *The New Savage Number: How Much Money Do You Really Need to Retire?* Hoboken, NJ: Wiley, 2009.

Schieber, Sylvester J., and John B. Shoven. *The Real Deal: The History and Future of Social Security*. New Haven, CT: Yale University Press, 1999.

Schultz, Patricia. *1,000 Places to See Before You Die*. New York: Workman Publishing Company, 2011.

Schwab-Pomerantz, Carrie. "When Is the Best Time to File for Social Security Benefits?" *Schwab.com*, April 28, 2014. Posted at schwab.com/public/schwab/nn/articles/When-Is-the-Best-Time-to-File-for-Social-Security-Benefits.

Shaviro, Daniel. *Making Sense of Social Security Reform.* Chicago: University of Chicago Press, 2000.

Sheedy, Rachel L. "Retiree Tax Burden Differs By State," *Kiplinger,* October 2012.

U.S. Social Security Administration. "Benefits for Children." SSA Publication No. 05-10085. August 2012.

———. "Disability Benefits." SSA Publication No. 05-10029. May 2014.

———. "How Work Affects Your Benefits." SSA Publication No. 05-10069. January 2014.

———. "Retirement Benefits." SSA Publication No. 05-10035. April 2013.

———. "Same-Sex Couples." Posted at ssa.gov/people/same-sexcouples.

———. "Survivors Benefits." SSA Publication No. 05-10084. July 2013.

———. "You May Be Able to Get Supplemental Security Income (SSI)." SSA Publication No. 05-11069. January 2014.

———. "Your Payments While Outside the United States." SSA Publication No. 05-10137. September 2013.

University of Texas at Austin. "Moderate Drinking Helps Middle-Aged and Older People Live Longer, Research Shows," Press release, August 27, 2010.

Wasik, John F. "Social Security at 62? Let's Run the Numbers." *The New York Times,* May 14, 2014. Posted at nytimes.com/2014/05/15/business/retirementspecial/social-security-at-62-lets-run-the-numbers.html.

Yager, Fred. "4 in 10 Americans Are Saving 0 for Retirement, Women Worrying More Than Men," *ConsumerAffairs,* October 18, 2010. Posted at consumeraffairs.com/news04/2010/10/surveys-show-4-in-10-americans-saving-0-for-retirement-women-worrying-more-than-men.html.

———. "Are Your Finances Driving You Nuts? Maybe You Need a Financial Therapist." January 3, 2011. Posted at consumeraffairs.com/news04/2011/01/are-your-finances-driving-you-crazy-maybe-you-need-a-financial-therapist.html.

Yager, Jan. *21 Ways to Beat a Financial Crisis.* New Delhi, India: Harper Collins, India, 2013.

———. "Boomers Becoming Their Own Bosses," *ConsumerAffairs,* 2010.

———. "Boomers Don't Outlive Your Money," *ConsumerAffairs,* June 20, 2010. Posted at consumeraffairs.com/boomerific/2010/016_boomers_outlive_money.html.

———. "Boomers Looking for Work." March 22, 2010. Posted at consumeraffairs.com/boomerific/2010/003_boomers_out_of_work.html.

———. "Digging Out of Debt and Surviving the Downturn," *Consumer Affairs,* March, 2010. Posted at consumeraffairs.com/boomerific/2010/002_digging_out_of_debt.html.

———. "Getting the Most Out of Social Security," *Consumer Affairs*, May 16, 2010. Posted at consumeraffairs.com/boomerific/2010/011_social_security.html.

———. "How Boomers Are Deciding Where to Spend the Rest of Their Lives," *Consumer Affairs*, April 19, 2010. Posted at consumeraffairs.com/boomerific/2010/007_where_to_live.html.

———. "How to Avoid Ponzi Schemes," *Consumer Affairs*, July 2010. Posted at consumeraffairs.com/boomerific/2010/018_avoiding_ponzi_schemes.html.

Zackham, Justin (screenwriter). *The Bucket List*. Directed by Rob Reiner. Movie produced by Warner Bros. *2007*.

Zelinski, Ernie. *How to Retire Happy, Wild, and Free*. Visions International Publishing, 2013.

Agencies, Organizations, Associations, and Companies

Inclusion in this listing does not imply an endorsement, nor does omission indicate a judgment about any agency, organization, association, company, or website that's missing. Furthermore, because information changes quickly, web addresses may have changed or even disappeared from the internet. Please send an email to yagerinquiries2@aol.com if you discover any outdated listings.

Government Agencies

U.S. Social Security Administration

Social Security Administration
Office of Public Inquiries
1100 West High Rise
6401 Security Boulevard
Baltimore, MD 21235
1-800-772-1213
www.ssa.gov

Do NOT send applications or any documents you've been requested to send to the above address. Call the toll-free number or contact your local Social Security office if you're unsure where to send your application or documents.

This is the main website for the U.S. Social Security Administration (SSA). You can find out more about eligibility requirements as well as apply online at this website. The information at the website is in English, but there are also numerous additional language versions available (including Spanish, French, Chinese, Korean, Vietnamese, and others).

In addition, you can actually create your own account and fill out and submit your application at socialsecurity.gov/myaccount. You can also view your annual statement.

In August 2014, the first "my Social Security Week" was initiated. The hope of the SSA is that it will be an annual event with activities throughout the United States encouraging Americans to create their own account at socialsecurity.gov/myaccount.

In addition to the website, there are local SSA offices. To locate your local office, go to ssa.gov/locator and enter in your zip code. You may also call the headquarters of the U.S. Social Security Administration to get your questions answered or to apply over the phone.

To view a free video on the history of Social Security, go to socialsecurity.gov/history/index. html.

Medicaid.gov

The U.S. government administers the Medicaid program which provides free health care to those who meet certain eligibility requirements in terms of their income level. In general, it's best to go to the Medicaid program website for the state you're currently residing in, as each state has its own set of eligibility rules.

Medicare.gov

This U.S. government program provides health-care services to Americans age 65 and older. You can find out what Medicare covers as well as how to submit claims or appeals by going to the website. You can also find out about costs and when your Open Enrollment Period begins and ends.

Administration on Aging (AoA)

aoa.gov

Part of the U.S. Department of Health and Human Services, this agency provides information as well as funding opportunities, programs, and activities related to aging.

Organizations

Privacy Rights Clearinghouse (PRC)

privacyrights.org

PRC is a California-based nonprofit organization with the tagline "Empowering Consumers, Protecting Privacy." Check out the detailed discussion with links and resources titled, "My Social Security Number—How Secure Is It?"

Debtors Anonymous (DA)

debtorsanonymous.org

Headquartered in Needham, Massachusetts, DA is founded on the principles of the Twelve Steps of Alcoholics Anonymous. Its focus, however, is on those who are addicted to spending. It is free and anonymous, with chapters holding local weekly meetings throughout the United States and internationally.

Associations

AARP

Washington, D.C.
aarp.org

This is the official site for AARP, the huge association for those 50 and over that covers everything from health care and travel to financial matters and where to live. You can read *The AARP Magazine* and the *AARP Bulletin* at the site, and find information on the Life@50+ biannual three-day events it sponsors. There are numerous articles on Social Security benefits and related topics.

American Geriatrics Society (AGS)

americangeriatrics.org

A not-for-profit organization of more than 6,700 health professionals concerned with older individuals.

National Association of Social Workers (NASW)

naswdc.org

The NASW offers information at its website about Social Security benefits, disability, and SSI benefits, including information for people living with HIV/AIDS.

National Organization of Social Security Claimants' Representatives (NOSSCR)

560 Sylvan Ave, Suite 2200
Englewood Cliffs, NJ 07632
nosscr.org

Founded in 1979, there are now more than 4,000 members of NOSSCR, lawyers and other advocates for Social Security and SSI claimants' representatives.

National Stroke Association

stroke.org

This website offers information on Social Security Disability Insurance (SSDI) for those who have had a stroke, including how to apply if eligible.

National Committee to Preserve Social Security and Medicare

ncpssm.org

A membership organization whose mission is to see that Social Security and Medicare continue for future generations of Americans.

Advancing Excellence in America's Nursing Homes

nhqualitycampaign.org

An organization dedicated to improving the quality of care and lifestyle of the more than 1.5 million residents of America's nursing homes.

Assisted Living Federation of America (ALFA)

alfa.org

A national membership organization focused on education and research related to assisted living.

National Association for Home Care and Hospice (NAHC)

nahc.org

A trade association for hospices, home health-care aide organizations, medical equipment suppliers, and home care agencies.

Companies

Social Security Solutions, Inc. and Retiree Inc.

SocialSecuritySolutions.com

A company founded by William Meyer and William Reichenstein to help their clients get more out of their Social Security benefits. You can sign up at their website for their free newsletter.

Social Security Central, LLC

socialsecuritycentral.com

This company is directed by Angela S. Deppe, CPA, and offers clients advice on when to take Social Security in addition to holding seminars regionally. You can sign up at their website for a benefits calculator to see a variety of scenarios based on when you might file and on what basis. The cost is only $9.99 annually per individual.

Franklin Chase Wealth Management

Charlotte, NC
fcwm.biz

Michael Turner, MBA, is Managing Director of this company, which offers financial planning for retirement and wealth management including Social Security benefits advice. Articles on business and personal financial issues, including Social Security, can be found at the website.

Premier Social Security Consulting, LLC

premiernssa.com

Started by CPA Marc Kiner and Jim Blair, who worked at the Social Security Administration for 35 years, this company offers information as well as certification to those looking to learn more about Social Security so they can advise others. It also runs National Social Security Association (NSSA).

Fisher Financial Group

Northbrook, IL
fisherfinancialgroupllc.com

Founded and led by financial planner Dan Fisher, this company provides clients with advice on Social Security including retirement and disability benefits.

The Mercury Group at Morgan Stanley

Atlanta, GA
morganstanleyfa.com/themercurygroup

This is a group of financial advisors who offer their clients advice on a range of financial concerns including retirement and Social Security benefits.

Research institutions and Education

Center for Retirement Research at Boston College

Boston, MA
crr.bc.edu

The center was created through a grant from the Social Security Administration to promote research on retirement issues and transmit the findings to policy makers, the research community, and the public. There is a free email list you can sign up for that will send you alerts about their research findings and upcoming events.

Gerontological Society of America (GSA)

geron.org

A multi-disciplined association concerned with education and research related to aging.

Websites and Apps

Note: Some of these websites or apps are also included in the previous listings for Organizations, Associations, Companies, and Government Agencies. However, to facilitate finding these especially useful websites and apps, the listings appear here as well.

Government Websites

benefits.gov

A U.S. government site offering information on various types of government benefits available, including Social Security, food, housing, unemployment, and grants.

disability.gov

A government website offering information on disability services and programs.

healthcare.gov

A government website about various health-care initiatives that are more geared to Health Insurance Marketplace issues. For senior health care and care related to low-income situations, go to the following websites.

medicare.gov

Its related site is cms.gov for the Center for Medicare and Medicaid Services.

medicaid.gov

This is the federal government site for Medicaid. For more information, go to the website for your own state's Medicaid program.

Social Security Advisory Board

ssab.gov

An independent, bipartisan board created by Congress and appointed by the president and the Congress to advise the president, Congress, and the Commissioner of Social Security on matters related to the Social Security and Supplemental Security Income (SSI) programs. As an advisory body, they have no authority to take any administrative actions and cannot resolve questions regarding individual claims.

USA.gov

usa.gov

The government's official web portal where you can find information on all the various programs and services. From this one site, if you click on "Benefits, Grants, and Loans," you can also be directed to the websites for everything from Social Security, disabilities, and seniors to Medicare and Medicaid.

Life Expectancy Calculator

socialsecurity.gov/oact/population/longevity.html

There are several such calculators available at the main government website for Social Security as well as at company or other association websites. The government calculator is very simple. You enter your gender and your date of birth, and it will tell your projected life expectancy. Remember, however, this is just based on actuarial tables. It doesn't take into account family history or genetics, unanticipated acts of nature or accidents that can cause premature death. The calculator shows how many years you can expect to live if you reach four different ages: 54, 62, 67, and 70.

Additional Nongovernmental Websites

Baby Boomer People Meet

babyboomerpeoplemeet.com

For single Boomers, this is a dating site that is partnered with Match.com and OurTime.com. (Of course, you want to be cautious about any new potential dates you meet over the internet, whatever site you might use.)

Better After 50

betterafter50.com

With the tag line "Real Women—Real Stories," this is a site for women over 50 founded by writer and entrepreneur Felice Shapiro. There are articles and blogs on topics ranging from food to relationships, as well as a section called Men's Room with contributions from men.

Boomer Authority

boomerauthority.com

This site describes itself as a "professional association for experts and associations that specialize in the 50+ Baby Boomer demographic." Founded by Martin D. Diano, there's a speakers bureau as well as a bookstore, blogs, related radio show, and videos.

Creditcards.com

creditcards.com

Comparison site for various credit card offers, including the terms, and a blog related to this topic at the site.

Day One Stories

dayonestories.com

You've probably seen some of the Day One TV advertisements or videos. This is an extensive site that Prudential put together related to its Day One retirement initiative, which offers financial advice focusing on how to prepare for that first day of retirement.

Disability Secrets

disabilitysecrets.com

A website developed and maintained by Nolo, a subsidiary of Internet Brands, Inc., and a legal educational website and publisher on everything related to legal concerns including receiving disability benefits or Social Security retirement benefits.

Fab Over Fifty

faboverfifty.com

A website for women founded in 2010 by Geri Brin, a former newspaper and magazine editor and publisher. This site emphasizes fashion and beauty, as well as career, relationships, and wellness.

HUFF/POST 50

huffingtonpost.com/50

This website offers blogs and articles for the 50+ age group on relationships, health issues, travel, recommended books, retiring overseas, and more.

Lawyers.com

lawyers.com

A website developed and maintained by Martinell-Hubbell, a source of information about the legal profession dating back 140 years. You can search for a lawyer by specialty and location on this site.

Nolo Law for All

950 Parker S.
Berkeley, CA 94710
nolo.com
nolo.com/lawyers

A website dedicated to legal information for the public, including how to file for Social Security and disability benefits and how to find a lawyer.

Road Scholar

roadscholar.org

Formerly known as Elderhostel, this was started in 1975 as an organization to help older people go on trips offering lifelong learning opportunities. Co-author Jan's parents went on numerous trips around the country through Elderhostel during their retirement years and they always had a rewarding experience. Now it's called Road Scholar, and there are many more international trips offered, but it's the same organization with the same mission.

Third Age

thirdage.com

Started back in 1997, this is one of the older internet information sites for those who are 50+. Here you'll find articles, blogs, and videos on health, relationships, aging, entertainment, and more.

Volunteer Match

volunteermatch.org

If you want to travel but you'd prefer to do it through a volunteer opportunity that's been set up by volunteer experts, this is a place to start.

Index

C

N

T

tax credits, electric or hybrid car, 247
tax-deferred annuities, 239
taxes, 179
  adjusted gross income, 181
  determining if benefits are taxable, 180
    additional income, 180
    average monthly benefit, 181
    combined income, 182
    deductions, 181
    joint return, 180
    living outside the United States, 182
    modified adjusted gross income, 180
    publication, 181
    total income, 180
  federal income tax responsibility, 188
  FICA, 93
  financial advisor, 186
  fixed income, 188
  return, 149
  Self-Employed Contributions Act, 93
  state taxes, 184
    exemption, 184
    federal government method, 185
    miscellaneous considerations, 186
    specified income, 185
    states with no income tax, 185
  voluntary withholding, 182
    accountant recommendation, 183
    decision, 183
    determination of taxable benefits, 182
    married filing separately, 183
    nest egg, 183
    nontaxed 1099 income, 183
    percentage, 183
    requesting the withholding of federal taxes, 183
    withholding taxes, 183
Taxpayer Identification Number (TIN), 17
technological advances in health care, 81
term life insurance, 169, 239
third rail of politics, 4, 234
Ticket to Hire program, 107
Ticket to Work program, 106, 209
TIN. *See* Taxpayer Identification Number
traditional IRA, 243
transportation, 192
Treasury bonds, 24
Trial Work Period (TWP), 106
TRICARE, 149
trust fund collections, 25
TWP. *See* Trial Work Period

U–V

Unicare, 148
United HealthCare, 148
U.S. Administration on Aging (AoA), 192
U.S. Department of Aging, Eldercare, 193
U.S. Department of Health and Human Services, 221
U.S. Department of Housing and Urban Development (HUD), 190, 195
U.S. Department of Labor, 143
U.S. Housing Act, 101
U.S. Postal Service, 8
U.S. Treasury, 25, 105, 145

variable annuities, 242
Veteran's Administration benefits, 104
video conference, hearing held via, 114
virtual villages, 228
vocational expert, 60
voluntary withholding (taxes), 182

W–X–Y–Z

wage caps, early retirement, 48
websites
  AARP, 226
  American Public Transportation Association, 193
  Bankrate.com, 80, 187, 221, 238
  CalFresh, 191
  creditcards.com, 250
  creditkarma.com, 248
  currentcodes.com, 245
  DisabilitySecrets.com, 117
  Eldercare, 193
  Electronic Transfer Account, 105
  freecreditscore.com, 248
  humana.com, 173
  Internal Revenue Service, 181, 183
  Kiplinger.com, 186
  livingto100.com, 80
  Mainstreet.com, 65
  Medicaid, 168
  Medicare Part D, 173
  Moneyrates.com, 198